DANGER, DANGER, EVERYWHERE

From the stratosphere where a hijacked atomic bomber steers a course for global disaster, to the depths of the Caribbean where sharks are the least of a skin diver's worries...

From a luxury casino where games of life and death are played with crooked cards, to a fabulous yacht where passengers are trapped on a diabolical voyage of death;

James Bond needs more than his usual skill and nerve.

He needs luck—and lots of it...

THUNDERBALL

IAN FLEMING
THUNDERBALL

CHARTER BOOKS, NEW YORK

This story is based on a screen treatment
by K. McClory, J. Whittingham,
and the author.

This Charter book contains the complete
text of the original hardcover edition.
It has been completely reset in a typeface
designed for easy reading, and was printed
from new film.

THUNDERBALL

A Charter Book / published by arrangement with
The Viking Press

PRINTING HISTORY
Viking edition / April 1961
Berkley edition / June 1982
Charter edition / July 1987

ISBN: 0-441-80863-8

Charter Books are published by The Berkley Publishing Group,
200 Madison Avenue, New York, New York 10016.
The name "CHARTER" and the "C" logo
are trademarks belonging to Charter Communications, Inc.

PRINTED IN THE UNITED STATES OF AMERICA

10   9   8   7   6   5   4   3   2   1

To Ernest Cuneo-Muse

CHAPTER 1

"Take It Easy, Mr. Bond"

It was one of those days when it seemed to James Bond that all life, as someone put it, was nothing but a heap of six to four against.

To begin with he was ashamed of himself—a rare state of mind. He had a hangover, a bad one, with an aching head and stiff joints. When he coughed—smoking too much goes with drinking too much and doubles the hangover—a cloud of small luminous black spots swam across his vision like amoebae in pond water. The one drink too many signals itself unmistakably. His final whisky and soda in the luxurious flat in Park Lane had been no different from the ten preceding ones, but it had gone down reluctantly and had left a bitter taste and an ugly sensation of surfeit. And, although he had taken in the message, he had agreed to play just one more rubber. Five pounds a hundred as it's the last one? He had agreed. And he had played the rubber like a fool. Even now he could see the queen of spades, with that stupid Mona Lisa smile on her fat face, slapping triumphantly down on his knave—the queen, as his partner had so sharply reminded him, that had been so infallibly marked with South, and that had made the difference between a grand slam redoubled (drunkenly) for him, and four hundred points above the line for the opposition. In the end it had been a twenty-point rubber, £100 against him—important money.

Again Bond dabbed with the bloodstained styptic pencil at the cut on his chin and despised the face that stared sullenly back at him from the mirror above the wash basin. Stupid, ignorant bastard! It all came from having nothing to do. More than a month of paper work—ticking off his number on stupid dockets, scribbling minutes that got spikier as the weeks passed, and snapping back down the telephone when some harmless section officer tried to argue with him. And then his secretary had gone down with the flu and he had been given a silly, and, worse, ugly bitch from the pool who called him "sir" and spoke to him primly through a mouth full of fruit stones. And now it was another Monday morning. Another week was beginning. The May rain thrashed at the windows. Bond swallowed down two Phensics and reached for the Eno's. The telephone in his bedroom rang. It was the loud ring of the direct line with Headquarters.

James Bond, his heart thumping faster than it should have done, despite the race across London and a fretful wait for the lift to the eighth floor, pulled out the chair and sat down and looked across into the calm, gray, damnably clear eyes he knew so well. What could he read in them?

"Good morning, James. Sorry to pull you along a bit early in the morning. Got a very full day ahead. Wanted to fit you in before the rush."

Bond's excitement waned minutely. It was never a good sign when M addressed him by his Christian name instead of by his number. This didn't look like a job—more like something personal. There was none of the tension in M's voice that heralded big, exciting news. M's expression was interested, friendly, almost benign. Bond said something noncommittal.

"Haven't seen much of you lately, James. How have you been? Your health, I mean." M picked up a sheet of paper, a form of some kind, from his desk, and held it as if preparing to read.

Suspiciously, trying to guess what the paper said, what all this was about, Bond said, "I'm all right, sir."

M said mildly, "That's not what the M.O. thinks, James. Just had your last Medical. I think you ought to hear what he has to say."

Bond looked angrily at the back of the paper. Now what the hell! He said with control, "Just as you say, sir."

M gave Bond a careful, appraising glance. He held the paper closer to his eyes. "'This officer,'" he read, "'remains basically physically sound. Unfortunately his mode of life is not such as is likely to allow him to remain in this happy state. Despite many previous warnings, he admits to smoking sixty cigarettes a day. These are of a Balkan mixture with a higher nicotine content than the cheaper varieties. When not engaged upon strenuous duty, the officer's average daily consumption of alcohol is in the region of half a bottle of spirits of between sixty and seventy proof. On examination, there continues to be little definite sign of deterioration. The tongue is furred. The blood pressure a little raised at 160/90. The liver is not palpable. On the other hand, when pressed, the officer admits to frequent occipital headaches and there is spasm in the trapezius muscles and so-called "fibrositis" nodules can be felt. I believe these symptoms to be due to this officer's mode of life. He is not responsive to the suggestion that overindulgence is no remedy for the tensions inherent in his professional calling and can only result in the creation of a toxic state which could finally have the effect of reducing his fitness as an officer. I recommend that No. 007 should take it easy for two to three weeks on a more abstemious regime, when I believe he would make a complete return to his previous exceptionally high state of physical fitness.'"

M reached over and slid the report into his OUT tray. He put his hands flat down on the desk in front of him and looked sternly across at Bond. He said, "Not very satisfactory, is it, James?"

Bond tried to keep impatience out of his voice. He said, "I'm perfectly fit, sir. Everyone has occasional headaches. Most week-end golfers have fibrositis. You get it from sweating and then sitting in a draft. Aspirin and embrocation get rid of them. Nothing to it, really, sir."

M said severely, "That's just where you're making a big mistake, James. Taking medicine only suppresses these symptoms of yours. Medicine doesn't get to the root of the trouble. It only conceals it. The result is a more highly poisoned condition which may become chronic disease. All drugs are harmful to the system. They are contrary to nature. The same applies to most of the food we eat—white bread with all the roughage removed, refined sugar with all the goodness machined out of it, pasteurized milk which has had most of the vitamins boiled away, everything overcooked and denaturized. Why"—M reached into his pocket for his notebook and consulted it—"do you know what our bread contains apart from a bit of over-ground flour?" M looked accusingly at Bond. "It contains large quantities of chalk, also benzol peroxide powder, chlorine gas, sal ammoniac, and alum." M put the notebook back in his pocket. "What do you think of that?"

Bond, mystified by all this, said defensively, "I don't eat all that much bread, sir."

"Maybe not," said M impatiently. "But how much stone-ground whole wheat do you eat? How much yoghurt? Uncooked vegetables, nuts, fresh fruit?"

Bond smiled. "Practically none at all, sir."

"It's no laughing matter." M tapped his forefinger on the desk for emphasis. "Mark my words. There is no way to health except the natural way. All your troubles"—Bond opened his mouth to protest, but M held up his hand—"the deep-seated toxemia revealed by your Medical, are the result of a basically unnatural way of life. Ever heard of Bircher-Brenner, for in-stance? Or Kneipp, Preissnitz, Rikli, Schroth, Gossman, Bilz?"

"No, sir."

"Just so. Well, those are the men you would be wise to study. Those are the great naturopaths—the men whose teach-ing we have foolishly ignored. Fortunately"—M's eyes gleamed enthusiastically—"there are a number of disciples of these men practicing in England. Nature cure is not beyond our reach."

James Bond looked curiously at M. What the hell had got into the old man? Was all this the first sign of senile decay? But M looked fitter than Bond had ever seen him. The cold gray eyes were clear as crystal and the skin of the hard, lined face was luminous with health. Even the iron-gray hair seemed to have new life. Then what was all this lunacy?

M reached for his IN tray and placed it in front of him in a preliminary gesture of dismissal. He said cheerfully, "Well, that's all, James. Miss Moneypenny has made the reservation. Two weeks will be quite enough to put you right. You won't know yourself when you come out. New man."

Bond looked across at M, aghast. He said in a strangled voice, "Out of where, sir?"

"Place called Shrublands. Run by quite a famous man in his line—Wain, Joshua Wain. Remarkable chap. Sixty-five. Doesn't look a day over forty. He'll take good care of you. Very up-to-date equipment, and he's even got his own herb garden. Nice stretch of country. Near Washington in Sussex. And don't worry about your work here. Put it right out of your mind for a couple of weeks. I'll tell 009 to take care of the Section."

Bond couldn't believe his ears. He said, "But, sir. I mean, I'm perfectly all right. Are you sure? I mean, is this really necessary?"

"No." M smiled frostily. "Not necessary. Essential. If you want to stay in the double-O Section, that is. I can't afford to have an officer in that section who isn't one-hundred-per-cent fit." M lowered his eyes to the basket in front of him and took out a signal file. "That's all, 007." He didn't look up. The tone of voice was final.

Bond got to his feet. He said nothing. He walked across the room and let himself out, closing the door with exaggerated softness.

Outside, Miss Moneypenny looked sweetly up at him.

Bond walked over to her desk and banged his fist down so that the typewriter jumped. He said furiously, "Now what the hell, Penny? Has the old man gone off his rocker? What's all this bloody nonsense? I'm damned if I'm going. He's absolutely nuts."

Miss Moneypenny smiled happily. "The manager's been terribly helpful and kind. He says he can give you the Myrtle room, in the annex. He says it's a lovely room. It looks right over the herb garden. They've got their own herb garden, you know."

"I know all about their bloody herb garden. Now look here, Penny," Bond pleaded with her, "be a good girl and tell me what it's all about. What's eating him?"

Miss Moneypenny, who often dreamed hopelessly about Bond, took pity on him. She lowered her voice conspiratorially. "As a matter of fact, I think it's only a passing phase. But it *is* rather bad luck on you getting caught up in it before it's passed. You know he's always apt to get bees in his bonnet about the efficiency of the Service. There was the time when all of us had to go through that physical-exercise course. Then he had that head-shrinker in, the psychoanalyst man—you missed that. You were somewhere abroad. All the Heads of Section had to tell him their dreams. He didn't last long. Some of their dreams must have scared him off or something. Well, last month M got lumbago and some friend of his at Blades, one of the fat, drinking ones I suppose"—Miss Moneypenny turned down her desirable mouth—"told him about this place in the country. This man swore by it. Told M that we were all like motor cars and that all we needed from time to time was to go to a garage and get decarbonized. He said he went there every year. He said it only cost twenty guineas a week, which was less than what he spent in Blades in one day, and it made him feel wonderful. Well, you know M always likes trying new things, and he went there for ten days and came back absolutely sold on the place. Yesterday he gave me a great talking-to all about it and this morning in the post I got a whole lot of tins of treacle and wheat germ and heaven knows what all. I don't know what to do with the stuff. I'm afraid my poor poodle'll have to live on it. Anyway, that's what's happened and I must say I've never seen him in such wonderful form. He's absolutely rejuvenated."

"He looked like that blasted man in the old Kruschen Salts advertisements. But why does he pick on me to go to this nuthouse?"

Miss Moneypenny gave a secret smile. "You know he thinks the world of you—or perhaps you don't. Anyway, as soon as he saw your Medical he told me to book you in." Miss Moneypenny screwed up her nose. "But, James, do you really drink and smoke as much as that? It can't be good for you, you know." She looked up at him with motherly eyes.

Bond controlled himself. He summoned a desperate effort at nonchalance, at the throw-away phrase. "It's just that I'd rather die of drink than of thirst. As for the cigarettes, it's really only that I don't know what to do with my hands." He heard the stale, hangover words fall like clinker in a dead grate. Cut out the schmaltz! What you need is a double brandy and soda.

Miss Moneypenny's warm lips pursed into a disapproving line. "About the hands—that's not what I've heard."

"Now don't you start on me, Penny." Bond walked angrily toward the door. He turned round. "Any more ticking-off from you and when I get out of this place I'll give you such a spanking you'll have to do your typing off a block of Dunlo-pillo."

Miss Moneypenny smiled sweetly at him. "I don't think you'll be able to do much spanking after living on nuts and lemon juice for two weeks, James."

Bond made a noise between a grunt and a snarl and stormed out of the room.

CHAPTER 2

Shrublands

James Bond slung his suitcase into the back of the old chocolate-brown Austin taxi and climbed into the front seat beside the foxy, pimpled young man in the black leather wind-cheater. The young man took a comb out of his breast pocket, ran it carefully through both sides of his duck-tail haircut, put the comb back in his pocket, then leaned forward and pressed the self-starter. The play with the comb, Bond guessed, was to assert to Bond that the driver was really only taking him and his money as a favor. It was typical of the cheap self-assertive-ness of young labor since the war. This youth, thought Bond, makes about twenty pounds a week, despises his parents, and would like to be Tommy Steele. It's not his fault. He was born into the buyers' market of the Welfare State and into the age of atomic bombs and space flight. For him, life is easy and meaningless. Bond said, "How far is it to Shrublands?"

The young man did an expert but unnecessary racing change round an island and changed up again. "'Bout half an hour." He put his foot down on the accelerator and neatly but rather dangerously overtook a lorry at an intersection.

"You certainly get the most out of your Bluebird."

The young man glanced sideways to see if he was being laughed at. He decided that he wasn't. He unbent fractionally. "My dad won't spring me something better. Says this old crate was okay for him for twenty years so it's got to be okay for me for another twenty. So I'm putting money by on my own. Halfway there already."

Bond decided that the comb play had made him over-censorious. He said, "What are you going to get?"

"Volkswagen Minibus. Do the Brighton races."

"That sounds a good idea. Plenty of money in Brighton."

"I'll say." The young man showed a trace of enthusiasm. "Only time I ever got there, a couple of bookies had me take them and a couple of tarts to London. Ten quid and a fiver tip. Piece of cake."

"Certainly was. But you can get both kinds at Brighton. You want to watch out for being mugged and rolled. There are some tough gangs operating out of Brighton. What's happened to The Bucket of Blood these days?"

"Never opened up again after that case they had. The one that got in all the papers." The young man realized that he was talking as if to an equal. He glanced sideways and looked Bond up and down with a new interest. "You going into the Scrubs or just visiting?"

"Scrubs?"

"Shrublands—Wormwood Scrubs—Scrubs," said the young man laconically. "You're not like the usual ones I get to take there. Mostly fat women and old geezers who tell me not to drive so fast or it'll shake up their sciatica or something."

Bond laughed. "I've got fourteen days without the option. Doctor thinks it'll do me good. Got to take it easy. What do they think of the place round here?"

The young man took the turning off the Brighton road and drove westward under the Downs through Poynings and Fulking. The Austin whined stolidly through the inoffensive countryside. "People think they're a lot of crackpots. Don't care for the place. All those rich folk and they don't spend any money in the area. Tearooms make a bit out of them—specially out of the cheats." He looked at Bond. "You'd be surprised. Grown people, some of them pretty big shots in the City and so forth, and they motor around in their Bentleys with their bellies empty and they see a tea shop and go in just for their cups of tea. That's all they're allowed. Next thing, they see some guy eating buttered toast and sugar cakes at the next table and they can't stand it. They order mounds of the stuff and hog it down just like kids who've broken into the larder—looking round all the time to see if they've been spotted. You'd think people like that would be ashamed of themselves."

"Seems a bit silly when they're paying plenty to take the cure or whatever it is."

"And that's another thing." The young man's voice was indignant. "I can understand charging twenty quid a week and giving you three square meals a day, but how do they get away with charging twenty quid for giving you nothing but hot water to eat? Doesn't make sense."

"I suppose there are the treatments. And it must be worth it to the people if they get well."

"Guess so," said the young man doubtfully. "Some of them do look a bit different when I come to take them back to the station." He sniggered. "And some of them change into real old goats after a week of nuts and so forth. Guess I might try it myself one day."

"What do you mean?"

The young man glanced at Bond. Reassured and remembering Bond's worldly comments on Brighton, he said, "Well, you see we got a girl here in Washington. Racy bird. Sort of local tart, if you see what I mean. Waitress at a place called The Honey Bee Tea Shop—or was, rather. She started most of us off, if you get my meaning. Quid a go and she knows a lot of French tricks. Regular sport. Well, this year the word got round up at the Scrubs and some of these old goats began patronizing Polly—Polly Grace, that's her name. Took her out in their Bentleys and gave her a roll in a deserted quarry up on the Downs. That's been her pitch for years. Trouble was they paid her five, ten quid and she soon got too good for the likes of us. Priced her out of our market, so to speak. Inflation, sort of. And a month ago she chucked up her job at The Honey Bee, and you know what?" The young man's voice was loud with indignation. "She bought herself a beat-up Austin Metropolitan for a couple of hundred quid and went mobile. Just like the London tarts in Curzon Street they talk about in the papers. Now she's off to Brighton, Lewes—anywhere she can find the sports, and in between whiles she goes to work in the quarry with these old goats from the Scrubs! Would you believe it!" The young man gave an angry blast on his klaxon at an inoffensive couple on a tandem bicycle.

Bond said seriously, "That's too bad. I wouldn't have thought these people would be interested in that sort of thing on nut cutlets and dandelion wine or whatever they get to eat at this place."

The young man snorted. "That's all you know. I mean"— he felt he had been too emphatic—"that's what we all thought. One of my pals, he's the son of the local doctor, talked the thing over with his dad—in a roundabout way, sort of. And his dad said no. He said that this sort of diet and no drink and plenty of rest, what with the massage and the hot and cold sitz baths and what have you, he said that all clears the blood stream and tones up the system, if you get my meaning. Wakes the old goats up—makes 'em want to start cutting the mustard again, if you know the song by that Rosemary Clooney."

Bond laughed. He said, "Well, well. Perhaps there's something to the place after all."

A sign on the right of the road said: " 'Shrublands.' Gateway to Health. First right. Silence please." The road ran through a wide belt of firs and evergreens in a fold of the Downs. A high wall appeared and then an imposing, mock-battlemented entrance with a Victorian lodge from which a thin wisp of smoke rose straight up among the quiet trees. The young man turned in and followed a gravel sweep between thick laurel bushes. An elderly couple cringed off the drive at a blare from his klaxon and then on the right there were broad stretches of lawn and neatly flowered borders and a sprinkling of slowly moving figures, alone and in pairs, and behind them a red-brick Victorian monstrosity from which a long glass sun parlor extended to the edge of the grass.

The young man pulled up beneath a heavy portico with a crenelated roof. Beside a varnished, iron-studded arched door stood a tall glazed urn above which a notice said: "No smoking inside. Cigarettes here please." Bond got down from the taxi and pulled his suitcase out of the back. He gave the young man a ten-shilling tip. The young man accepted it as no less than his due. He said, "Thanks. You ever want to break out, you can call me up. Polly's not the only one. And there's a tea shop on the Brighton road has buttered muffins. So long." He banged the gears into bottom and ground off back the way he had come. Bond picked up his suitcase and walked resignedly up the steps and through the heavy door.

Inside it was very warm and quiet. At the reception desk in the big oak-paneled hall a severely pretty girl in starched white welcomed him briskly. When he had signed the register she led him through a series of somberly furnished public rooms and down a neutral-smelling white corridor to the back of the building. Here there was a communicating door with the annex, a long, low, cheaply built structure with rooms on both sides of a central passage. The doors bore the names of flowers and shrubs. she showed him into Myrtle, told him that "the Chief" would see him in an hour's time, at six o'clock, and left him.

It was a room-shaped room with furniture-shaped furniture and dainty curtains. The bed was provided with an electric blanket. There was a vase containing three marigolds beside the bed and a book called *Nature Cure Explained* by Alan Moyle, M.N.B.A. Bond opened it and ascertained that the initials stood for "Member: British Naturopathic Association." He turned off the central heating and opened the windows wide. The herb garden, row upon row of small nameless plants round a central sundial, smiled up at him. Bond unpacked his things and sat down in the single armchair and read about eliminating the waste products from his body. He learned a great deal about foods he had never heard of, such as Potassium Broth, Nut Mince, and the mysteriously named Unmalted Slippery Elm. He had got as far as the chapter on massage and was reflecting on the injunction that this art should be divided into Effleurage, Stroking, Friction, Kneading, Petrissage, Tapotement, and Vibration, when the telephone rang. A girl's voice said that Mr. Wain would be glad to see him in Consulting Room A in five minutes.

Mr. Joshua Wain had a firm, dry handshake and a resonant, encouraging voice. He had a lot of bushy gray hair above an unlined brow, soft, clear brown eyes, and a sincere and Christian smile. He appeared to be genuinely pleased to see Bond and to be interested in him. He wore a very clean smocklike coat with short sleeves from which strong hairy arms hung relaxed. Below were rather incongruous pin-stripe trousers. He wore sandals over socks of conservative gray and when he moved across the consulting room his stride was a springy lope.

Mr. Wain asked Bond to remove all his clothes except his shorts. When he saw the many scars he said politely, "Dear me, you do seem to have been in the wars, Mr. Bond."

Bond said indifferently, "Near miss. During the war."

"Really! War between peoples is a terrible thing. Now, just breathe in deeply, please." Mr. Wain listened at Bond's back and chest, took his blood pressure, weighed him and recorded his height, and then, after asking him to lie face down on a surgical couch, handled his joints and vertebrae with soft, probing fingers.

While Bond replaced his clothes, Mr. Wain wrote busily at his desk. Then he sat back. "Well, Mr. Bond, nothing much to worry about here, I think. Blood pressure a little high, slight osteopathic lesions in the upper vertebrae—they'll probably be causing your tension headaches, by the way—and some right sacroiliac strain with the right ilium slightly displaced backwards. Due to a bad fall some time, no doubt." Mr. Wain raised his eyebrows for confirmation.

Bond said, "Perhaps." Inwardly he reflected that the "bad fall" had probably been when he had had to jump from the Arlberg Express after Heinkel and his friends had caught up with him around the time of the Hungarian uprising in 1956.

"Well, now." Mr. Wain drew a printed form toward him and thoughtfully ticked off items on a list. "Strict dieting for one week to eliminate the toxins in the blood stream. Massage to tone you up, irrigation, hot and cold sitz baths, osteopathic treatment, and a short course of traction to get rid of the lesions. That should put you right. And complete rest, of course. Just take it easy, Mr. Bond. You're a civil servant, I understand. Do you good to get away from all that worrying paper work for a while." Mr. Wain got up and handed the printed form to Bond. "Treatment rooms in half an hour, Mr. Bond. No harm in starting right away."

"Thank you." Bond took the form and glanced at it. "What's traction, by the way?"

"A mechanical device for stretching the spine. Very beneficial." Mr. Wain smiled indulgently. "Don't be worried by what some of the other patients tell you about it. They call it 'The Rack.' You know what wags some people are."

"Yes."

Bond walked out and along the white-painted corridor. People were sitting about, reading or talking in soft tones in the public rooms. They were all elderly, middle-class people, mostly women, many of whom wore unattractive quilted dressing gowns. The warm, close air and the frumpish women gave Bond claustrophobia. He walked through the hall to the main door and let himself out into the wonderful fresh air.

Bond walked thoughtfully down the trim narrow drive and smelled the musty smell of the laurels and the laburnums. Could he stand it? Was there any way out of this hell-hole short of resigning from the Service? Deep in thought, he almost collided with a girl in white who came hurrying round a sharp bend in the thickly hedged drive. At the same instant as she swerved out of his path and flashed him an amused smile, a mauve Bentley, taking the corner too fast, was on top of her. At one moment she was almost under its wheels, at the next, Bond, with one swift step, had gathered her up by the waist and, executing a passable Veronica, with a sharp swivel of his hips had picked her body literally off the hood of the car. He put the girl down as the Bentley dry-skidded to a stop in the gravel. His right hand held the memory of one beautiful breast. The girl said, "Oh!" and looked up into his eyes with an expression of flurried astonishment. Then she took in what had happened and said breathlessly, "Oh, thank you." She turned toward the car. A man had climbed unhurriedly down from the driving seat. He said calmly, "I am so sorry. Are you all right?" Recognition dawned on his face. He said silkily, "Why, if it isn't my friend Patricia. How are you, Pat? All ready for me?"

The man was extremely handsome—a dark-bronzed woman-killer with a neat mustache above the sort of callous mouth women kiss in their dreams. He had regular features that suggested Spanish or South American blood and bold, hard brown eyes that turned up oddly, or, as a woman would put it, intriguingly, at the corners. He was an athletic-looking six foot, dressed in the sort of casually well-cut beige herring-bone tweed that suggests Anderson and Sheppard. He wore a white silk shirt and a dark red polka-dot tie, and the soft dark brown V-necked sweater looked like vicuña. Bond summed him up as a good-looking bastard who got all the women he wanted and probably lived on them—and lived well.

The girl had recovered her poise. She said severely, "You really ought to be more careful, Count Lippe. You know there are always patients and staff walking down this drive. If it hadn't been for this gentleman"—she smiled at Bond—"you'd have run me over. After all, there *is* a big sign asking drivers to take care."

"I am so sorry, my dear. I was hurrying. I am late for my appointment with the good Mr. Wain. I am as usual in need of decarbonization—this time after two weeks in Paris." He turned to Bond. He said with a hint of condescension, "Thank you, my dear sir. You have quick reactions. And now, if you will forgive me—" He raised a hand, got back into the Bentley, and purred off up the drive.

The girl said, "Now I really must hurry. I'm terribly late." Together they turned and walked after the Bentley.

Bond said, examining her, "Do you work here?" She said that she did. She had been at Shrublands for three years. She liked it. And how long was he staying? The small-talk continued.

She was an athletic-looking girl whom Bond would have casually associated with tennis, or skating, or show-jumping. She had the sort of firm, compact figure that always attracted him and a fresh open-air type of prettiness that would have been commonplace but for a wide, rather passionate mouth and a hint of authority that would be a challenge to men. She was dressed in a feminine version of the white smock worn by Mr. Wain, and it was clear from the undisguised curves of her breasts and hips that she had little on underneath it. Bond asked her if she didn't get bored. What did she do with her time off?

She acknowledged the gambit with a smile and a quick glance of appraisal. "I've got one of those bubble cars. I get about the country quite a lot. And there are wonderful walks. And one's always seeing new people here. Some of them are very interesting. That man in the car, Count Lippe. He comes here every year. He tells me fascinating things about the Far East—China and so on. He's got some sort of a business in a place called Macao. It's near Hong Kong, isn't it?"

"Yes, that's right." So those turned-up eyes were a dash of Chinaman. It would be interesting to know his background. Probably Portuguese blood if he came from Macao.

They had reached the entrance. Inside the warm hall the girl said, "Well, I must run. Thank you again." She gave him a smile that, for the benefit of the watching receptionist, was entirely neutral. "I hope you enjoy your stay." She hurried off toward the treatment rooms. Bond followed, his eyes on the taut swell of her hips. He glanced at his watch and also went down the stairs and into a spotlessly white basement that smelled faintly of olive oil and an Aerosol disinfectant.

Beyond a door marked *"Gentlemen's Treatment"* he was taken in hand by an indiarubbery masseur in trousers and singlet. Bond undressed and with a towel round his waist followed the man down a long room divided into compartments by plastic curtains. In the first compartment, side by side, two elderly men lay, the perspiration pouring down their strawberry faces, in electric blanket-baths. In the next were two massage tables. On one, the pale, dimpled body of a youngish but very fat man wobbled obscenely beneath the pummeling of his masseur. Bond, his mind recoiling from it all, took off his towel and lay down on his face and surrendered himself to the toughest deep massage he had ever experienced.

Vaguely, against the jangling of his nerves and the aching of muscles and tendons, he heard the fat man heave himself off his table and, moments later, another patient take his place. He heard the man's masseur say, "I'm afraid we'll have to have the wrist-watch off, sir."

The urbane, silky voice that Bond at once recognized said with authority, "Nonsense, my dear fellow. I come here every year and I've been allowed to keep it on before. I'd rather keep it on, if you don't mind."

"Sorry, sir." The masseur's voice was politely firm. "You must have had someone else doing the treatment. It interferes with the flow of blood when I come to treat the arm and hand. If you don't mind, sir."

There was a moment's silence. Bond could almost feel Count Lippe controlling his temper. The words, when they came, were spat out with what seemed to Bond ludicrous violence. "Take it off then." The "Damn you" didn't have to be uttered. It hung in the air at the end of the sentence.

"Thank you, sir." There was a brief pause and then the massage began.

The small incident seemed odd to Bond. Obviously one had to take off one's wrist-watch for a massage. Why had the man wanted to keep it on? It seemed very childish.

"Turn over, please, sir."

Bond obeyed. Now his face was free to move. He glanced casually to his right. Count Lippe's face was turned away from him. His left arm hung down toward the floor. Where the sunburn ended, there was a bracelet of almost white flesh at the wrist. In the middle of the circle where the watch had been there was a sign tattooed on the skin. It looked like a small zigzag crossed by two vertical strokes. So Count Lippe had not wanted this sign to be seen! It would be amusing to ring up Records and see if they had a line on what sort of people wore this little secret recognition sign under their wrist-watches.

CHAPTER 3

The Rack

At the end of the hour's treatment Bond felt as if his body had been eviscerated and then run through a wringer. He put on his clothes and, cursing M, climbed weakly back up the stairs into what, by comparison with the world of nakedness and indignities in the basement, were civilized surroundings. At the entrance to the main lounge were two telephone booths. The switchboard put him through to the only Headquarters number he was allowed to call on an outside line. He knew that all such outside calls were monitored. As he asked for Records, he recognized the hollowness on the line that meant the line was bugged. He gave his number to Head of Records and put his question, adding that the subject was an Oriental probably of Portuguese extraction. After ten minutes Head of Records came back to him.

"It's a Tong sign." His voice sounded interested. "The Red Lightning Tong. Unusual to find anyone but a full-blooded Chinaman being a member. It's not the usual semi-religious organization. This is entirely criminal. Station H had dealings with it once. They're represented in Hong Kong, but their headquarters are across the bay in Macao. Station H paid big money to get a courier service running into Peking. Worked like a dream, so they gave the line a trial with some heavy stuff. It bounced, badly. Lost a couple of H's top men. It was a doublecross. Turned out that Redland had some sort of a deal with these people. Hell of a mess. Since then they've cropped up from time to time in drugs, gold smuggling to India, and top-bracket white slavery. They're big people. We'd be interested if you've got any kind of a line."

Bond said, "Thanks, Records. No, I've got nothing definite. First time I've heard of these Red Lightning people. Let you know if anything develops. So long."

Bond thoughtfully put back the receiver. How interesting! Now what the hell could this man be doing at Shrublands? Bond walked out of the booth. A movement in the next booth caught his eye. Count Lippe, his back to Bond, had just picked up the receiver. How long had he been in there? Had he heard Bond's inquiry? Or his comment? Bond had the crawling sensation at the pit of his stomach he knew so well—the signal that he had probably made a dangerous and silly mistake. He glanced at his watch. It was seven-thirty. He walked through the lounge to the sun parlor where "dinner" was being served. He gave his name to the elderly woman with a wardress face behind a long counter. She consulted a list and ladled hot vegetable soup into a plastic mug. Bond took the mug. He said anxiously, "Is that all?"

The woman didn't smile. She said severely, "You're lucky. You wouldn't be getting as much on Starvation. And you may have soup every day at midday and two cups of tea at four o'clock."

Bond gave her a bitter smile. He took the horrible mug over to one of the little café tables near the windows overlooking the dark lawn and sat down and sipped the thin soup while he watched some of his fellow inmates meandering aimlessly, weakly, through the room. Now he felt a grain of sympathy for the wretches. Now he was a member of their club. Now he had been initiated. He drank the soup down to the last neat cube of carrot and walked abstractedly off to his room, thinking of Count Lippe, thinking of sleep, but above all thinking of his empty stomach.

After two days of this, Bond felt terrible. He had a permanent slight nagging headache, the whites of his eyes had turned rather yellow, and his tongue was deeply furred. His masseur told him not to worry. This was as it should be. These were the poisons leaving his body. Bond, now a permanent prey to lassitude, didn't argue. Nothing seemed to matter any more but the single orange and hot water for breakfast, the mugs of hot soup, and the cups of tea which Bond filled with spoonfuls of brown sugar, the only variety that had Mr. Wain's sanction.

On the third day, after the massage and the shock of the sitz baths, Bond had on his program "Osteopathic Manipulation and Traction." He was directed to a new section of the base-ment, withdrawn and silent. When he opened the designated door he expected to find some hairy H-man waiting for him with flexed muscles. (H-man, he had discovered, stood for Health-man. It was the smart thing to call oneself if you were a naturopath.) He stopped in his tracks. The girl, Patricia some-thing, whom he had not set eyes on since his first day, stood waiting for him beside the couch. He closed the door behind him and said, "Good lord. Is this what you do?"

She was used to this reaction of the men patients and rather touchy about it. She didn't smile. She said in a business-like voice, "Nearly ten per cent of osteopaths are women. Take off your clothes, please. Everything except your shorts." When Bond had amusedly obeyed she told him to stand in front of her. She walked round him, examining him with eyes in which there was nothing but professional interest. Without com-menting on his scars she told him to lie face downward on the couch and, with strong, precise, and thoroughly practiced holds, went through the handling and joint-cracking of her profession.

Bond soon realized that she was an extremely powerful girl. His muscled body, admittedly unresistant, seemed to be easy going for her. Bond felt a kind of resentment at the neutrality of this relationship between an attractive girl and a half-naked man. At the end of the treatment she told him to stand up and clasp his hands behind her neck. Her eyes, a few inches away from his, held nothing but professional concentration. She hauled strongly away from him, presumably with the object of freeing his vertebrae. This was too much for Bond. At the end of it, when she told him to release his hands, he did nothing of the sort. He tightened them, pulled her head sharply toward him, and kissed her full on the lips. She ducked quickly down through his arms and straightened herself, her cheeks red and her eyes shining with anger. Bond smiled at her, knowing that he had never missed a slap in the face, and a hard one at that, by so little. He said, "It's all very well, but I just had to do it. You shouldn't have a mouth like that if you're going to be an osteopath."

The anger in her eyes subsided a fraction. She said, "The last time that happened, the man had to leave by the next train."

Bond laughed. He made a threatening move toward her. "If I thought there was any hope of being kicked out of this damn place I'd kiss you again."

She said, "Don't be silly. Now pick up your things. You've got half an hour's traction." She smiled grimly. "That ought to keep you quiet."

Bond said morosely, "Oh, all right. But only on condition you let me take you out on your next day off."

"We'll see about that. It depends how you behave at the next treatment." She held open the door. Bond picked up his clothes and went out, almost colliding with a man coming down the passage. It was Count Lippe, in slacks and a gay wind-cheater. He ignored Bond. With a smile and a slight bow he said to the girl, "Here comes the lamb to the slaughter. I hope you're not feeling too strong today." His eyes twinkled charmingly.

The girl said briskly, "Just get ready, please. I shan't be a moment putting Mr. Bond on the traction table." She moved off down the passage with Bond following.

She opened the door of a small anteroom, told Bond to put his things down on a chair, and pulled aside plastic curtains that formed a partition. Just inside the curtains was an odd-looking kind of surgical couch in leather and gleaming aluminum. Bond didn't like the look of it at all. While the girl fiddled with a series of straps attached to three upholstered sections that appeared to be on runners, Bond examined the contraption suspiciously. Below the couch was a stout electric motor on which a plate announced that this was the Hercules Motorized Traction Table. A power drive in the shape of articulated rods stretched upward from the motor to each of the three cushioned sections of the couch and terminated in tension screws to which the three sets of straps were attached. In front of the raised portion where the patient's head would lie, and approximately level with his face, was a large dial marked in lbs.-pressure up to 200. After 150 lbs. the numerals were in red. Below the headrest were grips for the patient's hands. Bond noted gloomily that the leather on the grips was stained with, presumably, sweat.

"Lie face downward here, please." The girl held the straps ready.

Bond said obstinately, "Not until you tell me what this thing does. I don't like the look of it."

The girl said patiently, "This is simply a machine for stretching your spine. You've got mild spinal lesions. It will help to free those. And at the base of your spine you've got some right sacroiliac strain. It'll help that too. You won't find it bad at all. Just a stretching sensation. It's very soothing, really. Quite a lot of patients fall asleep."

"This one won't," said Bond firmly. "What strength are you going to give me? Why are those top figures in red? Are you sure I'm not going to be pulled apart?"

The girl said with a touch of impatience, "Don't be silly. Of course if there was too much tension it might be dangerous. But I shall be starting you only at 90 pounds and in a quarter of an hour I shall come and see how you're getting on and probably put you up to 120. Now come along. I've got another patient waiting."

Reluctantly Bond climbed up on the couch and lay on his face with his nose and mouth buried in a deep cleft in the headrest. He said, his voice muffled by the leather, "If you kill me, I'll sue."

He felt the straps being tightened round his chest and then round his hips. The girl's skirt brushed the side of his face as she bent to reach the control lever beside the big dial. The motor began to whine. The straps tightened and then relaxed, tightened and relaxed. Bond felt as if his body was being stretched by giant hands. It was a curious sensation, but not unpleasant. With difficulty Bond raised his head. The needle on the dial stood at 90. Now the machine was making a soft iron hee-hawing, like a mechanical donkey, as the gears alternatively engaged and disengaged to produce the rhythmic traction.

"Are you all right?"

"Yes." He heard the girl pass through the plastic curtains and then the click of the outer door. Bond abandoned himself to the soft feel of the leather at his face, to the relentless intermittent haul on his spine and to the hypnotic whine and drone of the machine. It really wasn't too bad. How silly to have had nerves about it!

A quarter of an hour later he heard again the click of the outside door and the swish of the curtains.

"All right?"

"Fine."

The girl's hand came into his line of vision as she turned the lever. Bond raised his head. The needle crept up to 120. Now the pull was really hard and the voice of the machine was much louder.

The girl put her head down to his. She laid a reassuring hand on his shoulder. She said, her voice loud above the noise of the gears, "Only another quarter of an hour to go."

"All right." Bond's voice was careful. He was probing the new strength of the giant haul on his body. The curtains swished. Now the click of the outside door was drowned by the noise of the machine. Slowly Bond relaxed again into the arms of the rhythm.

It was perhaps five minutes later when a tiny movement of the air against his face made Bond open his eyes. In front of his eyes was a hand, a man's hand, reaching softly for the lever of the accelerator. Bond watched it, at first fascinated, and then with dawning horror as the lever was slowly depressed and the straps began to haul madly at his body. He shouted—something, he didn't know what. His whole body was racked with a great pain. Desperately he lifted his head and shouted again. On the dial, the needle was trembling at 200! His head dropped back, exhausted. Through a mist of sweat he watched the hand softly release the lever. The hand paused and turned slowly so that the back of the wrist was just below his eyes. In the center of the wrist was the little red sign of the zigzag and the two bisecting lines. A voice said quietly, close up against his ear, "You will not meddle again, my friend." Then there was nothing but the great whine and groan of the machine and the bite of the straps that were tearing his body in half. Bond began to scream, weakly, while the sweat poured from him and dripped off the leather cushions onto the floor.

Then suddenly there was blackness.

CHAPTER 4

Tea and Animosity

It is just as well that the body retains no memory of pain. Yes, it hurt, that abscess, that broken bone, but just how it hurt, and how much, is soon forgotten by the brain and the nerves. It is not so with pleasant sensations, a scent, a taste, the particular texture of a kiss. These things can be almost totally recalled. Bond, gingerly exploring his sensations as life came flooding back into his body, was astonished that the web of agony that had held his body so utterly had now completely dissolved. It was true that his whole spine ached as if it had been beaten, each vertebra separately, with wooden truncheons, but his pain was recognizable, something within his knowledge and therefore capable of control. The searing tornado that had entered his body and utterly dominated it, replacing his identity with its own, had gone. How had it been? What had it been like? Bond couldn't remember except that it had reduced him to something lower in the scale of existence than a handful of grass in the mouth of a tiger.

The murmur of voices grew more distinct.

"But what told you first that something was wrong, Miss Fearing?"

"It was the noise, the noise of the machine. I had just finished a treatment. A few minutes later I heard it. I'd never heard it so loud. I thought perhaps the door had been left open. I wasn't really worried but I came along to make sure. And there it was. The indicator up to 200! I tore down the lever and got the straps off and ran to the surgery and found the coramine and injected it into the vein—one c.c. The pulse was terribly weak. Then I telephoned you."

"You seem to have done everything possible, Miss Fearing. And I'm sure you bear no responsibility for this terrible thing." Mr. Wain's voice was doubtful. "It really is most unfortunate. I suppose the patient must have jerked the lever, somehow. Perhaps he was experimenting. He might easily have killed himself. We must tell the company about this and have some safety arrangements installed."

A hand gingerly clasped Bond's wrist, feeling for his pulse. Bond thought it was time to re-enter the world. He must quickly get himself a doctor, a real one, not one of these grated-carrot merchants. A sudden wave of anger poured through him. This was all M's fault. M was mad. He would have it out with him when he got back to Headquarters. If necessary he would go higher—to the Chiefs of Staff, the Cabinet, the Prime Minister. M was a dangerous lunatic—a danger to the country. It was up to Bond to save England. The weak, hysterical thoughts whirled through his brain, mixed themselves up with the hairy hand of Count Lippe, the mouth of Patricia Fearing, the taste of hot vegetable soup, and, as consciousness slipped away from him again, the diminishing voice of Mr. Wain: "No structural damage. Only considerable surface abrasion of the nerve ends. And of course shock. You will take personal charge of the case, Miss Fearing. Rest, warmth, and effleurage. Is that under . . . ?"

Rest, warmth, and effleurage. When Bond came round again, he was lying face downward on his bed and his whole body was bathed in exquisite sensation. Beneath him was the soft warmth of an electric blanket, his back glowed with the heat from two large sun lamps, and two hands, clad in what felt to be some particularly velvety fur, were rhythmically passing, one after the other, up and down the whole length of his body from his neck to the backs of his knees. It was a most gentle and almost piercingly luxurious experience, and Bond lay and bathed himself in it.

Presently he said sleepily, "Is that what they call effleurage?"

The girl's voice said softly, "I thought you'd come around. The whole tone of your skin suddenly changed. How are you feeling?"

"Wonderful. I'd be still better for a double whisky on the rocks."

The girl laughed. "Mr. Wain did say dandelion tea would be best for you. But I thought a little stimulant might be good, I mean just this once. So I brought the brandy with me. And there's plenty of ice as I'm going to give you an ice-pack presently. Would you really like some? Wait, I'll put your dressing gown over you and then you can see if you can turn over. I'll look the other way."

Bond heard the lamps being pulled away. Gingerly, he turned on his side. The dull ache returned, but it was already wearing off. He cautiously slipped his legs over the side of the bed and sat up.

Patricia Fearing stood in front of him, clean, white, comforting, desirable. In one hand was a pair of heavy mink gloves, but with the fur covering the palm instead of the back. In the other was a glass. She held out the glass. As Bond drank and heard the reassuring, real-life tinkle of the ice, he thought: This is a most splendid girl. I will settle down with her. She will give me effleurage all day long and from time to time a good tough drink like this. It will be a life of great beauty. He smiled at her and held out the empty glass and said, "More."

She laughed, mostly with relief that he was completely alive again. She took the glass and said, "Well, just one more, then. But don't forget it's on an empty stomach. It may make you dreadfully tight." She paused with the brandy bottle in her hand. Suddenly her gaze was cool, clinical. "And now you must try and tell me what happened. Did you accidentally touch the lever or something? You gave us all a dreadful fright. Nothing like that has ever happened before. The traction table's really perfectly safe, you know."

Bond looked candidly into her eyes. He said reassuringly, "Of course. I was just trying to get more comfortable. I heaved about and I do remember that my hand hit something rather hard. I suppose it must have been the lever. Then I don't remember any more. I must have been awfully lucky you came along so quickly."

She handed him the fresh drink. "Well, it's over now. And

thank heavens nothing's badly strained. Another two days of treatment and you'll be right as rain." She paused. She looked rather embarrassed. "Oh, and Mr. Wain asks if you could possibly keep all this, all this trouble, to yourself. He doesn't want the other patients to get worried."

I should think not, thought Bond. He could see the headlines. "PATIENT TORN NEARLY LIMB FROM LIMB AT NATURE CLINIC. RACK MACHINE GOES BERSERK. MINISTRY OF HEALTH STEPS IN." He said, "Of course I won't say anything. It was my fault, anyway." He finished his drink, handed back the glass, and cautiously lay back on the bed. He said, "That was marvelous. Now how about some more of the mink treatment. And by the way. Will you marry me? You're the only girl I've ever met who knows how to treat a man properly."

She laughed. "Don't be silly. And turn over on your face. It's your back that needs treatment."

"How do you know?"

Two days later, Bond was once more back in the half-world of the nature cure. The routine of the early morning glass of hot water, the orange, carefully sliced into symmetrical pigs by some ingenious machine wielded, no doubt, by the wardress in charge of diets, then the treatments, the hot soup, the siesta, and the blank, aimless walk or bus ride to the nearest tea shop for the priceless strength-giving cups of tea laced with brown sugar. Bond loathed and despised tea, that flat, soft, time-wasting opium of the masses, but on his empty stomach, and in his febrile state, the sugary brew acted almost as an intoxicant. Three cups, he reckoned, had the effect, not of hard liquor, but of just about half a bottle of champagne in the outside world, in real life. He got to know them all, these dainty opium dens—Rose Cottage, which he avoided after the woman charged him extra for emptying the sugar bowl; The Thatched Barn, which amused him because it was a real den of iniquity—large plates of sugar cakes put on one's table, the piercing temptation of the smell of hot scones; The Transport Café, where the Indian tea was black and strong and the lorry drivers brought in a smell of sweat and petrol and the great world (Bond found that all his senses, particularly his palate and nose, had miraculously become sharpened), and a dozen other cottagey, raftery nooks where elderly couples with Ford Populars and Morris Minors talked in muted tones about children called Len and Ron and Pearl and Ethel, and ate in small mouthfuls with the points of their teeth and made not a sound with the tea things. It was all a world whose ghastly daintiness and propriety would normally have sickened him. Now, empty, weak, drained of all the things that belonged to his tough, fast, basically dirty life, through banting, he had somehow regained some of the innocence and purity of childhood. In this frame of mind the naïveté and total lack of savor, surprise, excitement, of the dimity world of the Nice-Cup-of-Tea, of the Home-Made Cakes, and the One-Lump-or-Two, were perfectly acceptable.

And the extraordinary thing was that he could not remember when he had felt so well—not strong, but without any aches and pains, clear of eye and skin, sleeping ten hours a day and, above all, without that nagging sense of morning guilt that one is slowly wrecking one's body. It was really quite disturbing. Was his personality changing? Was he losing his edge, his point, his identity? Was he losing the vices that were so much part of his ruthless, cruel, fundamentally tough character? Who was he in process of becoming? A soft, dreaming, kindly idealist who would naturally leave the Service and become instead a prison visitor, interest himself in youth clubs, march with the H-bomb marchers, eat nut cutlets, try and change the world for the better?

James Bond would have been more worried, as day by day the H-cure drew his teeth, if it had not been for three obsessions which belonged to his former life and which would not leave him—a passionate longing for a large dish of Spaghetti Bolognese containing plenty of chopped garlic and accompanied by a whole bottle of the cheapest, rawest Chianti (bulk for his empty stomach and sharp tastes for his starved palate), an overwhelming desire for the strong, smooth body of Patricia Fearing, and a deadly concentration on ways and means to wring the guts of Count Lippe.

The first two would have to wait, though tantalizing schemes of consuming both dishes on the day of his release from Shrublands occupied much of his mind. So far as Count Lippe was concerned, work had started on the project from the moment Bond took up again the routine of the cure.

With the cold intensity he would have employed against an
enemy agent, say in a hotel in Stockholm or Lisbon during the
war, James Bond set about spying on the other man. He became
garrulous and inquisitive, chatting with Patricia Fearing about
the various routines at Shrublands. "But when do the staff find
time to have lunch?" "That man Lippe looks very fit. Oh, he's
worried about his waist-line! Aren't the electric blanket-baths
good for that? No, I haven't seen the Turkish Bath Cabinet.
Must have a look at it sometime." And to his masseur: "Haven't
seen that big chap about lately, Count something—Ripper?
Hipper? Oh yes, Lippe. Oh, noon every day? I think I must
try and get that time as well. Nice being clear for the rest of
the day. And I'd like to have a spell in the Turkish Bath thing
when you've finished the massage. Need a good sweat." In-
nocently, fragment by fragment, James Bond built up a plan
of operations—a plan that would leave him and Lippe alone
among the machinery of the soundproof treatment rooms.

For there would be no other opportunity. Count Lippe kept
to his room in the main building until his treatment time at
noon. In the afternoons he swished away in the violet Bentley—
to Bournemouth, it seemed, where he had "business." The
night porter let him in around eleven each night. One afternoon—in the siesta hour—Bond slipped the Yale lock on
Count Lippe's room with a straight piece of plastic cut off a
child's airplane he had bought for the purpose in Washington.
He went over the room meticulously and drew a blank. All he
learned—from the clothes—was that the Count was a much-
traveled man—shirts from Charvet, ties from Tripler, Dior,
and Hardy Amies, shoes from Peel, and raw-silk pajamas from
Hong Kong. The dark red morocco suitcase from Mark Cross
might have contained secrets, and Bond eyed the silk linings
and toyed with the Count's Wilkinson razor. But no! Better
that revenge, if it could be contrived, should come out of a
clear sky.

That same afternoon, drinking his treacly tea, Bond scraped
together the meager scraps of his knowledge of Count Lippe.
He was about thirty, attractive to women, and physically, to
judge from the naked body Bond had seen, very strong. His
blood would be Portuguese with a dash of Chinaman and he
gave the appearance of wealth. What did he do? What was his

profession? At first glance Bond would have put him down as a tough *maquereau* from the Ritz bar in Paris, the Palace at St. Moritz, the Carlton at Cannes—good at backgammon, polo, water-skiing, but with the yellow streak of the man who lives on women. But Lippe had heard Bond making inquiries about him and that had been enough for an act of violence—an inspired act that he had carried out swiftly and coolly when he finished his treatment with the Fearing girl and knew, from her remark, that Bond would be alone on the traction table. The act of violence might only have been designed to warn, but equally, since Lippe could only guess at the effect of a 200-pound pull on the spine, it might have been designed to kill. Why? Who was this man who had so much to hide? And what were his secrets? Bond poured the last of his tea on to a mound of brown sugar. One thing was certain—the secrets were big ones.

Bond never seriously considered telling Headquarters about Lippe and what he had done to Bond. The whole thing, against the background of Shrublands, was so unlikely and so utterly ridiculous. And somehow Bond, the man of action and re-source, came out of it all as something of a ninny. Weakened by a diet of hot water and vegetable soup, the ace of the Secret Service had been tied to some kind of a rack and then a man had come along and just pulled a lever up a few notches and reduced the hero of a hundred combats to a quivering jelly! No! There was only one solution—a private solution, man to man. Later perhaps, to satisfy his curiosity, it might be amusing to put through a good Trace on Count Lippe—with S.I.S. Records, with the C.I.D., with the Hong Kong Station. But for the time being Bond would stay quiet, keep out of Count Lippe's way, and plan meticulously for just the right kind of pay-off.

By the time the fourteenth day, the last day, came, Bond had it all fixed—the time, the place, and the method.

At ten o'clock Mr. Joshua Wain received Bond for his final checkup. When Bond came into the consulting room, Mr. Wain was standing by the open window doing deep-breathing exercises. With a final thorough exhalation through the nostrils he turned to greet Bond with an Ah! Bisto! expression on his healthily flushed face. His smile was elastic with good-fellow-ship. "And how's the world treating you, Mr. Bond? No ill effects from that unhappy little accident? No. Quite so. The body is a most remarkable piece of mechanism. Extraordinary power of recovery. Now then, shirt off, please, and we'll see what Shrublands has managed to do for you."

Ten minutes later, Bond, blood pressure down to 132/84, weight reduced by ten pounds, osteopathic lesions gone, clear of eye and tongue, was on his way down to the basement rooms for his final treatment.

As usual, it was clammily quiet and neutral-smelling in the white rooms and corridors. From the separate cubicles there came an occasional soft exchange between patient and staff, and, in the background, intermittent plumbing noises. The steady whir of the ventilation system created the impression of the deep innards of a liner in a dead calm. It was nearly twelve-thirty. Bond lay face down on the massage table and listened for the authoritative voice and the quick slap of the naked feet of his prey. The door at the end of the corridor sighed open and sighed shut again. "Morning, Beresford. All ready for me? Make it good and hot today. Last treatment. Three more ounces to lose. Right?"

"Very good, sir." The gym shoes of the chief attendant, followed by the slapping feet, came down the corridor outside the plastic curtain of the massage room and on to the end room of all, the electric Turkish bath. The door sighed shut and a few minutes later sighed again as the attendant, having installed Count Lippe, came back down the corridor. Twenty minutes went by. Twenty-five. Bond rolled off the table. "Well, thanks, Sam. You've done me a power of good. I'll be back to see you again one of these days, I expect. I'll just go along and have a final salt rub and a sitz bath. You cut along to your carrot cutlets. Don't worry about me. I'll let myself out when I've finished." Bond wrapped a towel round his waist and moved off down the corridor. There was a flurry of movement and voices as the attendants got rid of their patients and made their way through the staff door for the luncheon break. The last patient, a reformed drunk, called back from the entrance, "See you later, Irrigator!" Somebody laughed. Now the petty-officer voice of Beresford sounded down the corridor, making certain that everything was shipshape: "Windows, Bill? Okay.

Your next is Mr. Dunbar at two sharp. Len, tell the laundry we shall need more towels after lunch. Ted . . . Ted. You there, Ted? Well, then, Sam, look after Count Lippe, would you, Turkish bath."

Bond had listened to this routine for a whole week, noting the men that cut minutes off their duty and got off early to lunch, noting the ones that stayed to do their full share of the last chores. Now, from the open door of the empty shower room, he called back, in Sam's deep voice, "Okay, Mr. Beresford," and waited for the crisp squeak of the gym shoes on the linoleum. There it was! The brief pause halfway down the corridor and then the double sigh as the staff door opened and shut. Now there was dead silence save for the hum of the fans. The treatment rooms were empty. Now there was only James Bond and Count Lippe.

Bond waited a moment and then came out of the shower room and softly opened the door to the Turkish bath. He had had one session in the place, just to get the geography clear in his mind, and the scene was exactly as he remembered.

It was a white cubicle treatment room like all the others, but in this one the only object was a big cream metal-and-plastic box about five feet tall by four feet square. It was closed on all sides but the top. The front of the big cabinet was hinged to allow a patient to climb in and sit inside and there was a hole in the top with a foam-rubber support for the nape of the neck and the chin, through which the patient's head emerged. The rest of his body was exposed to the heat from many rows of naked electric bulbs inside the cabinet and the degree of heat was thermostatically controlled by a dial at the back of the cabinet. It was a simple sweat box, designed, as Bond had noticed on his previous visit to the room, by the Medikalischer Maschinenbau G.m.b.H., 44 Franziskanerstrasse, Ulm, Bavaria.

The cabinet faced away from the door. At the hiss of the hydraulic fastener, Count Lippe said angrily, "Goddammit, Beresford. Let me out of this thing. I'm sweating like a pig."

"You said you wanted it hot, sir." Bond's amiable voice was a good approximation to the chief attendant's.

"Don't argue, goddammit. Let me out of here."

"I don't think you quite realize the value of heat in the H-cure, sir. Heat resolves many of the toxins in the blood stream and for the matter of that in the muscle tissue also. A patient suffering from your condition of pronounced toxemia will find much benefit from the heat treatment." Bond found the H-lingo rattling quite easily off the tongue. He was not worried about the consequences to Beresford. He would have the solid alibi of luncheon in the staff canteen.

"Don't give me that crap. I tell you, let me out of here."

Bond examined the dial on the back of the machine. The needle stood at 120. What should he give the man? The dial ran up to 200 degrees. That much might roast him alive. This was only to be a punishment, not a murder. Perhaps 180 would be a just retribution. Bond clicked the knob up to 180. He said, "I think just half an hour of real heat will do you the world of good, sir." Bond dropped the sham voice. He added sharply, "And if you catch fire you can sue."

The dripping head tried to turn, failed. Bond moved toward the door. Count Lippe now had a new voice, controlled but desperate. He said woodenly, concealing the knowledge and the hate, "Give you a thousand pounds and we're quits." He heard the hiss of the open door. "Ten thousand. All right then, fifty."

Bond closed the door firmly behind him and walked quickly down the corridor to put on his clothes and get out. Behind him, deeply muffled, came the first shout for help. Bond closed his ears. There was nothing that a painful week in hospital and plenty of gentian violet or tannic acid jelly wouldn't cure. But it did cross his mind that a man who could offer a bribe of fifty thousand pounds must be either very rich or have some very urgent reason for needing freedom of movement. It was surely too much to pay just for avoidance of pain.

James Bond was right. The outcome of this rather childish trial of strength between two extremely tough and ruthless men, in the bizarre surroundings of a nature clinic in Sussex, was to upset, if only in a minute fashion, the exactly timed machinery of a plot that was about to shake the governments of the Western world.

CHAPTER 5

S.P.E.C.T.R.E.

The Boulevard Haussmann, in the VIIIth and IXth Arrondissements, stretches from the Rue du Faubourg St. Honoré to the Opéra. It is very long and very dull, but it is perhaps the solidest street in the whole of Paris. Not the richest—the Avenue d'Iéna has that distinction—but rich people are not necessarily solid people and too many of the landlords and tenants in the Avenue d'Iéna have names ending in "escu," "ovitch," "ski," and "stein," and these are sometimes not the endings of respectable names. Moreover, the Avenue d'Iéna is almost entirely residential. The occasional discreet brass plates giving the name of a holding company in Liechtenstein or in the Bahamas or the Canton de Vaud in Switzerland are there for tax purposes only—the cover names for private family fortunes seeking alleviation from the punitive burden of the Revenue, or, more briefly, tax-dodging. The Boulevard Haussmann is not like that. The massive, turn-of-the-century, bastard Second Empire buildings in heavily ornamented brick and stucco are the "sièges," the seats, of important businesses. Here are the head offices of the *gros industriels* from Lille, Lyons, Bordeaux, Clermont Ferrand, the *locaux* of the *gros légumes,* the "big vegetables" in cotton, artificial silk, coal, wine, steel, and shipping. If, among them, there are some fly-by-nights concealing a lack of serious capital—*des fonds sérieux*—behind a good address, it would only be fair to admit that such

men of paper exist also behind the even solider frontages of
Lombard and Wall Streets.

It is appropriate that among this extremely respectable company of tenants, suitably diversified by a couple of churches,
a small museum and the French Shakespeare Society, you
should also find the headquarters of charitable organizations.
At No. 136 *bis*, for instance, a discreetly glittering brass plate
says: *"F.I.R.C.O."* and, underneath: *"Fraternité Internation-
ale de la Résistance Contre l'Oppression."* If you were interested in this organization, either as an idealist or because you
were a salesman of, say, office furniture, and you pressed the
very clean porcelain bell button, the door would in due course
be opened by an entirely typical French concierge. If your
business was serious or obviously well-meaning, the concierge
would show you across a rather dusty hall to tall, bogus Di-
rectoire double doors adjoining the over ornamented cage of
a shaky-looking lift. Inside the doors you would be greeted by
exactly what you had expected to see—a large dingy room
needing a fresh coat of its café-au-lait paint, in which half a
dozen men sat at cheap desks and typed or wrote amidst the
usual accouterments of a busy organization—IN and OUT bas-
kets, telephones, in this case the old-fashioned standard ones
that are typical of such an office in this part of Paris, and dark
green metal filing cabinets in which drawers stand open. If you
were observant of small details, you might register that all the
men were of approximately the same age group, between thirty
and forty, and that in an office where you would have expected
to find women doing the secretarial work, there were none.

Inside the tall door you would receive the slightly defensive
welcome appropriate to a busy organization accustomed to the
usual proportion of cranks and time-wasters but, in response
to your serious inquiry, the face of the man at the desk near
the door would clear and become cautiously helpful. The aims
of the Fraternity? We exist, monsieur, to keep alive the ideals
that flourished during the last war among members of all Resistance groups. No, monsieur, we are entirely unpolitical. Our
funds? They come from modest subscriptions from our members and from certain private persons who share our aims. You
have perhaps a relative, a member of a Resistance group, whose
whereabouts you seek? Certainly, monsieur. The name? Gregor

Karlski, last heard of with Mihailovitch in the summer of 1943.
Jules! (He might turn to a particular man and call out.) Karlski,
Gregor. Mihailovitch, 1943. Jules would go to a cabinet and
there would be a brief pause. Then the reply might come back,
Dead. Killed in the bombing of the General's headquarters,
October 21st, 1943. I regret, monsieur. Is there anything further
we can do for you? Then perhaps you would care to have some
of our literature. Forgive me for not having time to spare to
give you more details of FIRCO myself. But you will find everything there. This happens to be a particularly busy day. This
is the International Refugee Year and we have many inquiries
such as yours from all over the world. Good afternoon, monsieur. *Pas de quoi*.

So, or more or less so, it would be and you would go out
on to the Boulevard satisfied and even impressed with an organization that was doing its excellent if rather vague work
with so much dedication and efficiency.

On the day after James Bond had completed his nature cure
and had left for London after, the night before, scoring a most
satisfactory left and right of Spaghetti Bolognese and Chianti
at Lucien's in Brighton and of Miss Patricia Fearing on the
squab seats from her bubble car high up on the Downs, an
emergency meeting of the trustees of FIRCO was called for seven
o'clock in the evening. The men, for they were all men, came
from all over Europe, by train or car or airplane, and they
entered No. 136 *bis* singly or in pairs, some by the front door
and some by the back, at intervals during the late afternoon
and evening. Each man had his allotted time for arriving at
these meetings—so many minutes, up to two hours, before
zero hour—and each man alternated between the back and the
front door from meeting to meeting. Now there were two "con-
cierges" for each door and other less obvious security measures—warning systems, closed-circuit television scanning of
the two entrances, and complete sets of dummy FIRCO minutes,
backed up one hundred per cent by the current business of the
FIRCO organization on the ground floor. Thus, if necessary, the
deliberations of the "trustees" could, in a matter only of seconds, be switched from clandestine to overt—as solidly overt
as any meeting of principals in the Boulevard Haussmann could
possibly be.

At seven o'clock precisely the twenty men who made up this organization strode, lounged, or sidled, each according to his character, into the workmanlike board room on the third floor. Their chairman was already in his seat. No greetings were exchanged. They were ruled by the chairman to be a waste of breath and, in an organization of this nature, hypocritical. The men filed round the table and took their places at their numbers, the numbers from one to twenty-one that were their only names and that, as a small security precaution, advanced round the rota by two digits at midnight on the first of every month. Nobody smoked—drinking was taboo and smoking frowned upon—and nobody bothered to glance down at the bogus FIRCO agenda on the table in front of him. They sat very still and looked up the table at the chairman with expressions of the sharpest interest and what, in lesser men, would have been obsequious respect.

Any man seeing No. 2, for that was the chairman's number of the month, even for the first time would have looked at him with some degree of the same feelings, for he was one of those men—one meets perhaps only two or three in a lifetime—who seem almost to suck the eyes out of your head. These rare men are apt to possess three basic attributes—their physical appearance is extraordinary, they have a quality of relaxation, of inner certainty, and they exude a powerful animal magnetism. The herd has always recognized the other-worldliness of these phenomena, and in primitive tribes you will find that any man singled out by nature in this fashion will also have been chosen by the tribe to be their chief. Certain great men of history, perhaps Genghis Khan, Alexander the Great, Napoleon, among the politicians, have had these qualities. Perhaps they even explain the hypnotic sway of an altogether more meager individual, the otherwise inexplicable Adolf Hitler, over eighty million of the most gifted nation in Europe. Certainly, No. 2 had these qualities and any man in the street would have recognized them—let alone these twenty chosen men. For them, despite the deep cynicism ingrained in their respective callings, despite their basic insensitivity toward the human race, he was, however reluctantly, their Supreme Commander—almost their god.

This man's name was Ernst Stavro Blofeld and he was born in Gdynia of a Polish father and a Greek mother on May 28th, 1908. After matriculating in economics and political history at the University of Warsaw he studied engineering and radionics at the Warsaw Technical Institute and at the age of twenty-five obtained a modest post in the central administration of the Ministry of Posts and Telegraphs. This would seem a curious choice for such a highly gifted youth, but Blofeld had come to an interesting conclusion about the future of the world. He had decided that fast and accurate communication lay, in a contracting world, at the very heart of power. Knowledge of the truth before the next man, in peace or war, lay, he thought, behind every correct decision in history and was the source of all great reputations. He was doing very well on this theory, watching the cables and radiograms that passed through his hands at the Central Post Office and buying or selling on margin on the Warsaw Bourse—only occasionally, when he was absolutely certain, but then very big—when the basic nature of the postal traffic changed. Now Poland was mobilizing for war and a spate of munition orders and diplomatic cables poured through his department. Blofeld changed his tactics. This was valuable stuff, worth nothing to him, but priceless to the enemy. Clumsily at first, and then more expertly, he contrived to take copies of cables, choosing, for the ciphers hid their contents from him, only those prefixed "MOST IMMEDIATE" or "MOST SECRET." Then, working carefully, he built up in his head a network of fictitious agents. These were real but small people in the various embassies and armament firms to whom most of the traffic was addressed—a junior cipher clerk in the British Embassy, a translator working for the French, private secretaries—real ones—in the big firms. These names were easily obtained from the diplomatic lists, by ringing up a firm and asking Inquiries for the name of the chairman's private secretary. He was speaking for the Red Cross. They wished to discuss the possibility of a donation from the chairman. And so on. When Blofeld had all his names right, he christened his network TARTAR and made a discreet approach to the German Military Attaché with one or two specimens of its work. He was rapidly passed on to the representative of AMT IV of the

Abwehr, and from then on things were easy. When this pot was bubbling merrily, and the money (he refused to accept payment except in American dollars) coming in (it came in fast; he explained that he had so many agents to pay off), he proceeded to widen his market. He considered the Russians but dismissed them, and the Czechs, as probable non-, or at any rate slow, payers. Instead he chose the Americans and the Swedes, and money positively showered in on him. He soon realized, for he was a man of almost mimosaic sensibility in matters of security, that the pace could not possibly last. There would be a leak: perhaps between the Swedish and German secret services, who he knew (for through his contacts with their spies he was picking up the gossip of his new trade) were working closely together in some territories; or through Allied counter-espionage or their cryptographic services; or else one of his notional agents would die or be transferred without his knowledge while he continued to use the name as a source. Anyway, by now he had $200,000 and there was the added spur that the war was getting too close for comfort. It was time for him to be off into the wide world—into one of the safe bits of it.

Blofeld carried out his withdrawal expertly. First he slowly petered off the service. Security, he explained, was being tightened up by the English and the French. Perhaps there had been a leak—he looked with mild reproof into the eyes of his contact—this secretary had had a change of heart, that one was asking too much money. Then he went to his friend on the Bourse and, after sealing his lips with a thousand dollars, had all his funds invested in Shell Bearer Bonds in Amsterdam and thence transferred to a Numbered Safe Deposit box with the Diskonto Bank in Zurich. Before the final step of telling his contacts that he was *brulé* and that the Polish Deuxième Bureau was sniffing at his heels, he paid a visit to Gdynia, called on the registrar and on the church where he had been baptized and, on the pretext of looking up details of an invented friend, neatly cut out the page recording his own name and birth. It remained only to locate the passport factory that operates in every big seaport and purchase a Canadian seaman's passport for $2,000. Then he was off to Sweden by the next boat. After a pause in Stockholm for a careful look round the world and some cool thinking about the probable course of the war, he flew to Turkey on his original Polish passport, transferred his money from Switzerland to the Ottoman Bank in Istanbul, and waited for Poland to fall. When, in due course, this happened, he claimed refuge in Turkey and spent a little money among the right officials in order to get his claim established. Then he settled down. Ankara Radio was glad to have his expert services and he set up RAHIR, another espionage service built on the lines of TARTAR, but rather more solidly. Blofeld wisely waited to ascertain the victor before selling his wares, and it was only when Rommel had been kicked out of Africa that he plumped for the Allies. He finished the war in a blaze of glory and prosperity and with decorations or citations from the British, Americans, and French. Then, with half a million dollars in Swiss banks and a Swedish passport in the name of Serge Angstrom, he slipped off to South America for a rest, some good food, and a fresh think.

And now Ernst Blofeld, the name to which he had decided it was perfectly safe to return, sat in the quiet room in the Boulevard Haussmann, gazed slowly round the faces of his twenty men, and looked for eyes that didn't squarely meet his. Blofeld's own eyes were deep black pools surrounded—totally surrounded, as Mussolini's were—by very clear whites. The doll-like effect of this unusual symmetry was enhanced by long silken black eyelashes that should have belonged to a woman. The gaze of these soft doll's eyes was totally relaxed and rarely held any expression stronger than a mild curiosity in the object of their focus. They conveyed a restful certitude in their owner and in their analysis of what they observed. To the innocent they exuded confidence, a wonderful cocoon of confidence in which the observed one could rest and relax, knowing that he was in comfortable, reliable hands. But they stripped the guilty or the false and made him feel transparent—as transparent as a fishbowl through whose sides Blofeld examined, with only the most casual curiosity, the few solid fish, the grains of truth, suspended in the void of deceit or attempted obscurity. Blofeld's gaze was a microscope, the window on the world of a superbly clear brain, with a focus that had been sharpened by thirty years of danger, and of keeping just one step ahead of it, and of an inner self-assurance built up on a lifetime of success in whatever he had attempted.

The skin beneath the eyes that now slowly, mildly, surveyed his colleagues was unpouched. There was no sign of debauchery, illness, or old age on the large, white, bland face under the square, wiry black crew-cut. The jaw line, going to the appropriate middle-aged fat of authority, showed decision and independence. Only the mouth, under a heavy, squat nose, marred what might have been the face of a philosopher or a scientist. Proud and thin, like a badly healed wound, the compressed, dark lips, capable only of false, ugly smiles, suggested contempt, tyranny, and cruelty—but to an almost Shakespearian degree. Nothing about Blofeld was small.

Blofeld's body weighed about two hundred and eighty pounds. It had once been all muscle—he had been an amateur weight-lifter in his youth—but in the past ten years it had softened and he had a vast belly that he concealed behind roomy trousers and well-cut double-breasted suits, tailored, that evening, out of beige doeskin. Blofeld's hands and feet were long and pointed. They were quick-moving when they wanted to be, but normally, as now, they were still and reposed. For the rest, he didn't smoke or drink and he had never been known to sleep with a member of either sex. He didn't even eat very much. So far as vices or physical weaknesses were concerned, Blofeld had always been an enigma to everyone who had known him.

The twenty men who looked up the long table at this man and waited patiently for him to speak were a curious mixture of national types. But they had certain characteristics in common. They were all in the thirty-to-forty age-group, they all looked extremely fit, and nearly all of them—there were two who were different—had quick, hard, predatory eyes, the eyes of the wolves and the hawks that prey upon the herd. The two who were different were both scientists with scientists' otherworldly eyes—Kotze, the East German physicist who had come over to the West five years before and had exchanged his secrets for a modest pension and retirement in Switzerland, and Maslov, formerly Kandinsky, the Polish electronics expert who, in 1956, had resigned as head of the radio research department of Philips AG of Eindhoven and had then disappeared into obscurity. The other eighteen men consisted of cells of three

(Blofeld accepted the Communist triangle system for security reasons) from six national groups and, within these groups, from six of the world's great criminal and subversive organizations. There were three Sicilians from the top echelon of the Unione Siciliano, the Mafia; three Corsican Frenchmen from the Union Corse, the secret society contemporary with and similar to the Mafia that runs nearly all organized crime in France; three former members of SMERSH, the Soviet organization for the execution of traitors and enemies of the State that had been disbanded on the orders of Khrushchev in 1958 and replaced by the Special Executive Department of the M.W.D.; three of the top surviving members of the former Sonderdienst of the Gestapo; three tough Yugoslav operatives who had resigned from Marshal Tito's Secret Police, and three highland Turks (the Turks of the plains are no good) formerly members of Blofeld's RAHIR and subsequently responsible for KRYSTAL, the important Middle East heroin pipeline whose outlet is Beirut. These eighteen men, all experts in conspiracy, in the highest ranges of secret communication and action and, above all, of silence, also shared one supreme virtue—every man had a solid cover. Every man possessed a valid passport with up-to-date visas for the principal countries in the world, and an entirely clean sheet with Interpol and with their respective national police forces. That factor alone, the factor of each man's cleanliness after a lifetime in big crime, was his highest qualification for membership of S.P.E.C.T.R.E.—The Special Executive for Counterintelligence, Terrorism, Revenge, and Extortion.

The founder and chairman of this private enterprise for private profit was Ernst Stavro Blofeld.

CHAPTER 6

Violet-Scented Breath

Blofeld completed his inspection of the faces. As he had anticipated, only one pair of eyes had slid away from his. He had known he was right. The double-checked reports had been entirely circumstantial, but his own eyes and his intuition had to be the seal. He slowly put both hands under the table. One hand remained flat on his thigh. The other went to a side pocket and drew out a thin gold vinaigrette and placed it on the table in front of him. He prised open the lid with his thumbnail, took out a violet-scented cachou, and slipped it into his mouth. It was his custom, when unpleasant things had to be said, to sweeten his breath.

Blofeld tucked the cachou under his tongue and began to talk in a soft, resonant, and very beautifully modulated voice.

"I have a report to make to members about The Big Affair, about Plan Omega." (Blofeld never prefixed his words with "Gentlemen," "Friends," "Colleagues," or the like. These were fripperies.) "But before I proceed to that matter, for security's sake I propose to touch upon another topic." Blofeld looked mildly round the table. The same pair of eyes evaded his. He continued in a narrative tone of voice: "The Executive will agree that the first three years of our experience have been successful. Thanks in part to our German section, the recovery of Himmler's jewels from the Mondsee was successfully accomplished in total secrecy, and the stones disposed of by our

Turkish section in Beirut. Income: £750,000. The disappearance of the safe with its contents intact from the M.W.D. headquarters in East Berlin has never been traced to our Russian section, and the subsequent sale to the American Central Intelligence Agency yielded $500,000. The interception of one thousand ounces of heroin in Naples, the property of the Pastori circuit, when sold to the Firpone interests in Los Angeles, brought in $800,000. The British Secret Service paid £100,000 for the Czech germ-warfare phials from the state chemical factory in Pilsen. The successful blackmail of former S.S. Gruppenführer Sonntag, living under the name of Santos in Havana, yielded a meager $100,000—unfortunately all the man possessed—and the assassination of Peringue, the French heavy-water specialist who went over to the Communists through Berlin added, thanks to the importance of his knowledge and the fact that we got him before he had talked, one billion francs from the Deuxième Bureau. In round sums, as the Special Executive knows from our accounts, the total income to date, not counting our last and undistributed dividend, has amounted to approximately one and a half million pounds sterling in the Swiss francs and Venezuelan bolivars in which for reasons of prudence—they continue to be the hardest currencies in the world—we convert all our takings. This income, as the Special Executive will be aware, has been distributed in accordance with our charter as to ten per cent for overheads and working capital, ten per cent to myself, and the remainder in equal shares of four per cent to the members—a profit to each member of approximately £60,000. This amount I regard as a barely adequate remuneration for members' services—£20,000 a year is not in accordance with our expectations—but you will be aware that Plan Omega will yield sufficient to provide each of us with a considerable fortune and will allow us, if we wish to do so, to wind up our organization and transfer our respective energies to other pursuits." Blofeld looked down the table. He said amiably, "Any questions?"

The twenty pairs of eyes, on this occasion all of them, gazed stolidly, unemotionally back at their chairman. Each man had made his own calculation, knew his own mind. There was no comment to be extracted from these good, though narrow, minds. They were satisfied, but it was not a part of their harsh personalities to say so. These were known things that their chairman had spoken. It was time for the unknown.

Blofeld slipped a second cachou into his mouth, maneuvered it under his tongue, and continued.

"Then so be it. And now to the last operation, completed a month ago and yielding one million dollars." Blofeld's eyes moved down the left-hand rank of members to the end of the row. He said softly, "Stand up, No. 7."

Marius Domingue of the Union Corse, a proud, chunky man with slow eyes, who was wearing ready-made, rather sharp clothes that probably came from the Galleries Barbes in Marseilles, got slowly to his feet. He looked squarely down the table at Blofeld. His big, rough hands hung relaxed at the seams of his trousers. Blofeld appeared to answer his gaze, but in fact he was noting the reaction of the Corsican next to No. 7, No. 12, Pierre Borraud. This man sat directly facing Blofeld at the far end of the long table. It was his eyes that had been evasive during the meeting. Now they were not. Now they were relaxed, assured. Whatever the eyes had feared had passed.

Blofeld addressed the company. "This operation, you will recall, involved the kidnaping of the seventeen-year-old daughter of Magnus Blomberg, owner of the Principality Hotel in Las Vegas and participant in other American enterprises through his membership of the Detroit Purple Gang. The girl was abducted from her father's suite in the Hotel de Paris in Monte Carlo and taken by sea to Corsica. This part of the operation was executed by the Corsican section. One million dollars ransom was demanded. Mr. Blomberg was willing and, in accordance with the instructions of SPECTRE, the money in an inflated life raft was dropped at dusk off the Italian coast near San Remo. At nightfall the raft was recovered by the ship operated by our Sicilian section. This section is to be commended for detecting the transistorized radio transmitter concealed in the raft which it was intended should allow a unit of the French Navy to direction-find our ship and hunt it down. On receipt of the ransom money, and in accordance with our undertaking, the girl was returned to her parents apparently suffering from no ill effects except for the hair dye that had been necessary to transfer her from Corsica to a *wagon-lit* in the Blue Train from Marseilles. I say 'apparently.' From a source in the police commissariat at Nice, I now learn that the girl was violated during her captivity in Corsica." Blofeld paused to allow this intelligence time to sink in. He continued. "It is the parents who maintain that she was violated. It is possible that only carnal knowledge, with her consent, was involved. No matter. This organization undertook that the girl would be returned undamaged. Without splitting hairs about the effect of sexual knowledge on a girl, I am of the opinion that, whether the act was voluntary or involuntary on the girl's part, she was returned to her parents in a damaged, or at least used, condition." Blofeld rarely employed gestures. Now he slowly opened the left hand that lay on the table. He said, in the same even tone of voice, "We are a large and powerful organization. I am not concerned with morals or ethics, but members will be aware that I desire, and most strongly recommend, that SPECTRE shall conduct itself in a superior fashion. There is no discipline in SPECTRE except self-discipline. We are a dedicated fraternity whose strength lies entirely in the strength of each member. Weakness in one member is the deathwatch beetle in the total structure. You are aware of my views in this matter, and on the occasions when cleansing has been necessary you have approved my action. In this case, I have already done what I considered necessary vis-à-vis this girl's family. I have returned half a million dollars with an appropriate note of apology. This despite the matter of the radio transmitter which was a breach of our contract with the family. I dare say they knew nothing of the ruse. It was typical police behavior—a pattern that I was expecting. The dividend for all of us from this operation will be correspondingly reduced. Regarding the culprit, I have satisfied myself that he is guilty. I have decided on the appropriate action."

Blofeld looked down the table. His eyes were fixed on the man standing—on No. 7. The Corsican, Marius Domingue, looked back at him steadily. He knew he was innocent. He knew who was guilty. His body was still with tension. But it was not fear. He had faith, as they all had, in the rightness of Blofeld. He could not understand why he had been singled out as a target for all the eyes that were now upon him, but Blofeld had decided, and Blofeld was always right.

Blofeld noted the man's courage and sensed the reasons for

it. He also observed the sweat shining on the face of No. 12, the man alone at the head of the table. Good! The sweat would improve the contact.

Under the table, Blofeld's right hand came up off his thigh, found the knob, and pulled the switch.

The body of Pierre Borraud, seized in the iron fist of 3000 volts, arced in the armchair as if it had been kicked in the back. The rough mat of black hair rose sharply straight up on his head and remained upright, a gollywog fringe for the contorted, bursting face. The eyes glared wildly and then faded. A blackened tongue slowly protruded between the snarling teeth and remained hideously extended. Thin wisps of smoke rose from under the hands, from the middle of the back, and from under the thighs where the concealed electrodes in the chair had made contact. Blofeld pulled back the switch. The lights in the room that had dimmed to orange, making a dull supernatural glow, brightened to normal. The roasted-meat and burned-fabric smell spread slowly. The body of No. 12 crumpled horribly. There was a sharp crack as the chin hit the edge of the table. It was all over.

Blofeld's soft, even voice broke the silence. He looked down the table at No. 7. He noted that the stanch, impassive stance had not quavered. This was a good man with good nerves. Blofeld said, "Sit down, No. 7. I am satisfied with your conduct." (Satisfaction was Blofeld's highest expression of praise.) "It was necessary to distract the attention of No. 12. He knew that he was under suspicion. There might have been an untidy scene."

Some of the men round the table nodded their understanding. As usual, Blofeld's reasoning made good sense. No one was greatly perturbed or surprised by what he had witnessed. Blofeld always exercised his authority, meted out justice, in full view of the members. There had been two previous occasions of this nature, both at similar meetings and both on security or disciplinary grounds which affected the cohesion, the inner strength, of the whole team. In one, the offender had been shot by Blofeld through the heart with a thick needle fired from a compressed-air pistol—no mean feat at around twelve paces. In the other, the guilty man, who had been seated next to Blofeld on his left hand, had been garroted with a wire noose casually flicked over his head and then, with two swift steps by Blofeld, pulled tight over the back of the man's chair. Those two deaths had been just, necessary. So had this death, the third. Now, the members, ignoring the heap of death at the end of the table, settled in their chairs. It was time to get back to business.

Blofeld snapped shut the gold vinaigrette and slipped it into a waistcoat pocket. "The Corsican section," he said softly, "will put forward recommendations for a replacement for No. 12. But that can wait until after completion of Plan Omega. On this matter, there are certain details to be discussed. Sub-operator G, recruited by the German section, has made an error, a serious error which radically affects our time table. This man, whose membership of the Red Lightning Tong in Macao should have made him expert in conspiracy, was instructed to make his headquarters at a certain clinic in the south of England, an admirable refuge for his purposes. His instructions were to keep intermittent contact with the airman Petacchi at the not-far-distant Boscombe Downs airfield where the bomber squadron is under training. He was to report at intervals on the airman's fitness and morale. His reports have been satisfactory, and the airman, by the way, continues to be willing. But Sub-operator G was also required to post the Letter on D plus One, or three days from now. Unfortunately this foolish man took it upon himself to become embroiled in a hotheaded fashion with some fellow patient at the clinic, as a result of which, and I need not go into details, he is now in Brighton Central Hospital suffering from second-degree burns. He is thus out of action for at least a week. This will involve an irritating but fortunately not a serious delay in Plan Omega. Fresh instructions have been issued. The airman Petacchi has been provided with a phial of influenza virus of sufficient strength for him to remain on the sick list for one week, during which he will be unable to accept his test flight. He will take the first flight after his recovery and alert us accordingly. The date of his flight will be communicated to Sub-operator G and he will by that time be recovered and will post the Letter according to plan. The Special Executive"—Blofeld glanced round the table—"will readjust their flight schedules to Area Zeta in accordance with the new operational schedule. As for

Sub-operator G"—Blofeld bent his gaze, one by one, on the three ex-Gestapo men—"this is an unreliable agent. The German section will make arrangements for his elimination within twenty-four hours of the posting of the Letter. Is that understood?"

The three German faces stood, unanimously to attention, "Yes, sir."

"For the rest," continued Blofeld, "all is in order. No. 1 has solidly established his cover in Area Zeta. The treasure-hunting myth continues to be built up and has already gained full credence. The crew of the yacht, all hand-picked sub-operators, are accepting the discipline and the security regulations better than had been expected. A suitable land base has been secured. It is remote and not easily accessible. It belongs to an eccentric Englishman the nature of whose friends and personal habits demands seclusion. Your arrival in Area Zeta continues to be minutely planned. Your wardrobe awaits you in Areas F and D, according to your various flight plans. This wardrobe, down to the smallest detail, will be in accordance with your identities as financial backers of the treasure hunt who have demanded to visit the scene and take part in the adventure. You are not gullible millionaires. You are the kind of rich, middle-class *rentiers* and businessmen who might be expected to be taken in by such a scheme. You are all shrewd, so you have come to watch over your investment and ensure that not one doubloon goes astray." (Nobody smiled.) "You are all aware of the part you have to play and I trust that you have studied your respective roles with close attention."

There was a careful nodding of heads round the table. These men were all satisfied that not too much had been asked of them in the matter of their cover. This one was a rich café proprietor from Marseilles. (He had been one. He could talk to anyone about the business.) That one had vineyards in Yugoslavia. (He had been brought up in Bled. He could talk vintages and crop sprays with a Calvet from Bordeaux.) That one had smuggled cigarettes from Tangier. (He had done so and would be just sufficiently discreet about it.) All of them had been given covers that would stand up at least to second-degree inspection.

"In the matter of aqualung training," continued Blofeld,

"I would like reports from each section." Blofeld looked at the Yugoslav section on his left.

"Satisfactory." "Satisfactory," echoed the German section, and the word was repeated round the table.

Blofeld commented, "The safety factor is paramount in all underwater operations. Has this factor received sufficient attention in your respective training schedules?" Affirmative. "And exercises with the new CO_2 underwater gun?" Again all sections reported favorably. "And now," continued Blofeld, "I would like a report from the Sicilian section on the preparations for the bullion drop."

Fidelio Sciacca was a gaunt, cadaverous Sicilian with a closed face. He might have been, and had been, a schoolmaster with communist leanings. He spoke for the section because his English, the compulsory language of the Special Executive, was the best. He said, in a careful, expository tone of voice, "The chosen area has been carefully reconnoitered. It is satisfactory. I have here"—he touched the briefcase on his lap—"the plans and detailed time table for the information of the Chairman and members. Briefly, the designated area, Area T, is on the northwest slopes of Mount Etna, above the tree line—that is to say between the altitudes of two thousand and three thousand meters. This is an uninhabited and uncultivated area of black lava on the upper slopes of the volcano more or less above the small town of Bronte. For the purpose of the drop, an area approximately two kilometers square will be marked out by the torches of the recovery team. In the center of this area will be positioned a Decca Aircraft Homing Signal as an additional navigational aid. The bullion flight, which I estimate conservatively will consist of five Mark IV Transport Comets, should make their run in at ten thousand feet at an air speed of three hundred miles per hour. Having regard to the weight of each consignment, multiple parachutes will be needed, and, owing to the harsh nature of the terrain, very careful packing in foam rubber will be essential. The parachutes and the packings should be coated in Dayglo or some phosphorescent paint to assist recovery. No doubt"—the man opened his hands —"the SPECTRE memorandum of dropping instructions will include these and other details, but very careful planning and coordination by those responsible for the flight will be necessary."

"And the recovery team?" Blofeld's voice probed softly but with an urgent edge to it.

"The Capo Mafiosi of the district is my uncle. He has eight grandchildren, to whom he is devoted. I have made it clear that the whereabouts of these children is known to my associates. The man understood. At the same time, as instructed, I made him the offer of one million pounds for total recovery and safe delivery to the depot at Catania. This is a most important sum for the funds of the Unione. The Capo Mafiosi agreed to these terms. He understands that the robbery of a bank is in question. He wishes to know no more. The delay that has been announced will not affect the arrangements. It will still be within the full-moon period. Sub-operator 52 is a most capable man. He has been provided with the Hallicraftor set issued to me for the purpose and he will listen on 18 megacycles in accordance with the schedule. Meanwhile he remains in touch with the Capo Mafiosi, to whom he is related by marriage."

Blofeld was silent for a long two minutes. He slowly nodded. "I am satisfied. So far as the next step is concerned, the disposal of the bullion, this will be in the hands of Sub-operator 201, of whom we have had full experience. He is a man to be trusted. The M.V. *Mercurial* will load at Catania and proceed through the Suez Canal to Goa, in Portuguese India. En route, at a designated cross-bearing in the Arabian Gulf, she will rendezvous with a merchant ship owned by a consortium of the chief Bombay bullion brokers. The bullion will be transferred to this ship in exchange for the equivalent value, at the ruling gold bullion price, in used Swiss francs, dollars, and bolivars. These large amounts of currency will be broken up into the allotted percentages and will then be transferred from Goa by chartered plane to twenty-two different Swiss banks in Zurich, where they will be placed in deposit boxes. The keys to these numbered boxes will be distributed to members after this meeting. From that moment on, and subject of course to the usual security regulations regarding injudicious spending and display, these deposits will be entirely at the disposal of members." Blofeld's slow, calm eyes surveyed the meeting. "Is this procedure considered satisfactory?"

There were cautious nods. No. 18, Kandinsky, the Polish electronics expert, spoke up. He spoke without diffidence. There was no diffidence between these men. "This is not my province," he said seriously. "But is there not danger that one of the navies concerned will intercept this ship, the *Mercurial*, and remove the bullion? It will be clear to the Western powers that the bullion will have to be removed from Sicily. Various patrols of the air and sea would be an easy matter."

"You forget"—Blofeld's voice was patient—"that neither the first, nor if need be the second, bomb will be rendered safe until the money is in the Swiss banks. There will be no risk on that score. Nor, another possibility that I had envisaged, is there likely to be danger of our ship being pirated on the high seas by some independent operator. I envisage that complete secrecy will be enforced by the Western powers. Any leakage would result in panic. Any other questions?"

Bruno Bayer, one of the German Section, said stiffly, "It is fully understood that No. 1 will be in immediate control in Area Zeta. Is it correct that he will have full powers delegated by yourself? Is it that he will, so to speak, be Supreme Commander in the field?"

How typical, thought Blofeld. The Germans will always obey orders, but they wish to be quite clear where final authority resides. The German generals would only obey the Supreme Command if they knew Hitler approved the Supreme Command. He said firmly, "I have made it clear to the Special Executive, and I repeat: No. 1 is already, by your unanimous vote, my successor in case of my death or incapacity. So far as Plan Omega is concerned, he is deputy Supreme Commander of SPECTRE, and since I shall remain at Headquarters to keep watch over reactions to the Letter, No. 1 will be Supreme Commander in the field. His orders will be obeyed as if they were my own. I hope we are fully agreed in this matter." Blofeld's eyes, sharply focused, swept the meeting. Everyone signified his agreement.

"So," said Blofeld. "Then the meeting is now closed. I will instruct the disposal squad to take care of the remains of No. 12. No. 18, please connect me with No. 1 on 20 megacycles. That waveband will have been unoccupied by the French Post Office since eight o'clock."

Bond said cheerfully, "I know, May. You're quite right. But at least I've got them down to ten a day."

"I'm not talking about yer wee bitty smoke. I'm talking 'bout this"—May gestured at the tray—"this pap." The word was spat out with disdain. Having got this off her chest, May gathered steam. "It's no recht for a man to be eating bairns' food and slops and suchlike. Ye needn't worry that I'll talk, Mister James, but I'm knowing more about yer life than mebbe ye were wishing I did. There's been times when they're brought ye home from hospital and there's talk you've been in a motoring accident or some such. But I'm not the old fule ye think I am, Mister James. Motoring accidents don't make one small hole in yer shoulder or yer leg or somewhere. Why, ye've got scars on ye the noo—ach, ye needn't grin like that, I've seen them—that could only be made by buellets. And these guns and knives and things ye carry around when ye're off abroad. Ach!" May put her hands on her hips. Her eyes were bright and defiant. "Ye can tell me to mind my ain business and pack me off back to Glen Orchy, but before I go I'm telling ye, Mister James, that if ye get yerself into anuither fight and ye've got nothing but yon muck in yer stomach, they'll be bringing ye home in a hearse. That's what they'll be doing."

In the old days, James Bond would have told May to go to hell and leave him in peace. Now, with infinite patience and good humor, he gave May a quick run through the basic tenets of "live" as against "dead" foods. "You see, May," he said reasonably, "all these denaturized foods—white flour, white sugar, white rice, white salts, whites of egg—these are dead foods. Either they're dead anyway like whites of egg or they've had all the nourishment refined out of them. They're slow poisons, like fried foods and cakes and coffee and heaven knows how many of the things I used to eat. And anyway, look how wonderfully well I am. I feel absolutely a new man since I took to eating the right things and gave up drink and so on. I sleep twice as well. I've got twice as much energy. No headaches. No muscle pains. No hangovers. Why, a month ago there wasn't a week went by but that on at least one day I couldn't eat anything for breakfast but a couple of aspirins and a prairie oyster. And you know quite well that that used to make you cluck and tut-tut all over the place like an old hen.

Well"—Bond raised his eyebrows amiably—"what about that?"

May was defeated. She picked up the tray and, with a stiff back, made for the door. She paused on the threshold and turned round. Her eyes were bright with angry tears. "Well, all I can say is, Mr. James, that mebbe ye're right and mebbe ye're wrong. What worries the life out of me is that ye're not yersel' any more." She went out and banged the door.

Bond sighed and picked up the paper. He said the magical words that all men say when a middle-aged woman makes a temperamental scene, "change of life," and went back to reading about the latest reasons for not having a Summit meeting.

The telephone, the red one that was the direct line with Headquarters, gave its loud, distinctive jangle. Bond kept his eyes on the page and reached out a hand. With the Cold War easing off, it was not like the old days. This would be nothing exciting. Probably canceling his shoot at Bisley that afternoon with the new F.N. rifle.

"Bond speaking."

It was the Chief of Staff. Bond dropped his paper on the floor. He pressed the receiver to his ear, trying, as in the old days, to read behind the words.

"At once please, James. M."

"Something for me?"

"Something for everyone. Crash dive, and ultra hush. If you've got any dates for the next few weeks, better cancel them. You'll be off tonight. See you." The line went dead.

Bond had the most selfish car in England. It was a Mark II Continental Bentley that some rich idiot had married to a telegraph pole on the Great West Road. Bond had bought the bits for £1500 and Rolls had straightened the bend in the chassis and fitted new clockwork—the Mark IV engine with 9.5 compression. Then Bond had gone to Mulliners with £3000, which was half his total capital, and they had sawn off the old cramped sports saloon body and had fitted a trim, rather square convertible two-seater affair, power-operated, with only two large armed bucket seats in black leather. The rest of the blunt end was all knife-edged, rather ugly, trunk. The car was painted in rough, not gloss, battleship gray and the upholstery was black morocco. She went like a bird and a bomb and Bond loved her more than all the women at present in his life rolled, if that were feasible, together.

But Bond refused to be owned by any car. A car, however splendid, was a means of locomotion (he called the Continental "the locomotive" . . . "I'll pick you up in my locomotive") and it must at all times be ready to locomote—no garage doors to break one's nails on, no pampering with mechanics except for the quick monthly service. The locomotive slept out of doors in front of his flat and was required to start immediately, in all weathers, and after that, stay on the road.

The twin exhausts—Bond had demanded two-inch pipes; he hadn't liked the old soft flutter of the marque—growled solidly as the long gray nose topped by a big octagonal silver bolt instead of the winged B, swerved out of the little Chelsea square and into King's Road. It was nine o'clock, too early for the bad traffic, and Bond pushed the car fast up Sloane Street and into the park. It would also be too early for the traffic police, so he did some fancy driving that brought him to the Marble Arch exit in three minutes flat. Then there came the slow round-the-houses into Baker Street and so into Regents Park. Within ten minutes of getting the Hurry call he was going up in the lift of the big square building to the eighth and top floor.

Already, as he strode down the carpeted corridor, he smelled emergency. On this floor, besides M's offices, was housed Communications, and from behind the gray closed doors there came a steady zing and crackle from the banks of transmitters and a continuous machine-gun rattle and clack from the cipher machines. It crossed Bond's mind that a General Call was going out. What the hell had happened?

The Chief of Staff was standing over Miss Moneypenny. He was handing her signals from a large sheaf and giving her routing instructions. "CIA Washington, Personal for Dulles. Cipher Triple X by Teleprinter. Mathis. Deuxième Bureau. Same prefix and route. Station F for Head of NATO Intelligence. Personal. Standard route through Head of Section. This one by Safe Hand to Head of M.I.5, Personal, copy to Commissioner of Police, Personal, and these"—he handed over a thick batch—"Personal to Heads of Stations from M. Cipher Double

X by Whitehall Radio and Portishead. All right? Clear them
as quick as you can, there's a good girl. There'll be more
coming. We're in for a bad day."

Miss Moneypenny smiled cheerfully. She liked what she
called the shot-and-shell days. It reminded her of when she had
started in the Service as a junior in the Cipher Department. She
leaned over and pressed the switch on the intercom. "007's
here, sir." She looked up at Bond. "You're off." The Chief of
Staff grinned and said, "Fasten your lap-strap." The red light
went on above M's door. Bond walked through.

Here it was entirely peaceful. M sat relaxed, sideways to
his desk, looking out of the broad window at the distant glittering fretwork of London's skyline. He glanced up. "Sit down,
007. Have a look at these." He reached out and slid some
foolscap-sized photostats across the desk. "Take your time."
He picked up his pipe and began to fill it, absent-minded fingers
dipping into the shell-base tobacco jar at his elbow.

Bond picked up the top photostat. It showed the front and
back of an addressed envelope, dusted for fingerprints, which
were all over its surface.

M glanced sideways. "Smoke if you like."

Bond said, "Thanks, sir. I'm trying to give it up."

M said, "Humpf," put his pipe in his mouth, struck a match,
and inhaled a deep lungful of smoke. He settled himself deeper
in his chair. The gray sailor's eyes gazed through the window
introspectively, seeing nothing.

The envelope, prefixed "PERSONAL AND MOST IMMEDIATE,"
was addressed to the Prime Minister, by name, at No. 10,
Downing Street, Whitehall, London, SW1. Every detail of the
address was correct down to the final "P.C." to denote that the
Prime Minister was a Privy Councillor. The punctuation was
meticulous. The stamp was postmarked Brighton, 8:30 a.m.
on June 3. It crossed Bond's mind that the letter might therefore
have been posted under cover of night and that it would probably have been delivered some time in the early afternoon of
the same day, yesterday. A typewriter with a bold, rather elegant type had been used. This fact, together with the generous
5-by-7½-inch envelope and the spacing and style of the address, gave a solid, businesslike impression. The back of the

envelope showed nothing but fingerprints. There was no sealing wax.

The letter, equally correct and well laid out, ran as follows:

Mr. Prime Minister,

You should be aware, or you will be if you communicate with the Chief of the Air Staff, that, since approximately 10 p.m. yesterday, 2nd June, a British aircraft carrying two atomic weapons is overdue on a training flight. The aircraft is Villiers Vindicator O/NBR from No. 5 R.A.F. Experimental Squadron based at Boscombe Down. The Ministry of Supply Identification Numbers on the atomic weapons are MOS/bd/654/Mk V. and MOS/bd/655/Mk V. There are also U.S.A.F. Identification Numbers in such profusion and of such prolixity that I will not weary you with them.

This aircraft was on a NATO training flight with a crew of five and one observer. It carried sufficient fuel for ten hours' flying at 600 m.p.h. at a mean altitude of 40,000 feet.

This aircraft, together with the two atomic weapons, is now in the possession of this organization. The crew and the observer are deceased and you have our authority to inform the next-of-kin accordingly, thus assisting you in preserving, on the grounds that the aircraft has crashed, the degree of secrecy you will no doubt wish to maintain and which will be equally agreeable to ourselves.

The whereabouts of this aircraft and of the two atomic weapons, rendering them possible of recovery, will be communicated to you in exchange for the equivalent of £100,000,000 in gold bullion, one thousand, or not less than nine hundred and ninety-nine, fine. Instructions for the delivery of the gold are contained in the attached memorandum. A further condition is that the recovery and disposal of the gold will not be hampered and that a free pardon, under your personal signature and that of the President of the United States, will be issued in the name of this organization and all its members.

Failure to accept these conditions within seven days from 5 p.m. G.M.T. on June 3rd, 1959—i.e. not later than 5 p.m. G.M.T. on June 10th, 1959—will have the following consequences. Immediately after that date a piece of property belonging to the Western Powers, valued at not less than the aforesaid £100,000,000, will be destroyed. There will be loss of life. If, within 48 hours after this warning, willingness to accept our terms is still not communicated, there will ensue, without further warning, the destruction of a major city situated in an undesignated country of the world. There will be very great loss of life. Moreover, between the two occurrences, this organization will reserve to itself the right to communicate to the world the 48-hour time limit. This measure, which will cause widespread panic in every major city, will be designed to hasten your hand.

This, Mr. Prime Minister, is a single and final communication. We shall await your reply, every hour on the hour G.M.T., on the 16-megacycle waveband.

Signed
S.P.E.C.T.R.E.
(The Special Executive for Counterintelligence, Terrorism, Revenge, and Extortion)

James Bond read through the letter again and put it carefully down on the desk in front of him. He then turned to the second page, a detailed memorandum for the delivery of the gold. "Northwestern slopes of Mount Etna in Sicily...Decca Navigational Aid transmitting on...Full moon period...between midnight and 0100 G.M.T....individual quarter-ton consignments packed in one-foot-thick foam rubber...minimum of three parachutes per consignment...nature of planes and flight schedule to be communicated on the 16-megacycle waveband not later than 24 hours before the operation...Any countermeasures initiated will be considered a breach of contract and will result in the detonation of Atomic Weapon No. 1 or No. 2 as the case may be." The typed signature was the same. Both pages had one last line: "Copy to the President of the United States of America, by Registered Airmail, posted simultaneously."

Bond laid the photostat quietly down on top of the others. He reached into his hip pocket for the gunmetal cigarette case that now contained only nine cigarettes, took one, and lit it, drawing the smoke deep down into his lungs and letting it out with a long, reflective hiss.

M swiveled his chair round so they were facing each other. "Well?"

Bond noticed that M's eyes, three weeks before so clear and vital, were now bloodshot and strained. No wonder! He said, "If this plane, and the weapons, really are missing, I think it stands up, sir. I think they mean it. I think it's a true bill."

M said, "So does the War Cabinet. So do I." He paused. "Yes, the plane with the bombs is missing. And the stock numbers on the bombs are correct."

CHAPTER 8

"Big Fleas Have Little Fleas..."

Bond said, "What is there to go on, sir?"

"Damned little, practically speaking nothing. Nobody's ever heard of these SPECTRE people. We know there's some kind of independent unit working in Europe—we've bought some stuff from them, so have the Americans, and Mathis admits now that Goltz, the French heavy-water scientist who went over last year, was assassinated by them, for big money, as a result of an offer he got out of the blue. No names were mentioned. It was all done on the radio, the same 16 megacycles that's mentioned in the letter. To the Deuxième Communications section. Mathis accepted on the off-chance. They did a neat job. Mathis paid up—a suitcase full of money left at the Michelin road sign on N1. But no one can tie them in with these SPECTRE people. When we and the Americans dealt, there were endless cutouts, really professional ones, and anyway we were more interested in the end product than the people involved. We both paid a lot of money, but it was worth it. If it's the same group working this, they're a serious outfit and I've told the P.M. so. But that's not the point. The plane is missing and the two bombs, just as the letter says. All details exactly correct. The Vindicator was on a NATO training flight south of Ireland and out into the Atlantic." M reached for a bulky folder and turned over some pages. He found what he wanted. "Yes, it was to be a six-hour flight leaving Boscombe Down at eight

p.m. and due back at two a.m. There was an R.A.F. crew of
five and a NATO observer, an Italian, man called Petacchi,
Giuseppe Petacchi, squadron leader in the Italian Air Force,
seconded to NATO. Fine flyer, apparently, but they're checking
on his background now. He was sent over here on a normal
tour of duty. The top pilots from NATO have been coming over
for months to get used to the Vindicator and the bomb-release
routines. This plane's apparently going to be used for the NATO
long-range striking force. Anyway"—M turned over a page—
"the plane was watched on the screen as usual and all went
well until it was west of Ireland at about forty thousand feet.
Then, contrary to the drill, it came down to around thirty
thousand and got lost in the transatlantic air traffic. Bomber
Command tried to get in touch, but the radio couldn't or
wouldn't answer. The immediate reaction was that the Vindicator had hit one of the transatlantic planes and there was
something of a panic. But none of the companies reported any
trouble or even a sighting." M looked across at Bond. "And
that was the end of it. The plane just vanished."

Bond said, "Did the American DEW line pick it up—their
Defense Early Warning system?"

"There's a query on that. The only grain of evidence we've
got. Apparently about five hundred miles east of Boston there
was some evidence that a plane had peeled off the inward route
to Idlewild and turned south. But that's another big traffic
lane—for the northern traffic from Montreal and Gander down
to Bermuda and the Bahamas and South America. So these
DEW operators just put it down as a B.O.A.C. or Trans-Canada
plane."

It certainly sounds as if they've got the whole thing worked
out pretty well, hiding in these traffic lanes. Could the plane
have turned northwards in the middle of the Atlantic and made
for Russia?"

"Yes, or southwards. There's a big block of space about
five hundred miles out from both shores that's out of radar
range. Better still, it could have turned on its tracks and come
back to Europe on any of two or three air lanes. In fact it could
be almost anywhere in the world by now. That's the point."

"But it's a huge plane. It must need special runways and
so on. It must have come down somewhere. You can't hide
a plane of that size."

"Just so. All these things are obvious. By midnight last night the R.A.F. had checked with every single airport, every one in the world that could have taken it. Negative. But the C.A.S. says of course it could be crash-landed in the Sahara, for instance, or on some other desert, or in the sea, in shallow water."

"Wouldn't that explode the bombs?"

"No. They're absolutely safe until they're armed. Apparently even a direct drop, like that one from the B-47 over North Carolina in 1958, would only explode the T.N.T trigger to the thing. Not the plutonium."

"How are these SPECTRE people going to explode them, then?"

M spread his hands. "They explained all this at the War Cabinet meeting. I don't understand it all, but apparently an atomic bomb looks just like any other bomb. The way it works is that the nose is full of ordinary T.N.T. with the plutonium in the tail. Between the two there's a hole into which you screw some sort of a detonator, a kind of plug. When the bomb hits, the T.N.T ignites the detonator and the detonator sets off the plutonium."

"So these people would have to drop the bomb to set it off?"

"Apparently not. They would need a man with good physics knowledge who understood the thing, but then all he'd have to do would be to unscrew the nose cone on the bomb—the ordinary detonator that sets off the T.N.T.—and fix on some kind of time fuse that would ignite the T.N.T. without it being dropped. That would set the thing off. And it's not a very bulky affair. You could get the whole thing into something only about twice the size of a big golf bag. Very heavy, of course. But you could put it into the back of a big car, for instance, and just run the car into a town and leave it parked with the time fuse switched on. Give yourself a couple of hours' start to get out of range—at least a hundred miles away—and that would be that."

Bond reached in his pocket for another cigarette. It couldn't be, yet it was so. Just what his Service and all the other intelligence services in the world had been expecting to happen. The anonymous little man in the raincoat with a heavy suitcase—or golf bag, if you like. The left luggage office, the parked car, the clump of bushes in a park in the center of a big town. And there was no answer to it. In a few years' time, if the experts were right, there would be even less answer to it. Every tin-pot little nation would be making atomic bombs in their backyards, so to speak. Apparently there was no secret now about the things. It had only been the prototypes that had been difficult—like the first gunpowder weapons for instance, or machine guns or tanks. Today these were everybody's bows and arrows. Tomorrow, or the day after, the bows and arrows would be atomic bombs. And this was the first blackmail case. Unless SPECTRE was stopped, the word would get round and soon every criminal scientist with a chemical set and some scrap iron would be doing it. If they couldn't be stopped in time there would be nothing for it but to pay up. Bond said so.

"That's about it," commented M. "From every point of view, including politics, not that they matter all that much. But neither the P.M. nor the President would last five minutes if anything went wrong. But whether we pay or don't pay, the consequences will be endless—and all bad. That's why absolutely everything has got to be done to find these people and the plane and stop the thing in time. The P.M. and the President are entirely agreed. Every intelligence man all over the world who's on our side is being put on to this operation—Operation *Thunderball* they're calling it. Planes, ships, submarines—and of course money's no object. We can have everything, whenever we want it. The Cabinet have already set up a special staff and a war room. Every scrap of information will be fed into it. The Americans have done the same. Some kind of a leak can't be helped. It's being put about that all the panic, and it is panic, is because of the loss of the Vindicator—bombs included, whatever fuss that may cause politically. Only the letter will be absolutely secret. All the usual detective work—fingerprints, Brighton, writing paper—these'll be looked after by Scotland Yard with the F.B.I., Interpol, and all the NATO intelligence organizations, helping where they can. Only a segment of the paper and the typing will be used—a few innocent words. This will all be quite separate from the search for the plane. That'll be handled as a top espionage matter. No one should be able to connect the two investigations. M.I.5 will handle the background to all the crew members and the Italian observer. That will be a natural part of the search for the plane.

As for the Service, we've teamed up with the C.I.A. to cover the world. Allen Dulles is putting every man he's got onto it and so am I. Just sent out a General Call. Now all we can do is sit back and wait."

Bond lit another cigarette, his sinful third in one hour. He said, putting unconcern into his voice, "Where do I come in, sir?"

M looked vaguely at Bond, as if seeing him for the first time. Then he swiveled his chair and gazed again through the window at nothing. Finally he said, in a conversational tone of voice, "I have committed a breach of faith with the P.M. in telling you all this, 007. I was under oath to tell no one what I have just told you. I decided to do what I have done because I have an idea, a hunch, and I wish this idea to be pursued by a"—he hesitated—"by a reliable man. It seemed to me that the only grain of possible evidence in this case was the DEW radar plot, a doubtful one I admit, of the plane that left the east-west air channel over the Atlantic and turned south towards Bermuda and the Bahamas. I decided to accept this evidence, although it has not aroused much interest elsewhere. I then spent some time studying a map and charts of the Western Atlantic and I endeavored to put myself in the minds of SPECTRE—or rather, for there is certainly a master mind behind all this, in the mind of the chief of SPECTRE: my opposite number, so to speak. And I came to certain conclusions. I decided that a favorable target for Bomb No. 1, and for Bomb No. 2, if it comes to that, would be in America rather than in Europe. To begin with, the Americans are more bomb-conscious than we in Europe and therefore more susceptible to persuasion if it came to using Bomb No. 2. Installation worth more than £100,000,000, and thus targets for Bomb No. 1, are more numerous in America than in Europe, and finally, guessing that SPECTRE is a European organization, from the style of the letter and from the paper, which is Dutch by the way, and also from the ruthlessness of the plot, it seemed to me at least possible that an American rather than a European target might have been chosen. Anyway, going on these assumptions, and assuming that the plane could not have landed in America itself or off American shores—the coastal radar network is too good—I looked for a neighboring area which might be suitable. And"—M glanced round at Bond and away again—"I decided on the Bahamas, the group of islands, many of them uninhabited, surrounded mostly by shoal water over sand and possessing only one simple radar station—and that one concerned only with civilian air traffic and manned by local civilian personnel. South, towards Cuba, Jamaica, and the Caribbean, offers no worthwhile targets. Anyway it is too far from the American coastline. Northwards towards Bermuda has the same disadvantages. But the nearest of the Bahama group is only two hundred miles—only six or seven hours in a fast motorboat or yacht—from the American coastline."

Bond interrupted. "If you're right, sir, why didn't SPECTRE send their letter to the President instead of the P.M.?"

"For the sake of obscurity. To make us do what we are doing—hunting all round the world instead of only in one part of it. And for maximum impact. SPECTRE would realize that the arrival of the letter right on top of the loss of the bomber would hit us in the solar plexus. It might, they would reason, even shake the money out of us without any further effort. The next stage of their operation, attacking target No. 1, is going to be a nasty business for them. It's going to expose their whereabouts to a considerable extent. They'd like to collect the money and close the operation as quickly as possible. That's what we've got to gamble on. We've got to push them as close to the use of No. 1 bomb as we dare in the hope that something will betray them in the next six and three-quarter days. It's a slim chance. I'm pinning my hopes on my guess"—M swung his chair round to the desk—"and on you. Well?" He looked hard at Bond. "Any comments? If not, you'd better get started. You're booked on all New York planes from now until midnight. Then on by B.O.A.C. I thought of using an R.A.F. Canberra, but I don't want your arrival to make any noise. You're a rich young man looking for some property in the islands. That'll give you an excuse to do as much prospecting as you want. Well?"

"All right, sir." Bond got to his feet. "I'd rather have had somewhere more interesting—the Iron Curtain beat, for instance. I can't help feeling this is a bigger operation than a small unit could take on. For my money this looks more like a Russian job. They get the experimental plane and the bombs—they obviously want them—and throw dust in our eyes with all this SPECTRE ballyhoo. If SMERSH was still in business, I'd say they'd got a finger in it somewhere. Just their style. But the Eastern Stations may pick up something on that if there's anything in the idea. Anything else, sir? Who do I cooperate with in Nassau?"

"The Governor knows you're coming. They've got a well-trained police force. C.I.A. are sending down a good man, I gather. With a communications outfit. They've got more of that sort of machinery than we have. Take a cipher machine with the Triple X setting. I want to hear every single detail you turn up. Personal to me. Right?"

"Right, sir." Bond went to the door and let himself out. There was nothing more to be said. This looked like the biggest job the Service had ever been given, and in Bond's opinion, for he didn't give much for M's guess, he had been relegated to the back row of the chorus. So be it. He would get himself a good sunburn and watch the show from the wings.

When Bond walked out of the building, carrying the neat leather cipher case, an expensive movie camera perhaps, slung over his shoulder, the man in the beige Volkswagen stopped scratching the burn-scab under his shirt, loosened, for the tenth time, the long-barrelled .45 in the holster under his arm, started the car, and put it in gear. He was twenty yards behind Bond's parked Bentley. He had no idea what the big building was. He had simply obtained Bond's home address from the receptionist at Shrublands and, as soon as he got out of the Brighton hospital, he had carefully tailed Bond. The car was hired, under an assumed name. When he had done what had to be done he would go straight to London Airport and take the first plane out to any country on the Continent. Count Lippe was a sanguine individual. The job, the private score he had to settle, presented no problem to him. He was a ruthless, vengeful man and he had eliminated many obstreperous and perhaps dangerous people in his life. He reasoned that, if they ever came to hear of this, SPECTRE would not object. The overheard telephone conversation on that first day at the clinic showed that his cover had been broached, however slightly, and it was just conceivable that he could be traced through his membership in the Red Lightning Tong. From there to SPECTRE was a long step, but Sub-operator G knew that once a cover began to run, it ran like an old sock. Apart from that, this man must be paid off. Count Lippe had to be quits with him.

Bond was getting into his car. He had slammed the door. Sub-operator G watched the blue smoke curl from the twin exhausts. He got moving.

On the other side of the road, and a hundred yards behind the Volkswagen SPECTRE No. 6 slipped his goggles down over his eyes, stamped the 500-c.c. Triumph into gear, and accelerated down the road. He swerved neatly through the traffic— he had been a test rider for D.K.W. at one time in his postwar career—and stationed himself ten yards behind the off rear wheel of the Volkswagen and just out of the driver's line of vision in the windscreen mirror. He had no idea why Sub-operator G was following the Bentley, nor whom the Bentley belonged to. His job was to kill the driver of the Volkswagen. He put his hand into the leather satchel he carried slung over his shoulder, took out the heavy grenade—it was twice the normal military size—and watched the traffic ahead for the right pattern to allow his getaway.

Sub-operator G was watching for a similar pattern. He also noted the spacing on the lampposts on the pavement in case he might be blocked and have to run off the road. Now the cars ahead were sparse. He stamped his foot into the floor and, driving with his left hand, drew out the Colt with his right. Now he was up with the Bentley's rear bumper. Now he was alongside. The dark profile was a sitting target. With a last quick glance ahead, he raised the gun.

It was the cheeky iron rattle of the Volkswagen's air-cooled engine that made Bond turn his head, and it was this minute reduction of the target area that saved his jaw. If he had then accelerated, the second bullet would have got him, but some blessed instinct made his foot stamp the brake at the same time as his head ducked so swiftly that his chin hit the horn button, nearly knocking him out. Almost simultaneously, instead of a third shot, there came the roar of an explosion and the remains of his windshield, already shattered, cascaded around him. The Bentley had stopped, the engine stalled. Brakes screamed. There were shouts and the panicky screams of horns. Bond shook his head and cautiously raised it. The Volkswagen, one wheel still spinning lay on its side in front and broadside to the Bentley. Most of the roof had been blown off. Inside, and half sprawling into the road, was a horrible, glinting mess. Flames were licking at the blistered paintwork. People were gathering. Bond pulled himself together and got quickly out of his car. He shouted, "Stand back. The petrol tank'll go." Almost as he said the words there came a dull boom and a cloud of black smoke. The flames spurted. In the distance, sirens sounded. Bond edged through the people and strode quickly back toward his headquarters, his thoughts racing.

The inquiry made Bond lose two planes to New York. By the time the police had put out the fire and had transported the bits of man and the bits of machinery and bomb casing to the morgue it was quite clear that they would have nothing to go on but the shoes, the number on the gun, some fibers and shreds of clothing, and the car. The car-hire people remembered nothing but a man with dark glasses, a driver's license in the name of Johnston, and a handful of fivers. The car had been hired three days before for one week. Plenty of people remembered the motorcyclist, but it seemed that he had no rear number plate. He had gone like a bat out of hell toward Baker Street. He wore goggles. Medium build. Nothing else.

Bond had not been able to help. He had seen nothing of the Volkswagen driver. The roof of the Volkswagen had been too low. There had only been a hand and the glitter of a gun.

The Secret Service asked for a copy of the police report and M instructed that this should be sent to the Thunderball war room. He saw Bond briefly again, rather impatiently, as if it had all been Bond's fault. Then he told Bond to forget about it—it was probably something to do with one of his past cases. A hangover of some kind. The police would get to the bottom of it in time. The main thing was operation Thunderball. Bond had better get a move on.

By the time Bond left the building for the second time, it had begun to rain. One of the mechanics from the car pool at the back of the building had done what he could, knocking out the remains of the Bentley's windscreen and cleaning the bits out of the car, but when he got home at lunch time Bond was soaked to the skin. He left the car in a nearby garage, telephoned

Rolls and his insurance company (he had got too close to a lorry carrying steel lengths, for reinforced concrete presumably. No, he had not got the lorry's number. Sorry, but you know how it is when these things happen all of a sudden), and then went home and had a bath and changed into his dark blue tropical worsted. He packed carefully—one large suitcase and a hold-all for his underwater swimming gear—and went through to the kitchen.

May was looking rather contrite. It seemed as if she might make another speech. Bond held up his hand. "Don't tell me, May. You were right. I can't do my work on carrot juice. I've got to be off in an hour and I need some proper food. Be an angel and make me your kind of scrambled eggs—four eggs. Four rashers of that American hickory-smoked bacon if we've got any left, hot buttered toast—your kind, not whole-meal—and a big pot of coffee, double strength. And bring in the drink tray."

May looked at him, relieved but aghast. "Whatever happened, Mr. James?"

Bond laughed at the expression on her face. "Nothing, May. It just occurred to me that life's too short. Plenty of time to watch the calories when one gets to heaven."

Bond left May tut-tutting at this profanity, and went off to look to his armament.

CHAPTER 9

Multiple Requiem

So far as SPECTRE was concerned, Plan Omega had gone exactly as Blofeld had known it would and Phases I to III to their entirety had been completed on schedule and without a hitch.

Giuseppe Petacchi, the late Giuseppe Petacchi, had been well chosen. At the age of eighteen he had been co-pilot of a Focke-wulf 200 from the Adriatic anti-submarine patrol, one of the few hand-picked Italian airmen who had been allowed to handle these German planes. The group was issued with the latest German pressure mines charged with the new Hexogen explosive just when the tide had turned in the Allied battle up the spine of Italy. Petacchi had known where his destiny lay and had gone into business for himself. On a routine patrol, he had shot the pilot and the navigator, very carefully, with one .38 bullet in the back of the head for each of them, and had brought the big plane skimming in, just above the waves to avoid the antiaircraft fire, to the harbor of Bari. Then he had hung his shirt out of the cockpit as a token of surrender and had waited for the R.A.F. launch. He had been decorated by the English and the Americans for this exploit and had been awarded £10,000 from special funds for his presentation to the Allies of the pressure mine. He had told a highly colored story to the Intelligence people of having been a one-man resistance ever since he had been old enough to join the Italian Air Force, and he emerged at the end of the war as one of Italy's most gallant resistance heroes. From then on life had been easy—pilot and later captain in Alitalia when it got going again, and then back into the new Italian Air Force as colonel. His secondment to NATO followed and then his appointment as one of the six Italians chosen for the Advance Striking Force. But he was now thirty-four, and it occurred to him that he had had just about enough of flying. He especially did not care for the idea of being part of the spearhead of NATO defenses. It was time for younger men to provide the heroics. And all his life he had had a passion for owning things—flashy, exciting, expensive things. He had most of what he desired—a couple of gold cigarette cases, a solid gold Rolex Oyster Perpetual Chronometer on a flexible gold bracelet, a white convertible Lancia Gran Turismo, plenty of sharp clothes, and all the girls he wanted (he had once been briefly married but it had not been a success). Now he desired, and what he desired he often got, a particular Ghia-bodied 3500 G.T. Maserati he had seen at the Milan motor show. He also wanted Out—out of the pale green corridors of NATO, out of the Air Force, and, therefore, off to new worlds with a new name. Rio de Janeiro sounded just right. But all this meant a new passport, plenty of money, and "organismo"—the vital "organismo."

The organismo turned up, and turned up bearing just those gifts that Petacchi lusted for. It came in the shape of an Italian named Fonda who was at that time No. 4 in SPECTRE and who had been casing the personnel of NATO, via Versailles and Paris night clubs and restaurants, for just such a man. It had taken one whole very careful month to prepare the bait and inch it forward toward the fish and, when it was finally presented, No. 4 had been almost put off by the greed with which it had been gobbled. There was delay while the possibility of a double-cross was probed by SPECTRE, but finally all the lights were green and the full proposition was laid out for inspection. Petacchi was to get on the Vindicator training course and highjack the plane. (There was no mention of atomic weapons. This was a Cuban revolutionary group who wanted to call attention to its existence and aims by a dramatic piece of self-advertisement. Petacchi closed his ears to this specious tale. He didn't mind in the least who wanted the plane so long as he was paid.) In exchange, Petacchi would receive $1,000,000, a new passport in any name and nationality he chose, and immediate onward passage from the point of delivery to Rio de Janeiro. Many details were discussed and perfected, and when, at eight o'clock in the evening of that June 2nd, the Vindicator screamed off down the runway and out over St. Alban's Head, Petacchi was tense but confident.

For the training flights, a couple of ordinary civil aircraft seats had been fixed inside the roomy fuselage just back of the large cockpit, and Petacchi sat quietly for a whole hour and watched the five men at work at the crowded dials and instruments. When it came his turn to fly the plane he was quite satisfied that he could dispense with all five of them. Once he had set George, there would be nothing to do but stay awake and make certain from time to time that he was keeping exactly at 32,000 feet, just above the transatlantic air channel. There would be a tricky moment when he turned off the east-west channel on to the North-South for the Bahamas, but this had all been worked out for him and every move he would have to make was written down in the notebook in his breast pocket. The landing was going to need very steady nerves, but for $1,000,000 the steady nerves would be summoned.

For the tenth time Petacchi consulted the Rolex. Now! He verified and tested the oxygen mask in the bulkhead beside him and laid it down ready. Next he took the little red-ringed cylinder out of his pocket and remembered exactly how many turns to give the release valve. Then he put it back in his pocket and went through into the cockpit.

"Hullo, Seppy. Enjoying the flight?" The pilot liked the Italian. They had gone out together on one or two majestic thrashes in Bournemouth.

"Sure, sure." Petacchi asked some questions, verified the course set on George, checked the air speed and altitude. Now everyone in the cockpit was relaxed, almost drowsy. Five more hours to go. Rather a bind missing *North by Northwest* at the Odeon. But one would catch up with it at Southampton. Petacchi stood with his back to the metal map rack that held the log and the charts. His right hand went to his pocket, felt for the release valve, and gave it three complete turns. He eased the cylinder out of his pocket and slipped it behind him and down behind the books.

Petacchi stretched and yawned. "Is time for a zizz," he said amiably. He had got the slang phrase pat. It rolled easily off his tongue.

The navigator laughed. "What do they call it in Italian—Zizzo?"

Petacchi grinned cheerfully. He went through the open hatch, got back to his chair, clamped on his oxygen mask, and turned the control regulator to 100 per cent oxygen to cut out the air bleed. Then he made himself comfortable and watched.

They had said it would take under five minutes. Sure enough, in about two minutes, the man nearest to the map rack, the navigator, suddenly clutched his throat and fell forward, gargling horribly. The radio operator dropped his earphones and started forward, but with his second step he was down on his knees. He lurched sideways and collapsed. Now the three other men began to fight for air, briefly, terribly. The co-pilot and the flight engineer writhed off their stools together. They clawed vaguely at each other and then fell back, spread-eagled. The pilot groped up toward the microphone above his head, said something indistinctly, got half to his feet, turned slowly so that his bulging eyes, already dead, seemed to stare through the hatchway into Petacchi's, and then thudded down on top of the body of his co-pilot.

Petacchi glanced at his watch. Four minutes flat. Give them one more minute. When the minute was up, he took rubber gloves out of his pocket, put them on, and, pressing the oxygen mask tight against his face and trailing the flexible tube behind him, went forward, reached down into the map rack, and closed the valve on the cylinder of cyanide. He verified George and adjusted the cabin pressurization to help clear the poison gas. He then went back to his seat to wait for fifteen minutes.

They had said fifteen would be enough, but at the last moment he gave it another ten and then, still with his oxygen mask on, he went forward again and began slowly, for the oxygen made him rather breathless, to pull the bodies back into the fuselage. When the cockpit was clear, he took a small phial of crystals out of his trousers pocket, took out the cork, and sprinkled the cabin floor with them. He went down on his knees and watched the crystals. They kept their white color. He eased his oxygen mask away and took a small cautious sniff. There was no smell. But still, when he took over the controls and began easing the plane down to 32,000 and then slightly north-west-by-west to get into the traffic lane, he kept the mask on.

The giant plane whispered on into the night. The cockpit, bright with the yellow eyes of the dials, was quiet and warm. In the deafening silence in the cockpit of a big jet in flight there was only the faint buzz of an invector. As he verified the dials, the click of each switch seemed as loud as a small-caliber pistol shot.

Petacchi again checked George with the gyro and verified each fuel tank to see that they were all feeding evenly. One tank pump needed adjustment. The jet-pipe temperatures were not overheating.

Satisfied, Petacchi settled himself comfortably in the pilot's seat and swallowed a benzedrine tablet and thought about the future. One of the headphones scattered on the floor of the cockpit began to chirrup loudly. Petacchi glanced at his watch. Of course! Boscombe Air Traffic Control was trying to raise the Vindicator. He had missed the third of the half-hourly calls. How long would Air Control wait before alerting Air Sea Rescue, Bomber Command, and the Air Ministry? There would first be checks and double-checks with the Southern Rescue Center. They would probably take another half hour, and by that time he would be well out over the Atlantic.

The chirrup of the headphones went quiet. Petacchi got up from his seat and took a look at the radar screen. He watched it for some time, noting the occasional "blip" of planes being overhauled below him. Would his own swift passage above the air corridor be noted by the planes as he passed above them? Unlikely. The radar on commercial planes has a limited field of vision in a forward cone. He would almost certainly not be spotted until he crossed the Defense Early Warning line, and DEW would probably put him down as a commercial jet that had strayed above its normal channel.

Petacchi went back to the pilot's seat and again minutely checked the dials. He weaved the plane gently to get the feel of the controls. Behind him, the bodies on the floor of the fuselage stirred uneasily. The plane answered perfectly. It was like driving a beautiful quiet motor car. Petacchi dreamed briefly of the Maserati. What color? Better not his usual white, or anything spectacular. Dark blue with a thin red line along

the coachwork. Something quiet and respectable that would fit
in with his new, quiet identity. It would be fun to run her in
some of the trials and road races—even the Mexican "2000."
But that would be too dangerous. Supposing he won and his
picture got into the papers! No. He would have to cut out
anything like that. He would only drive the car really fast when
he wanted to get a girl. They melted in a fast car. Why was
that? The sense of surrender to the machine, to the man whose
strong, sunburned hands were on the wheel? But it was always
so. You turned the car into a wood after ten minutes at 150
and you would almost have to lift the girl out and lay her down
on the moss, her limbs would be so trembling and soft.

Petacchi pulled himself out of the daydream. He glanced
at his watch. The Vindicator was already four hours out. At
600 m.p.h. one certainly covered the miles. The coastline of
America should be on the screen by now. He got up and had
a look. Yes, there, 500 miles away, was the coastline map
already in high definition, the bulge that was Boston, and the
silvery creek of the Hudson River. No need to check his position
with weather ships Delta or Echo that would be somewhere
below him. He was dead on course and it would soon be time
to turn off the East-West channel.

Petacchi went back to his seat, munched another benzedrine tablet, and consulted his chart. He got his hands to the
controls and watched the eerie glow of the gyro compass. Now!
He eased the controls gently round in a fairly tight curve, then
he flattened out again, edged the plane exactly on to its new
course, and reset George. Now he was flying due south, now
he was on the last lap, a bare three hours to go. It was time
to start worrying about the landing.

Petacchi took out his little notebook. "Watch for the lights
of Grand Bahama to port, and Palm Beach to starboard. Be
ready to pick up the navigational aids from No. 1's yacht—
dot-dot-dash; dot-dot-dash, jettison fuel, lose height to around
1000 feet for the last quarter of an hour, kill speed with the
air brakes, and lose more height. Watch out for the flashing
red beacon and prepare for the final approach. Flaps down only
at the check altitude with about 140 knots indicated. Depth of
water will be 40 feet. You will have plenty of time to get out
of the escape hatch. You will be taken on board No. 1's yacht.

There is a Bahamas Airways flight to Miami at 8:30 on the next morning and then Braniff or Real Airlines for the rest of the way. No. 1 will give you the money in 1000-dollar bills or in Travellers Cheques. He will have both available, also the passport in the name of Enrico Valli, Company Director."

Petacchi checked his position, course, and speed. Only one more hour to go. It was three a.m. G.M.T., nine p.m. Nassau time. A full moon was coming up and the carpet of clouds 10,000 feet below was a snowfield. Petacchi dowsed the collision lights on his wingtips and fuselage. He checked the fuel: 2000 gallons including the reserve tanks. He would need 500 for the last four hundred miles. He pulled the release valve on the reserve tanks and lost 1000 gallons. With the loss of weight the plane began to climb slowly and he corrected back to 32,000. Now there was twenty minutes to go—time to begin the long descent. . . .

Down through the cloud base, the moments of blindness and then, far below, the sparse lights of North and South Bimini winked palely against the silver sheen of the moon on the quiet sea. There were no whitecaps. The met. report he had picked up from Vero Beach on the American mainland had been right: "Dead calm, light airs from the northeast, visibility good, no immediate likelihood of change," and a check on the fainter Nassau Radio had confirmed. The sea looked as smooth and as solid as steel. This was going to be all right. Petacchi dialed Channel 67 on the pilot's command set to pick up No.1's navigational aid. He had a moment's panic when he didn't hit it at once, but then he got it, faint but clear—dot-dot-dash, dot-dot-dash. It was time to get right down. Petacchi began to kill his speed with the air brakes and cut down the four jets. The great plane began a shallow dive. The radio altimeter became vocal, threatening. Petacchi watched it and the sea of quicksilver below him. He had a moment when the horizon was lost. There was so much reflection off the moonlit water. Then he was on and over a small dark island. It gave him confidence in the 2000 feet indicated on the altimeter. He pulled out of the shallow dive and held the plane steady.

Now No. 1's beacon was coming in loud and clear. Soon he would see the red flashing light. And there it was, perhaps five miles dead ahead. Petacchi inched the great nose of the plane down. Any moment now! It was going to be easy! His fingers played with the controls as delicately as if they were the erotic trigger points on a woman. Five hundred feet, four hundred, three, two ... There was the pale shape of the yacht, lights dowsed. He was dead on line with the red flash of the beacon. Would he hit it? Never mind. Inch her down, down, down. Be ready to switch off at once. The belly of the plane gave a jolt. Up with the nose! Crash! A leap in the air and then ... crash again!

Petacchi unhinged his cramped fingers from the controls, and gazed numbly out of the window at the foam and small waves. By God he had done it! He, Giuseppe Petacchi, had done it!

Now for the applause! Now for the rewards!

The plane was settling slowly and there was a hiss of steam from the submerging jets. From behind him came the rip and crack of tearing metal as the tail section gaped open where the back of the plane had broken. Petacchi went through into the fuselage. The water swirled around his feet. The filtering moonlight glittered white on the upturned face of one of the corpses now soggily awash in the rear of the plane. Petacchi broke the perspex cover to the handle of the port side emergency exit and jerked the handle down. The door fell outward and Petacchi stepped through and walked out along the wing.

The big jolly-boat was almost up with the plane. There were six men in it. Petacchi waved and shouted delightedly. One man raised a hand in reply. The faces of the men, milk-white under the moon, looked up at him quietly, curiously. Petacchi thought: These men are very serious, very businesslike. It is right so. He swallowed his triumph and also looked grave.

The boat came alongside the wing, now almost awash, and one man climbed up on to the wing and walked toward him. He was a short, thick man with a very direct gaze. He walked carefully, his feet well apart and his knees flexed to keep his balance. His left hand was hooked in his belt.

Petacchi said happily, "Good evening. Good evening. I am delivering one plane in good condition." (He had thought the joke out long before.) "Please sign here." He held out his hand.

The man from the jolly-boat took the hand in a strong grasp, braced himself, and pulled sharply. Petacchi's head was flung back by the quick jerk and he was looking full into the eyes of the moon as the stiletto flashed up and under the offered chin, through the roof of the mouth, into the brain. He knew nothing but a moment's surprise, a sear of pain, and an explosion of brilliant light.

The killer held in the knife for a moment, the back of hand feeling the stubble on Petacchi's chin, then lowered the body onto the wing and withdrew the knife. He carefully rinsed the knife in the sea water and wiped the blade on Petacchi's back and put the knife away. Then he hauled the body along the wing and thrust it under water beside the escape hatch.

The killer waded back along the wing to the waiting jollyboat and laconically raised a thumb. By now four of the men had pulled on their aqualungs. One by one, with a last adjustment of their mouthpieces, they clumsily heaved themselves over the side of the rocking boat and sank in a foam of small bubbles. When the last man had gone, the mechanic at the engine carefully lowered a huge underwater searchlight over the side and paid out the cable. At a given moment he switched the light on and the sea and the great sinking hulk of the plane were lit up with a mist of luminescence. The mechanic slipped the idling motor into gear and backed away, paying out cable as he went. At twenty yards, out of range of the suction of the sinking plane, he stopped and switched off his engine. He reached into his overalls and took out a packet of Camels. He offered one to the killer, who took it, broke it carefully in half, put one half behind his ear, and lit the other half.

The killer was a man who rigidly controlled his weaknesses.

CHAPTER 10

The Disco Volante

On board the yacht, No. 1 put down his night glasses, took a Charvet handkerchief out of the breast pocket of his white sharkskin jacket and dabbed gently at his forehead and temples. The musky scent of Schiaparelli's Snuff was reassuring, reminding him of the easy side of life, of Dominetta who would now be sitting down to dinner—everyone kept Spanish hours in Nassau and cocktails would not have finished before ten—with the raffish but rather gay Saumurs and their equally frivolous guests, of the early game that would already be under way at the Casino, of the calypsos thudding into the night from the bars and night clubs on Bay Street. He put the handkerchief back in his pocket. But this also was good—this wonderful operation! Like clockwork! He glanced at his watch. Just ten-fifteen. The plane had been a bare thirty minutes late, a nasty half-hour to have to wait, but the landing had been perfect. Vargas had done a good quick job on the Italian pilot— what was his name?—so that now they were running only fifteen minutes late. If the recovery group didn't have to use oxyacetylene cutters to get out the bombs, they would soon make that up. But one mustn't expect no hitch at all. There was a good eight hours of darkness to go. Calm, method, efficiency, in that order. Calm, method, efficiency. No. 1 ducked down off the bridge and went into the radio cabin. It smelled of sweat and tension. Anything from the Nassau control tower? Any report of a low-flying plane? Of a possible crash into the sea off Bimini? Then keep watching and get me No. 2. Quick, please. It's just on the quarter.

No. 1 lit a cigarette and watched the yacht's big brain get to work, scanning the ether, listening, searching. The operator played the dials with insect fingers, pausing, verifying, hastening on through the sound waves of the world. Now he suddenly stopped, checked, minutely adjusted the volume. He raised his thumb. No. 1 spoke into the sphere of wire mesh that rose before his mouth from the base of the headset. "No. 1 speaking."

"No. 2 listening." The voice was hollow. The words waxed and waned. But it was Blofeld, all right. No. 1 knew that voice better than he remembered his father's.

"Successful. Ten-fifteen. Next phase ten-forty-five. Continuing. Over."

"Thank you. Out." The sound waves went dead. The interchange had taken forty-five seconds. No conceivable fear of interception in that time, on that waveband.

No. 1 went through the big stateroom and down into the hold. The four men of B team, their aqualungs beside them, were sitting around smoking. The wide underwater hatch just above the keel of the yacht was open. Moonlight, reflected off the white sand under the ship, shone up through the six feet of water in the hold. Stacked on the grating beside the men was the thick pile of tarpaulin painted a very pale café-au-lait with occasional irregular blotches of dark green and brown. No. 1 said, "All is going very well. The recovery team is at work. It should not be long now. How about the chariot and the sled?"

One of the men jerked his thumb downward. "They are down there. Outside on the sand. So it will be quicker."

"Correct." No. 1 nodded toward the cranelike contraption fastened to a bulkhead above the hold. "The derrick took the strain all right?"

"That chain could handle twice the weight."

"The pumps?"

"In order. They will clear the hold in seven minutes."

"Good. Well, take it easy. It will be a long night." No. 1 climbed the iron ladder out of the hold and went up on deck.

He didn't need his night glasses. Two hundred yards away to starboard the sea was empty save for the jolly-boat riding at anchor above the golden submarine glow. The red marker light had been taken into the boat. The rattle of the little generator making current for the big searchlight was loud. It would carry far across a sea as still as this. But accumulators would have been too bulky and might have exhausted themselves before the work was finished. The generator was a calculated risk and a small one at that. The nearest island was five miles away and uninhabited unless someone was having a midnight picnic on it. The yacht had stopped and searched it on the way to the rendezvous. Everything had been done that could be done, every precaution taken. The wonderful machine was running silently and full out. There was nothing to worry about now except the next step. No. 1 went through the hatch into the enclosed bridge and bent over the lighted chart table.

Emilio Largo, No. 1, was a big, conspicuously handsome man of about forty. He was a Roman and he looked like a Roman, not from the Rome of today, but from the Rome of the ancient coins. The large, long face was sunburned a deep mahogany brown and the light glinted off the strong rather hooked nose and the clean-cut lantern jaw that had been meticulously shaved before he had started out late that afternoon. In contrast to the hard, slow-moving brown eyes, the mouth, with its thick, rather down-curled lips, belonged to a satyr. Ears that, from dead in front, looked almost pointed, added to an animalness that would devastate women. The only weakness in the fine centurion face lay in the overlong sideburns and the too carefully waved black hair that glistened so brightly with pomade that it might almost have been painted onto the skull. There was no fat on the big-boned frame—Largo had fought for Italy in the Olympic foils, was almost an Olympic-class swimmer with the Australian crawl, and only a month before had won the senior class in the Nassau water-ski championships—and the muscles bulged under the exquisitely cut shark-skin jacket. An aid to his athletic prowess were his hands. They were almost twice the normal size, even for a man of his stature, and now, as they walked across the chart holding a ruler and a pair of dividers, they looked, extruding from the white sleeves that rested on the white chart, almost like large brown furry animals quite separate from their owner.

Largo was an adventurer, a predator on the herd. Two hundred years before he would have been a pirate—not one of the jolly ones of the story books, but a man like Blackbeard, a blood-stained cutthroat who scythed his way through people toward gold. But Blackbeard had been too much of a bully and a roughneck, and wherever he went in the world he left behind a tell-tale shambles. Largo was different. There was a cool brain and an exquisite finesse behind his actions that had always saved him from the herd's revenge—from his postwar debut as head of the black market in Naples, through five lucrative years smuggling from Tangier, five more master-minding the wave of big jewel robberies on the French Riviera, down to his last five with SPECTRE. Always he got away with it. Always he had seen the essential step ahead that would have been hidden from lesser men. He was the epitome of the gentleman crook—a man of the world, a great womanizer, a high liver with the entrée to café society in four continents, and the last survivor, conveniently enough, of a once famous Roman family whose fortune, so he said, he had inherited. He also benefited from having no wife, a spotless police record, nerves of steel, a heart of ice, and the ruthlessness of a Himmler. He was the perfect man for SPECTRE, and the perfect man, rich Nassau playboy and all, to be Supreme Commander of Plan Omega.

One of the crew knocked on the hatch and came in. "They have signaled. The chariot and sled are on the way."

"Thank you." In the heat and excitement of any operation, Largo always created calm. However much was at stake, however great the dangers and however urgent the need for speed and quick decisions, he made a fetish of calm, of the pause, of an almost judolike inertia. This was an act of will to which he had trained himself. He found it had an extraordinary effect on his accomplices. It tied them to him and invoked their obedience and loyalty more than any other factor in leadership. That he, a clever and cunning man, should show unconcern at particularly bad, or, as in this case, particularly good news, meant that he already knew that what had happened would happen. With Largo, consequences were foreseen. One could depend on him. He never lost balance. So now, at this splendid news, Largo deliberately picked up his dividers again and made a trace, an imaginary trace, on the chart for the sake of the crew member. He then put down the dividers and strolled out of the air-conditioning into the warm night.

A tiny worm of underwater light was creeping out toward the jolly-boat. It was a two-man underwater chariot identical with those used by the Italians during the war and bought, with improvements, from Ansaldo, the firm that had originally invented the one-man submarine. It was towing an underwater sled, a sharp prowed tray with negative buoyancy used for the recovery and transport of heavy objects under the sea. The worm of light merged with the luminescence from the searchlight and, minutes later, reemerged on its way back to the ship. It would have been natural for Largo to have gone down to the hold to witness the arrival of the two atomic weapons. Typically, he did nothing of the sort. In due course the little headlight reappeared, going back over its previous course. Now the sled would be loaded with the huge tarpaulin, camouflaged to merge in with just this piece of underwater terrain, with its white sand and patches of coral outcrop, that would be spread so as to cover every inch of the wrecked plane and pegged all round with corkscrew iron stanchions that would not be shifted by the heaviest surface storm or groundswell. In his imagination, Largo saw every move of the eight men who would now be working far below the surface on the reality for which there had been so much training, so many dummy exercises. He marveled at the effort, the incredible ingenuity, that had gone into Plan Omega. Now all the months of preparation, of sweat and tears, were being repaid.

There came a bright blink of light on the surface of the water not far from the jolly-boat—then another and another. The men were surfacing. As they did so, the moon caught the glass of their masks. They swam to the boat—Largo verified that all eight were there—and clumsily heaved up the short ladder and over the side. The mechanic and Brandt, the German killer, helped them off with their gear, the underwater light was switched off and hauled inboard and, instead of the rattle of the generator, there came the muffled roar of the twin Johnstons. The boat sped back to the yacht and to the waiting arms of the derricks. The couplings were made firm and verified and, with a shrill electric whine, the boat, complete with passengers, was swung up and inboard.

The captain came and stood at Largo's side. He was a big, sullen, rawboned man who had been cashiered from the Canadian Navy for drunkenness and insubordination. He had been a slave to Largo ever since Largo had called him to the stateroom one day and broken a chair over his head on account of a questioned command. That was the kind of discipline he understood. Now he said, "The hold's clear. Okay to sail?"

"Are both the teams satisfied?"

"They say so. Not a hitch."

"First see they all get one full jigger of whisky. Then tell them to rest. They will be going out again in just about an hour. Ask Kotze to have a word with me. Be ready to sail in five minutes."

"Okay."

The eyes of the physicist, Kotze, were bright under the moon. Largo noticed that he was trembling slightly as if with fever. He tried to instill calm into the man. He said cheerfully, "Well, my friend. Are you pleased with your toys? The toy shop has sent you everything you want?"

Kotze's lips trembled. He was on the verge of excited tears. He said, his voice high, "It is tremendous! You have no idea. Weapons such as I had never dreamed of. And of a simplicity— a safety! Even a child could handle these things without danger."

"The cradles were big enough for them? You have room to do your work?"

"Yes, yes." Kotze almost flapped his hands with enthusiasm. "There are no problems, none at all. The fuses will be off in no time. It will be a simple matter to replace them with the time mechanism. Maslov is already at work correcting the threads. I am using lead screws. They are more easy to machine."

"And the two plugs—these ignitors you were telling me about? They are safe? Where did the divers find them?"

"They were in a leaden box under the pilot's seat. I have verified them. Perfectly simple when the time comes. They will of course be kept apart in the hiding place. The rubber bags are splendid. Just what was needed. I have verified that they seal completely watertight."

"No danger from radiation?"

"Not now. Everything is in the leaden cases." Kotze shrugged. "I may have picked up a little while I was working on the monsters but I wore the harness. I will watch for signs. I know what to do."

"You are a brave man, Kotze. I won't go near the damned things until I have to. I value my sex life too much. So you are satisfied with everything? You have no problems? Nothing has been left on the plane?"

Kotze had got himself under control. He had been bursting with the news, with his relief that the technical problems were within his power. Now he felt empty, tired. He had voided himself of the tensions that had been with him for weeks. After all this planning, all these dangers, supposing his knowledge had not been enough! Supposing the bloody English had invented some new safety device, some secret control, of which he knew nothing! But when the time came, when he unwrapped the protective webbing and got to work with his jeweler's tools, then triumph and gratitude had flooded into him. No, now there were no problems. Everything was all right. Now there was only routine. Kotze said dully, "No. There are no problems. Everything is there. I will go and get the job finished."

Largo watched the thin figure shamble off along the deck. Scientists were queer fish. They saw nothing but science. Kotze couldn't visualize the risks that still had to be run. For him the turning of a few screws was the end of the job. For the rest of the time he would be a useless supercargo. It would be easier to get rid of him. But that couldn't be done yet. He would have to be kept on just in case the weapons had to be used. But he was a depressing little man and a near hysteric. Largo didn't like such people near him. They lowered his spirits. They smelled of bad luck. Kotze would have to be found some job in the engine room where he would be kept busy and, above all, out of sight.

Largo went into the cockpit bridge. The captain was sitting at the wheel, a light aluminum affair consisting only of the bottom half of a circle. Largo said, "Okay. Let's go." The captain reached out his hand to the bank of buttons at his side and pressed the one that said *"Start Both."* There came a low, hollow rumble from amidships. A light blinked on the panel to show that both engines were firing properly. The captain pulled the electromagnetic gear shift to *"Slow Ahead Both"* and the yacht began to move. The captain made it *"Full Ahead Both"* and the yacht trembled and settled a little in the stern. The captain watched the revolution counter, his hand on a squat lever at his side. At twenty knots the counter showed 5000. The captain inched back the lever that depressed the great steel scoop below the hull. The revolutions remained the same, but the finger of the speedometer crawled on round the dial until it said forty knots. Now the yacht was half flying, half planing across the glittering sheet of still water, the hull supported four feet above the surface on the broad, slightly uptilted metal skid and with only a few feet of the stern and the two big screws submerged. It was a glorious sensation and Largo, as he always did, thrilled to it.

The motor yacht, *Disco Volante,* was a hydrofoil craft, built for Largo with SPECTRE funds by the Italian constructors Leopoldo Rodrigues of Messina, the only firm in the world to have successfully adapted the Shertel-Sachsenberg system to commercial use. With a hull of aluminum and magnesium alloy, two Daimler-Benz four-stroke Diesels supercharged by twin Brown-Boveri turbo superchargers, the *Disco Volante* could move her hundred tons at around fifty knots, with a cruising range at that speed of around four hundred miles. She had cost £200,000, but she had been the only craft in the world with the speed, cargo-, and passenger-space, and with the essential shallow draft for the job required of her in Bahamian waters.

The constructors claim of this type of craft that it has a particular refinement that SPECTRE had appreciated. Having high stability and a shallow draft, *Aliscafos,* as they are called in Italy, do not determine magnetic field variation, nor do they cause pressure waves—both desirable characteristics, in case the *Disco Volante* might wish, some time in her career, to escape detection.

Six months before, the *Disco* had been shipped out to the Florida Keys by the South Atlantic route. She had been a sensation in Florida waters and among the Bahamas, and had vastly helped to make Largo the most popular "millionaire" in a corner of the world that crawls with millionaires who "have everything." And the fast and mysterious voyages he made in the *Disco*, with all those underwater swimmers and occasionally with a two seater Lycoming-engined folding-wing amphibian mounted on the roof of the streamlined superstructure had aroused just the right amount of excited comment. Slowly, Largo had let the secret leak out—through his own indiscretions at dinners and cocktail parties, through carefully primed members of the crew in the Bay Street bars. This was a treasure hunt, an important one. There was a pirates' map, a sunken galleon thickly overgrown with coral. The wreck had been located. Largo was only waiting for the end of the winter tourist season and for the calms of early summer and then his shareholders would be coming out from Europe and work would begin in earnest. And two days before, the shareholders, nineteen of them, had duly come trickling in to Nassau by different routes—from Bermuda, from New York, from Miami. Rather dull-looking people to be sure, just the sort of hard-headed, hard-working businessmen who would be amused by a gamble like this, a pleasant sunshine gamble with a couple of weeks' holiday in Nassau to make up for it if the doubloons were after all not in the wreck. And that evening, with all the visitors on board, the engines of the *Disco* had begun to murmur, just when they should have, the harbor folk agreed, just when it was getting dark, and the beautiful dark blue and white yacht had slid out of harbor. Once in the open sea, the engines had started up their deep booming that had gradually diminished to the southeast, toward, the listeners agreed, an entirely appropriate hunting ground.

The southerly course was considered appropriate because it is among the Southern Bahamas that the great local treasure troves are expected to be found. It was through the southerly passages through these islands—the Crooked Island, the Mayaguana and the Caicos passages—that the Spanish treasure ships would try to dodge the pirates and the French and British fleets as they made for home. Here, it is believed, lie the remains of the *Porto Pedro*, sunk in 1668, with a million pounds of bullion on board. The *Santa Cruz*, lost in 1694, carried twice as much, and the *El Capitan* and *San Pedro*, both sunk in 1719, carried a million, and half a million, pounds of treasure respectively.

Every year, treasure hunts for these and other ships are

carried out among the Southern Bahamas. No one can guess
how much, if anything, has been recovered, but everyone in
Nassau knows of the 72-lb. silver bar recovered by two Nassau
businessmen off Gorda Cay in 1950, and since presented to the
Nassau Development Board, in whose offices it is permanently
on view. So all Bahamians know that treasure is there for the
finding, and when the harbor folk of Nassau heard the deep
boom of the *Disco*'s engines dying away to the south, they
nodded wisely.

But once the *Disco* was well away and the moon had not
yet risen, with all lights doused, she swung away in a wide
circle toward the west and toward the rendezvous point she
was now leaving. Now she was a hundred miles, two hours,
away from Nassau. But it would be almost dawn when, after
one more vital call, Nassau would again hear the boom of her
engines coming in from the false southern trail.

Largo got up and bent over the chart table. They had covered
the course many times and in all weathers. It was really no
problem. But Phases I and II had gone so well that double care
must be taken over Phase III. Yes, all was well. They were
dead on course. Fifty miles. They would be there in an hour.
He told the captain to keep the yacht as she was, and went
below to the radio room. Eleven-fifteen was just coming up.
It was call time.

The small island, Dog Island, was no bigger than two tennis
courts. It was a hunk of dead coral with a smattering of seagrape
and battered screw palm that grew on nothing but pockets of
brackish rainwater and sand. It was the point where the Dog
Shoal broke the surface, a well-known navigational hazard that
even the fishing boats kept well away from. In daylight, Andros
Island showed to eastward, but at night it was as safe as houses.

The *Disco* came up fast and then slowly lowered herself
back into the water and slid up to within a cable's length of
the rock. Her arrival brought small waves that lapped and
sucked at the rock and then were still. The anchor slipped
silently down forty feet and held. Down in the hold, Largo and
the disposal team of four waited for the underwater hatch to
be opened.

The five men wore aqualungs. Largo held nothing but a
powerful underwater electric torch. The four others were di-

vided into two pairs. They wore webbing slung between them and they sat on the edge of the iron grating with their frogmen's feet dangling, waiting for the water to swirl in and give them buoyancy. On the webbing, between each pair, rested a six-foot-long tapering object in an obscene gray rubber envelope.

The water seeped, rushed, and then burst into the hold, submerging the five men. They slipped off their seats and trudged out through the hatchway, Largo in the lead and the two pairs behind him at precisely tested intervals.

Largo did not at first switch on his torch. It was not necessary and it would bring stupid, dazed fish that were a distraction. It might even bring shark or barracuda, and, though they would be no more than a nuisance, one of the team, despite Largo's assurances, might lose his nerve.

They swam on in the soft moonlit mist of the sea. At first there was nothing but a milky void below them, but then the coral shelf of the island showed up, climbing steeply toward the surface. Sea fans, like small shrouds in the moonlight, waved softly, beckoning, and the clumps and trees of coral were gray and enigmatic. It was because of these things, the harmless underwater mysteries that make the skin crawl on the inexperienced, that Largo had decided to lead the disposal teams himself. Out in the open, where the plane had foundered, the eye of the big searchlight made, with the known object of the plane itself, the underwater world into the semblance of a big room. But this was different. This gray-white world needed the contempt of a swimmer who had experienced these phantom dangers a thousand times before. That was the main reason why Largo led the teams. He also wanted to know exactly how the two gray sausages were stored away. It could happen, if things went wrong, that he would have to salvage them himself.

The underpart of the small island had been eroded by the waves so that, seen from below, it resembled a thick mushroom. Under the umbrella of coral there was a wide fissure, a dark wound in the side of the stem. Largo made for it and, when he was close, switched on his torch. Beneath the umbrella of coral it was dark. The yellow light of the torch showed up the minute life of an inshore coral community—the pale sea urchins and the fierce black spines of sea eggs, the shifting underbrush of seaweeds, the yellow and blue seeking antennae of a langouste, the butterfly and angel fish, fluttering like moths in the light, a coiled *bêche de mer,* a couple of meandering sea caterpillars and the black and green jelly of a sea hare.

Largo lowered the black fins on his feet, got his balance on a ledge, and looked round, shining his torch on the rock so that the two teams could get a foothold. Then he waved them on and into the smooth broad fissure that showed a glimmer of moonlight at its far end inside the center of the rock. The underwater cave was only about ten yards long. Largo led the teams one after the other through and into the small chamber that might once perhaps have been a wonderful repository for a different kind of treasure. From the chamber a narrow fissure led to the upper air, and this would certainly become a fine blow-hole in a storm, though it would be unlikely that fishermen would be close enough to the Dog Shoal in a storm to see the water fountaining out of the center of the island. Above the present water line in the chamber, Largo's men had hammered stanchions into the rock to form cradles for the two atomic weapons with leather straps to hold them secure against any weather. Now, one by one, the two teams lifted the rubber packages up onto the iron bars and made them secure. Largo examined the result and was satisfied. The weapons would be ready for him when he needed them. In the meantime such radiation as there was would be quarantined within this tiny rock a hundred miles from Nassau and his men and his ship would be clean and innocent as snow.

The five men trudged calmly back to the ship and into the hold through the hatch. To the boom of the engines the bows of the *Disco* lifted slowly out of the water and the beautiful ship, streamlined like the gondola of some machine of the air rather than of the sea, skimmed off on the homeward journey.

Largo stripped off his equipment and, with a towel round his slim waist, went forward to the radio cabin. He had missed the midnight call. It was now one-fifteen—seven-fifteen in the morning for Blofeld.

Largo thought of this while contact was being made. Blofeld would be sitting there, haggard perhaps, probably unshaven. There would be coffee beside him, the last of an endless chain of cups. Largo could smell it. Now Blofeld would be able to take a taxi to the Turkish baths in the Rue Aubert, his resort when there were tensions to be dissipated. And there, at last, he would sleep.

"Number 1 speaking."

"Number 2 listening."

"Phase III completed. Phase III completed. Successful. One a.m. here. Closing down."

"I am satisfied."

Largo stripped off the earphones. He thought to himself, "So am I! We are more than three-quarters home. Now only the devil can stop us."

He went into the stateroom and carefully made himself a tall glass of his favorite drink—crème de menthe frappé with a maraschino cherry on top.

He sipped it delicately to the end and ate the cherry. Then he took one more cherry out of the bottle, slipped it into his mouth, and went up on the bridge.

CHAPTER 11

Domino

The girl in the sapphire blue MG two-seater shot down the slope of Parliament Street and at the junction with Bay Street executed an admirable racing change through third into second. She gave a quick glance to the right, correctly estimated the trot of the straw-hatted horse in the shafts of the rickety cab with the gay fringe, and swerved out of the side street left-handed. The horse jerked back his head indignantly and the coachman stamped his foot up and down on the big Bermuda bell. The disadvantage of the beautiful deep ting-tong, ting-tong of the Bermuda carriage bell is that it cannot possibly sound angry, however angrily you may sound it. The girl gave a cheerful wave of a sunburned hand, raced up the street in second, and stopped in front of the Pipe of Peace, the Dunhills of Nassau.

Not bothering to open the low door of the MG, the girl swung one brown leg and then the other over the side of the car, showing her thighs under the pleated cream cotton skirt almost to her waist, and slipped to the pavement. By now the cab was alongside. The cabby reined in. He was mollified by the gaiety and beauty of the girl. He said, "Missy, you done almost shaved de whiskers off of Old Dreamy here. You wanna be more careful."

The girl put her hands on her hips. She didn't like being told anything by anyone. She said sharply, "Old Dreamy yourself. Some people have got work to do. Both of you ought to be put out to grass instead of cluttering up the streets getting in everyone's way."

The ancient Negro opened his mouth, thought better of it, said a pacifying "Hokay, Missy. Hokay," flicked at his horse, and moved on, muttering to himself. He turned on his seat to get another look at the she-devil, but she had already disappeared into the shop. "Dat's a fine piece of gal," he said inconsequentially, and put his horse into an ambling trot.

Twenty yards away, James Bond had witnessed the whole scene. He felt the same way about the girl as the cabby did. He also knew who she was. He quickened his step and pushed through the striped sun blinds into the blessed cool of the tobacconist's.

The girl was standing at a counter arguing with one of the assistants. "But I tell you I don't want Senior Service. I tell you I want a cigarette that's so disgusting that I shan't want to smoke it. Haven't you got a cigarette that stops people smoking? Look at all that." She waved a hand toward the stacked shelves. "Don't tell me some of those don't taste horrible."

The man was used to crazy tourists, and anyway the Nassavian doesn't get excited. He said, "Well, Ma'am . . ." and turned and languidly looked along the shelves.

Bond said sternly to the girl, "You can choose between two kinds of cigarette if you want to smoke less."

She looked sharply up at him. "And who might you be?"

"My name's Bond, James Bond. I'm the world's authority on giving up smoking. I do it constantly. You're lucky I happen to be handy."

The girl looked him up and down. He was a man she hadn't seen before in Nassau. He was about six feet tall and somewhere in his middle thirties. He had dark, rather cruel good looks and very clear blue-gray eyes that were now observing her inspection sardonically. A scar down his right cheek showed pale against a tan so mild that he must have only recently come to the island. He was wearing a very dark blue lightweight single-breasted suit over a cream silk shirt and a black knitted silk tie. Despite the heat, he looked cool and clean, and his only concession to the tropics appeared to be the black saddle-stitched sandals on his bare feet.

It was an obvious attempt at a pick-up. He had an exciting face, and authority. She decided to go along. But she wasn't going to make it easy. She said coldly, "All right. Tell me."

"The only way to stop smoking is to stop it and not start again. If you want to *pretend* to stop for a week or two, it's no good trying to ration yourself. You'll become a bore and think about nothing else. And you'll snatch at a cigarette every time the hour strikes or whatever the intervals may be. You'll behave greedily. That's unattractive. The other way is to have cigarettes that are either too mild or too strong. The mild ones are probably the best for you." Bond said to the attendant, "A carton of Dukes, king-size with filter." Bond handed them to the girl. "Here, try these. With the compliments of Faust."

"Oh, but I can't. I mean . . ."

But Bond had already paid for the carton and for a packet of Chesterfields for himself. He took the change and followed her out of the shop. They stood together under the striped awning. The heat was terrific. The white light on the dusty street, the glare reflected back off the shop fronts opposite and off the dazzling limestone of the houses made them both screw up their eyes. Bond said, "I'm afraid smoking goes with drinking. Are you going to give them both up or one by one?"

She looked at him quizzically. "This is very sudden, Mr.—er—Bond. Well, all right. But somewhere out of the town. It's too hot here. Do you know the Wharf out beyond the Fort Montague?" Bond noticed that she looked quickly up and down the street. "It's not bad. Come on. I'll take you there. Mind the metal. It'll raise blisters on you."

Even the white leather of the upholstery burned through to Bond's thighs. But he wouldn't have minded if his suit had caught fire. This was his first sniff at the town and already he had got hold of the girl. And she was a fine girl at that. Bond caught hold of the leather-bound safety grip on the dashboard as the girl did a sharp turn up Frederick Street and another one onto Shirley.

Bond settled himself sideways so that he could look at her. She wore a gondolier's broadrimmed straw hat, tilted impudently down over her nose. The pale blue tails of its ribbon streamed out behind. On the front of the ribbon was printed in gold "M/Y DISCO VOLANTE." Her short-sleeved silk shirt was in half-inch vertical stripes of pale blue and white and, with the pleated cream skirt, the whole get-up reminded Bond vaguely of a sunny day at Henley Regatta. She wore no rings and no jewelery except for a rather masculine square gold wristwatch with a black face. Her flat-heeled sandals were of white doeskin. They matched her broad white doeskin belt and the sensible handbag that lay, with a black and white striped silk scarf, on the seat between them. Bond knew a good deal about her from the immigration form, one among a hundred, which he had been studying that morning. Her name was Dominetta Vitali. She had been born in Bolzano in the Italian Tyrol and therefore probably had as much Austrian as Italian blood in her. She was twenty-nine and gave her profession as "actress." She had arrived six months before in the *Disco* and it was entirely understood that she was mistress to the owner of the yacht, an Italian called Emilio Largo. "Whore," "tart," "prostitute" were not words Bond used about women unless they were professional streetwalkers or the inmates of a brothel, and when Harling, the Commissioner of Police, and Pitman, Chief of Immigration and Customs, had described her as an "Italian tart" Bond had reserved judgment. Now he knew he had been right. This was an independent, a girl of authority and character. She might like the rich, gay life but, so far as Bond was concerned, that was the right kind of girl. She might sleep with men, obviously did, but it would be on her terms and not on theirs.

Women are often meticulous and safe drivers, but they are very seldom first-class. In general Bond regarded them as a mild hazard and he always gave them plenty of road and was ready for the unpredictable. Four women in a car he regarded as the highest danger potential, and two women as nearly as lethal. Women together cannot keep silent in a car, and when women talk they have to look into each other's faces. An exchange of words is not enough. They have to see the other person's expression, perhaps in order to read behind the other's words or to analyze the reaction to their own. So two women in the front seat of a car constantly distract each other's attention from the road ahead and four women are more than doubly dangerous, for the driver has to hear, and see, not only what her companion is saying but also, for women are like that, what the two behind are talking about.

But this girl drove like a man. She was entirely focused on the road ahead and on what was going on in her driving mirror, an accessory rarely used by women except for making up their faces. And, equally rare in a woman, she took a man's pleasure in the feel of her machine, in the timing of her gear changes, and the use of her brakes.

She didn't talk to Bond or seem to be aware of him, and this allowed him to continue his inspection without inhibition. She had a gay, to-hell-with-you face that, Bond thought, would become animal in passion. In bed she would fight and bite and then suddenly melt into hot surrender. He could almost see the proud, sensual mouth bare away from the even white teeth in a snarl of desire and then, afterward, soften into a half-pout of loving slavery. In profile the eyes were soft charcoal slits such as you see on some birds, but in the shop Bond had seen them full face. Then they had been fierce and direct with a golden flicker in the dark brown that held much the same message as the mouth. The profile, the straight, small uptilted nose, the determined set of the chin, and the clean-cut sweep of the jaw line were as decisive as a royal command, and the way the head was set on the neck had the same authority—the poise one associates with imaginary princesses. Two features modified the clean-cut purity of line—a soft, muddled Brigitte Bardot haircut that escaped from under the straw hat in an endearing disarray, and two deeply cut but soft dimples which could only have been etched by a sweet if rather ironic smile that Bond had not yet seen. The sunburn was not overdone and her skin had none of that dried, exhausted sheen that can turn the texture of even the youngest skin into something more like parchment. Beneath the gold, there was an earthy warmth in the cheeks that suggested a good healthy peasant strain from the Italian Alps, and her breasts, high riding and deeply V-ed, were from the same stock. The general impression, Bond decided, was of a willful, high-tempered, sensual girl—a beautiful Arab mare who would only allow herself to be ridden by a horseman with steel thighs and velvet hands, and then only

with curb and saw bit—and then only when he had broken her
to bridle and saddle. Bond thought that he would like to try
his strength against hers. But that must be for some other time.
For the moment another man was in the saddle. He would first
have to be unhorsed. And anyway, what the hell was he doing
fooling with these things? There was a job to be done. The
devil of a job.

The MG swept out of Shirley Street on to Eastern Road and
followed the coast. Across the wide harbor entrance were the
emerald and turquoise shoals of Athol Island. A deep-sea fishing boat was passing over them, the two tall antennae of her
twelve-foot rods streaming their lines astern. A fast motorboat
came hammering by close inshore, the water-skier on the line
behind her executing tight slaloms across the waves of her
wake. It was a sparkling, beautiful day and Bond's heart lifted
momentarily from the trough of indecision and despondency
created by an assignment that, particularly since his arrival at
dawn that day, seemed increasingly time-wasting and futile.

The Bahamas, the string of a thousand islands that straggle
five hundred miles southeast from just east of the coast of
Florida to just north of Cuba, from latitude 27° down to latitude
21°, were, for most of three hundred years, the haunt of every
famous pirate of the western Atlantic, and today tourism makes
full use of the romantic mythology. A road-sign said *"Blackbeard's Tower I mile"* and another *"Gunpowder Wharf. Sea
Food. Native Drinks. Shady Garden. First Left."*

A sand track showed on their left. The girl took it and pulled
up in front of a ruined stone warehouse against which leaned
a pink clapboard house with white window frames and a white
Adam-style doorway over which hung a brightly painted inn
sign of a powder keg with a skull and crossbones on it. The
girl drove the MG into the shade of a clump of casuarinas and
they got out and went through the door and through a small
dining room with red and white checked covers and out onto
a terrace built on the remains of a stone wharf. The terrace was
shaded by sea-almond trees trimmed into umbrellas. Trailed
by a shuffling colored waiter with soup stains down his white
coat, they chose a cool table on the edge of the terrace looking
over the water. Bond glanced at his watch. He said to the girl,
"It's exactly midday. Do you want to drink solid or soft?"

The girl said, "Soft. I'll have a double Bloody Mary with plenty of Worcester sauce."

Bond said, "What do you call hard? I'll have a vodka and tonic with a dash of bitters." The waiter said, "Yassuh" and mooched away.

"I call vodka-on-the-rocks hard. All that tomato juice makes it soft." She hooked a chair toward her with one foot and stretched out her legs on it so that they were in the sun. The position wasn't comfortable enough. She kicked off her sandals and sat back, satisfied. She said, "When did you arrive? I haven't seen you about. When it's like this, at the end of the season, one expects to know most of the faces."

"I got in this morning. From New York. I've come to look for a property. It struck me that now would be better than in the season. When all the millionaires are here the prices are hopeless. They may come down a bit now they're gone. How long have you been here?"

"About six months. I came out in a yacht, the *Disco Volante*. You may have seen her. She's anchored up the coast. You probably flew right over her coming in to land at Windsor Field."

"A long low streamlined affair? Is she yours? She's got beautiful lines."

"She belongs to a relative of mine." The eyes watched Bond's face.

"Do you stay on board?"

"Oh, no. We've got a beach property. Or rather we've taken it. It's a place called Palmyra. Just opposite where the yacht is. It belongs to an Englishman. I believe he wants to sell it. It's very beautiful. And it's a long way away from the tourists. It's at a place called Lyford Key."

"That sounds the sort of place I'm looking for."

"Well, we'll be gone in about a week."

"Oh." Bond looked into her eyes. "I'm sorry."

"If you've got to flirt, don't be obvious." Suddenly the girl laughed. She looked contrite. The dimples remained. "I mean, I didn't really mean that—not the way it sounded. But I've spent six months listening to that kind of thing from these silly old rich goats and the only way to shut them up is to be rude. I'm not being conceited. There's no one under sixty in this place. Young people can't afford it. So any woman who hasn't got a harelip or a mustache—well not even a mustache would put them off. They'd probably like it. Well, I mean absolutely any girl makes these old goats get their bifocals all steamed up." She laughed again. She was getting friendly. "I expect you'll have just the same effect on the old women with pince-nez and blue rinses."

"Do they eat boiled vegetables for lunch?"

"Yes, and they drink carrot juice and prune juice."

"We won't get on, then. I won't sink lower than conch chowder."

She looked at him curiously. "You seem to know a lot about Nassau."

"You mean about conch being an aphrodisiac? That's not only a Nassau idea. It's all over the world where there are conchs."

"Is it true?"

"Island people have it on their wedding night. I haven't found it to have any effect on me."

"Why?" She looked mischievous. "Are you married?"

"No." Bond smiled across into her eyes. "Are you?"

"No."

"Then we might both try some conch soup some time and see what happens."

"That's only a little better than the millionaires. You'll have to try harder."

The drinks came. The girl stirred hers with a finger, to mix in the brown sediment of Worcester sauce, and drank half of it. She reached for the carton of Dukes, broke it open, and slit a packet with her thumbnail. She took out a cigarette, sniffed it cautiously, and lit it with Bond's lighter. She inhaled deeply and blew out a long plume of smoke. She said doubtfully, "Not bad. At least the smoke looks like smoke. Why did you say you were such an expert on giving up smoking?"

"Because I've given it up so often." Bond thought it time to get away from the small talk. He said, "Why do you talk such good English? Your accent sounds Italian."

"Yes, my name's Dominetta Vitali. But I was sent to school in England. To the Cheltenham Ladies College. Then I went to RADA to learn acting. The English kind of acting. My parents thought that was a ladylike way to be brought up. Then they were both killed in a train crash. I went back to Italy to earn my living. I remembered my English but"—she laughed without bitterness—"I soon forgot most of the rest. You don't get far in the Italian theater by being able to walk about with a book balanced on your head."

"But this relative with the yacht." Bond looked out to sea. "Wasn't he there to look after you?"

"No." The answer was curt. When Bond made no comment she added, "He's not exactly a relative, not a close one. He's a sort of close friend. A guardian."

"Oh, yes."

"You must come and visit us on the yacht." She felt that a bit of gush was needed. "He's called Largo, Emilio Largo. You've probably heard. He's here on some kind of a treasure hunt."

"Really?" Now it was Bond's turn to gush. "That sounds rather fun. Of course I'd like to meet him. What's it all about? Is there anything in it?"

"Heaven knows. He's very secretive about it. Apparently there's some kind of a map. But I'm not allowed to see it and I have to stay ashore when he goes off prospecting or whatever he does. A lot of people have put up money for it, sort of shareholders. They've all just arrived. As we're going in a week or so, I suppose everything's ready and the real hunt's going to start any moment now."

"What are the shareholders like? Do they seem sensible sort of people? The trouble with most treasure hunts is that either someone's been there before and sneaked off with the treasure or the ship's so deep in the coral you can't get at it."

"They seem all right. Very dull and rich. Terribly serious for something as romantic as treasure hunting. They seem to spend all their time with Largo. Plotting and planning, I suppose. And they never seem to go out in the sun or go bathing or anything. It's as if they didn't want to get sunburned. As far as I can gather, none of them have ever been in the tropics before. Just a typical bunch of stuffy businessmen. They're probably better than that. I haven't seen much of them. Largo's giving a party for them at the Casino tonight."

"What do you do all day?"

"Oh, I fool around. Do a bit of shopping for the yacht. Drive around in the car. Bathe on other people's beaches when their houses are empty. I like underwater swimming. I've got an aqualung and I take one of the crew out or a fisherman. The crew are better. They all do it."

"I used to do it a bit. I've brought my gear. Will you show me some good bits of reef sometime?"

The girl looked pointedly at her watch. "I might do. It's time I went." She got up. "Thanks for the drink. I'm afraid I can't take you back. I'm going the other way. They'll get you a taxi here." She shuffled her feet into her sandals.

Bond followed the girl through the restaurant to her car. She got in and pressed the starter. Bond decided to risk another snub. He said, "Perhaps I'll see you at the Casino tonight, Dominetta."

"Praps." She put the car pointedly into gear. She took another look at him. She decided that she did want to see him again. She said, "But for God's sake don't call me Dominetta. I'm never called that. People call me Domino." She gave him a brief smile, but it was a smile into the eyes. She raised a hand. The rear wheels spat sand and gravel and the little blue car whirled out along the driveway to the main road. It paused at the intersection and then, as Bond watched, turned right-handed toward Nassau.

Bond smiled. He said, "Bitch," and walked back into the restaurant to pay his bill and have a taxi called.

CHAPTER 12

The Man from the C.I.A.

The taxi took Bond out to the airport at the other end
of the island by the Interfield Road. The man from the Central
Intelligence Agency was due in by Pan American at one-fifteen.
His name was Larkin, F. Larkin. Bond hoped he wouldn't be
a muscle-bound ex-college man with a crew-cut and a desire
to show up the incompetence of the British, the backwardness
of their little Colony, and the clumsy ineptitude of Bond, in
order to gain credit with his chief in Washington. Bond hoped
that at any rate he would bring the equipment he had asked for
before he left London through Section A, who looked after the
liaison with C.I.A. This was the latest transmitter and receiver
for agents in the field, so that the two of them could be independent of cable offices, and have instant communication
with London and Washington, and the most modern portable
Geiger counters for operating both on land and under water.
One of the chief virtues of C.I.A., in Bond's estimation, was
the excellence of their equipment, and he had no false pride
about borrowing from them.

New Providence, the island containing Nassau, the capital
of the Bahamas, is a drab sandy slab of land fringed with some
of the most beautiful beaches in the world. But the interior is
nothing but a waste of low-lying scrub, casuarinas, mastic, and
poison-wood with a large brackish lake at the western end.

111

There are birds and tropical flowers and palm trees, imported fully grown from Florida, in the beautiful gardens of the millionaires round the coast, but in the middle of the island there is nothing to attract the eye but the skeleton fingers of spidery windmill pumps sticking up above the pine barrens, and Bond spent the ride to the airport reviewing the morning.

He had arrived at seven a.m. to be met by the Governor's A.D.C.—a mild error of security—and taken to the Royal Bahamian, a large old-fashioned hotel to which had recently been applied a thin veneer of American efficiency and tourist gimmicks—ice water in his room, a Cellophane-wrapped basket of dingy fruit "with the compliments of the Manager," and a strip of "sanitized" paper across the lavatory seat. After a shower and a tepid, touristy breakfast on his balcony overlooking the beautiful beach, he had gone up to Government House at nine o'clock for a meeting with the Commissioner of Police, the Chief of Immigration and Customs, and the Deputy Governor. It was exactly as he had imagined it would be. The MOST IMMEDIATES and the TOP SECRETS had made a superficial impact and he was promised full cooperation in every aspect of his assignment, but the whole business was clearly put down as a ridiculous flap and something that must not be allowed to interfere with the normal routine of running a small, sleepy colony, nor with the comfort and happiness of the tourists. Roddick, the Deputy Governor, a careful, middle-of-the-way man with a ginger mustache and gleaming pince-nez, had put the whole affair in a most sensible light. "You see, Commander Bond, in our opinion—and we have most carefully debated all the possibilities, all the, er, angles, as our American friends would say—it is inconceivable that a large four-engined plane could have been hidden anywhere within the confines of the Colony. The only airstrip capable of taking such a plane—am I right, Harling?—is here in Nassau. So far as a landing on the sea is concerned, a, er, ditching I think they call it, we have been in radio contact with the Administrators on all the larger outer islands and the replies are all negative. The radar people at the meteorological station..."

Bond had interrupted at this point. "Might I ask if the radar screen is manned round the clock? My impression is that the airport is very busy during the day, but that there is very little traffic at night. Would it be possible that the radar is not so closely watched at night?"

The Commissioner of Police, a pleasant, very military-looking man in his forties, the silver buttons and insignia on whose dark blue uniform glittered as they can only when spit and polish is a main activity and there are plenty of batmen around, said judiciously, "I think the Commander has a point there, sir. The airport commandant admits that things do slacken off a bit when there's nothing scheduled. He hasn't got all that amount of staff and of course most of them are locals, sir. Good men, but hardly up to London Airport standards. And the radar at the met. station is only a G.C.A. set with a low horizon and range—mostly used for shipping."

"Quite, quite." The Deputy Governor didn't want to be dragged into a discussion about radar sets or the merits of Nassavian labor. "There's certainly a point there. No doubt Commander Bond will be making his own inquiries. Now there was a request from the Secretary of State"—the title rolled sonorously forth—"for details and comments on recent arrivals in the island, suspicious characters, and so forth. Mr. Pitman?"

The Chief of Immigration and Customs was a sleek Nassavian with quick brown eyes and an ingratiating manner. He smiled pleasantly. "Nothing out of the ordinary, sir. The usual mixture of tourists and businessmen and local people coming home. We were asked to have details for the past two weeks, sir." He touched the briefcase on his lap. "I have all the immigration forms here, sir. Perhaps Commander Bond would care to go through them with me." The brown eyes flicked toward Bond and away. "All the big hotels have house detectives. I could probably get him further details on any particular name. All passports were checked in the normal manner. There were no irregularities and none of these people was on our Wanted List."

Bond said, "Might I ask a question?"

The Deputy Governor nodded enthusiastically. "Of course. Of course. Anything you like. We're all here to help."

"I'm looking for a group of men. Probably ten or more. They probably stick together a good deal. Might be as many as twenty or thirty. I guess they would be Europeans. They probably have a ship or a plane. They may have been here for months or only a few days. I gather you have plenty of conventions coming to Nassau—salesmen, tourist associations, religious groups, heaven knows what all. Apparently they take a block of rooms in some hotel and hold meetings and so forth for a week or so. Is there anything like that going on at the moment?"

"Mr. Pitman?"

"Well, of course we do have plenty of those sort of gatherings. Very welcome to the Tourist Board." The Chief of Immigration smiled conspiratorially at Bond as if he had just given away a closely guarded secret. "But in the last two weeks we've only had a Moral Rearmament Group at the Emerald Wave and the Tiptop Biscuit people at the Royal Bahamian. They've gone now. Quite the usual convention pattern. All very respectable."

"That's just it, Mr. Pitman. The people I'm looking for, the people who may have arranged to steal this plane, will certainly take pains to look respectable and behave in a respectable fashion. We're not looking for a bunch of flashy crooks. We think these must be very big people indeed. Now, is there anything like that on the island, a group of people like that?"

"Well"—the Chief of Immigration smiled broadly—"of course we've got our annual treasure hunt going on."

The Deputy Governor barked a quick, deprecating laugh. "Now, steady on, Mr. Pitman. Surely we don't want them to get mixed up in all this, or heaven knows where we shall end. I can't believe Commander Bond wants to bother his head over a lot of rich beachcombers."

The Commissioner of Police said doubtfully, "The only thing is, sir—they do have a yacht, and a small plane for the matter of that. And I did hear that a lot of shareholders in the swindle had come in lately. Those points do tally with what the Commander was asking about. I admit it's ridiculous, but this man Largo's respectable enough for Commander Bond's requirements and his men have never once given us trouble. Unusual to have not even one case of drunkenness in a ship's crew in nearly six months."

And Bond had leaped at the flimsy thread and had pursued it for another two hours—in the Customs building and in the Commissioner's office—and, as a result, he had gone walking in the town to see if he could get a look at Largo or any of his party or pick up any other shreds of gossip. As a result he had got a good look at Domino Vitali.

And now?

The taxi had arrived at the airport. Bond told the driver to wait and walked into the long low entrance hall just as the arrival of Larkin's flight was being announced over the Tannoy. He knew there would be the usual delay for customs and immigration. He went to the souvenir shop and bought a copy of the *New York Times*. In its usual discreet headlines it was still leading with the loss of the Vindicator. Perhaps it knew also about the loss of atom bombs, because Arthur Krock, on the editorial page, had a heavyweight column about the security aspects of the NATO alliance. Bond was halfway through this when a quiet voice in his ear said, "007? Meet No. 000."

Bond swung round. It was! It was Felix Leiter!

Leiter, his C.I.A. companion on some of the most thrilling cases in Bond's career, grinned and thrust the steel hook that was his right hand under Bond's arm. "Take it easy, friend. Dick Tracy will tell all when we get out of here. Bags are out front. Let's go."

Bond said, "Well God damn it! You old so-and-so! Did you know it was going to be me?"

"Sure. C.I.A. knows all."

At the entrance Leiter had his luggage, which was considerable, put aboard Bond's taxi, and told the driver to take it to the Royal Bahamian. A man standing beside an undistinguished-looking black Ford Consul sedan left the car and came up. "Mr. Larkin? I'm from the Hertz company. This is the car you ordered. We hope she's what you want. You did specify something conventional."

Leiter glanced casually at the car. "Looks all right. I just want a car that'll go. None of those ritzy jobs with only room for a small blonde with a sponge bag. I'm here to do property work—not jazz it up."

"May I see your New York license, sir? Right. Then if you'll just sign here . . . and I'll make a note of the number of your Diner's Club card. When you go, leave the car anywhere you like and just notify us. We'll collect it. Have a good holiday, sir."

They got into the car. Bond took the wheel. Leiter said that he'd have to practice a bit on what he called "this Limey southpaw routine" of driving on the left, and anyway he'd be interested to see if Bond had improved his cornering since their last drive together.

When they were out of the airport Bond said, "Now go ahead and tell. Last time we met you were with Pinkertons. What's the score?"

"Drafted. Just damned well drafted. Hell, anyone would think there was a war on. You see, James, once you've worked for C.I.A., you're automatically put on the reserve of officers when you leave. Unless you've been cashiered for not eating the code book under fire or something. And apparently my old Chief, Allen Dulles that is, just didn't have the men to go round when the President sounded the fire alarm. So I and twenty or so other guys were just pulled in—drop everything, twenty-four hours to report. Hell! I thought the Russians had landed! And then they tell me the score and to pack my bathing trunks and my spade and bucket and come on down to Nassau. So of course I griped like hell. Asked them if I shouldn't brush up on my Canasta game and take some quick lessons in the cha-cha. So then they unbuttoned and told me I was to team up with you down here and I thought maybe if that old bastard of yours, N or M or whatever you call him, had sent you down here with your old equalizer, there might be something cooking in the pot after all. So I picked up the gear you'd asked for from Admin., packed the bow and arrows instead of the spade and bucket, and here I am. And that's that. Now you tell, you old sonofabitch. Hell, it's good to see you."

Bond took Leiter through the whole story, point by point from the moment he had been summoned to M's office the morning before. When he came to the shooting outside his headquarters, Leiter stopped him.

"Now what do you make of that, James? In my book that's a pretty funny coincidence. Have you been fooling around with anybody's wife lately? Sounds more like around the Loop in Chicago than a mile or so from Piccadilly."

Bond said seriously, "It makes no sense to me, and none to anyone else. The only man who might have had it in for me, recently that is, is a crazy bastard I met down at a sort of

clinic place I had to go to on some blasted medical grounds."
Bond, to Leiter's keen pleasure, rather sheepishly gave details
of his "cure" at Shrublands. "I bowled this man out as a member
of a Chinese Tong, one of their secret societies, the Red Lightning Tong. He must have heard me getting the gen on his outfit
from Records—on an open line from a call box in the place.
Next thing, he damned near managed to murder me. Just for
a lark, and to get even, I did my best to roast him alive." Bond
gave the details. "Nice quiet place, Shrublands. You'd be surprised how carrot juice seems to affect people."

"Where was this lunatic asylum?"

"Place called Washington. Modest little place compared
with yours. Not far from Brighton."

"And the letter was posted from Brighton."

"That's the hell of a long shot."

"I'll try another. One of the points our chaps brought up
was that if a plane was to be stolen at night and landed at night,
a full moon would be the hell of an aid to the job. But the
plane was taken five days after the full. Just supposing your
roast chicken was the letter-sender. And supposing the roasting
forced him to delay sending the letter while he recovered. His
employers would be pretty angry. Yes?"

"I suppose so."

"And supposing they gave orders for him to be rubbed for
inefficiency. And supposing the killer got to him just as he got
to you to settle his private account. From what you tell me he
wouldn't have lain down under what you did to him. Well,
now. Just supposing all that. It adds up, doesn't it?"

Bond laughed, partly in admiration. "You've been taking
mescalin or something. It's a damned good sequence for a
comic strip, but these things don't happen in real life."

"Planes with atom bombs don't get stolen in real life. Except
that they do. You're slowing down, James. How many people
would believe the files on some of the cases you and I have
got mixed up in? Don't give me that crap about real life. There
ain't no such animal."

Bond said seriously, "Well, look here, Felix. Tell you what
I'll do. There's just enough sense in your story, so I'll put it
on the machine to M tonight and see if the Yard can get anywhere with it. They could check with the clinic and the hospital

in Brighton, if that's where he was taken, and they may be able to get on from there. Trouble is, wherever they get, there's nothing left of the man but his shoes, and I doubt if they'll catch up with the man on the motorbike. It looked a real pro job to me."

"Why not? These highjackers sound like pros. It's a pro plan. It all fits all right. You go ahead and put it on the wire and don't be ashamed of saying it was my idea. My medal collection has got to looking a bit thin since I left the outfit."

They pulled up under the portico of the Royal Bahamian and Bond gave the keys to the parking attendant. Leiter checked in and they went up to his room and sent for two double dry martinis on the rocks and the menu.

From the pretentious dishes, "For Your Particular Consideration," printed in Ornamental Gothic, Bond chose Native Seafood Cocktail Supreme followed by Disjointed Home Farm Chicken, Sauté au Cresson, which was described in italics as "Tender Farm Chicken, Broiled to a Rich Brown, Basted with Creamery Butter and Disjointed for Your Convenience. Price 38/6 or dollars 5.35." Felix Leiter went for the Baltic Herring in Sour Cream followed by "Chopped Tenderloin of Beef, French Onion Rings (Our Renowned Beef is Chef-Selected from the Finest Corn-fed, Mid-Western Cattle, and Aged to Perfection to Assure You of the Very Best). Price 40/3 or dollars 5.65."

When they had both commented sourly and at length about the inflated bogosity of tourist-hotel food and particularly the mendacious misuse of the English language to describe materials which had certainly been in various deep-freezes for at least six months, they settled down on the balcony to discuss Bond's findings of the morning.

Half an hour and one more double dry martini later, their luncheon came. The whole thing amounted to about five shillings' worth of badly cooked rubbish. They ate in a mood of absent-minded irritation, saying nothing. Finally Leiter threw down his knife and fork. "This is hamburger and bad hamburger. The French onion rings were never in France, and what's more"—he poked at the remains with a fork—"they're not even rings. They're oval." He looked belligerently across at Bond. "All right, Hawkshaw. Where do we go from here?"

"The major decision is to eat out in future. The next is to pay a visit to the *Disco*—now." Bond got up from the table. "When we've done that, we'll have to decide whether or not these people are hunting pieces of eight or £100,000,000 Then we'll have to report progress." Bond waved at the packing cases in a corner of the room. "I've got the loan of a couple of rooms on the top floor of police headquarters here. The Commissoner's cooperative and a solid character. These Colonial Police are good, and this one's a cut above the rest. We can set up the radio there and make contact this evening. Tonight there's this party at the Casino. We'll go to that and see if any of these faces mean anything to either of us. The first thing's to see if the yacht's clean or not. Can you break that Geiger counter out?"

"Sure. And it's a honey." Leiter went to the cases, selected one, and opened it. He came back carrying what looked like a Rolleiflex camera in a portable leather case. "Here, give me a hand." Leiter took off his wristwatch and strapped on what appeared to be another watch. He slung the "camera" by its strap over his left shoulder. "Now run those wires from the watch up my sleeve and down inside my coat. Right. Now these two small plugs go through these holes in my coat pocket and into the two holes in the box. Got it? Now we're all fixed." Leiter stood back and posed. "Man with a camera and a wristwatch." He unbuttoned the flap of the camera. "See? Perfectly good lenses and all that. Even a button to press in case you have to seem to take a picture. But in back of the make-believe there's a metal valve, a circuit, and batteries. Now take a look at this watch. And it is a watch." He held it under Bond's eyes. "Only difference is that it's a very small watch mechanism and that sweep second-hand is a meter that takes the radioactive count. Those wires up the sleeve hitch it on to the machine. Now then. You're still wearing that old wristwatch of yours with the big phosphorus numerals. So I walk round the room for a moment to get the background count. That's basic. All sorts of things give off radiation of some sort. And I take an occasional glance at my watch—nervous type, and I've got an appointment coming up. Now here, by the bathroom, all that metal is giving off something and my watch is registering positive, but very little. Nothing else in the room and I've established the amount of background interference I'll have to discount when I start to get hot. Right? Now I come close up to you and my camera's only a few inches away from your hand. Here, take a look. Put your watch right up against the counter. See! The sweephand is getting all excited. Move your watch away and it loses interest. It's those phosphorus numerals of yours. Remember the other day one of the watch companies withdrew an air pilots' watch from the market because the Atomic Energy people got fussy? Same thing. They thought this particular pilots' watch, with the big phosphorescent numerals, was giving off too much radiation to be good for the wearer. Of course"—Leiter patted the camera case—"this is a special job. Most types give off a clicking sound, and if you're prospecting for uranium, which is the big market for these machines, you wear earphones to try and pick up the stuff underground. For this job we don't need anything so sensitive. If we get near where those bombs are hidden, this damned sweephand'll go right off the dial. Okay? So let's go hire ourselves a sixpenny sick and pay a call on the ocean greyhound."

CHAPTER 13

"My Name Is Emilio Largo"

Leiter's "sixpenny sick" was the hotel launch, a smart Chrysler-engined speedboat that said it would be $20 an hour. They ran out westward from the harbor, past Silver Cay, Long Cay and Balmoral Island and round Delaporte Point. Five miles farther down the coast, encrusted with glittering seashore properties the boatman said cost £400 per foot of beach frontage, they rounded Old Fort Point and came upon the gleaming white and dark blue ship lying with two anchors out in deep water just outside the reef. Leiter whistled. He said in an awestruck voice, "Boy, is that a piece of boat! I'd sure like to have one of those to play with in my bath."

Bond said, "She's Italian. Built by a firm called Rodrigues at Messina. Thing called an *Aliscafo*. She's got a hydrofoil under the hull and when she gets going you let this sort of skid down and she rises up and practically flies. Only the screws and a few feet of the stern stay in the water. The Police Commissioner says she can do fifty knots in calm water. Only good for inshore work of course, but they can carry upwards of a hundred passengers when they're designed as fast ferries. Apparently this one's been designed for about forty. The rest of the space is taken up with the owner's quarters and cargo space. Must have cost damned near a quarter of a million."

The boatman broke in. "They say on Bay Street that she goin' go after the treasure these next few days or so. All the people that own share in the gold come in a few days ago. Then she spen' one whole night doin' a final recce. They say is down Exhuma way, or over by Watlings Island. Guess you folks know that's where Columbus make him first landfall on this side of the Atlantic. Around fourteen ninety somethin'. But could be anywhere down there. They's always been talk of treasure down 'mongst the Ragged Islands—even as far as Crooked Island. Fact is she sail out southward. Hear her myself, right until her engines died away. East by southeast, I'da say." The boatman spat discreetly over the side. "Must be plenty heap of treasure with the cost of that ship and all the money they throwing 'way. Every time she go to the Hoiling Wharf they say the bill's five hundred pound."

Bond said casually, "Which night was it they did the final recce?"

"Night after she hoiled. That'd be two nights ago. Sail round six."

The blank portholes of the ship watched them approach. A sailor polishing brass round the curve of the enclosed dome that was the bridge walked through the hatch into the bridge and Bond could see him talking into a mouthpiece. A tall man in white ducks and a very wide mesh singlet appeared on deck and observed them through binoculars. He called something to the sailor, who came and stood at the top of the ladder down the starboard side. When their launch came alongside, the man cupped his hands and called down, "What is your business, please? Have you an appointment?"

Bond called back, "It's Mr. Bond, Mr. James Bond. From New York. I have my attorney here. I have an inquiry to make about Palmyra, Mr. Largo's property."

"One moment, please." The sailor disappeared and returned accompanied by the man in white ducks and singlet. Bond recognized him from the police description. He called down cheerfully, "Come aboard, come aboard." He gestured for the sailor to go down and help fend the launch. Bond and Leiter climbed out of the launch and went up the ladder.

Largo held out a hand. "My name is Emilio Largo. Mr. Bond? And . . . ?"

"Mr. Larkin, my attorney from New York. Actually I'm

English, but I have property in America." They shook hands. "I'm sorry to bother you, Mr. Largo, but it's about Palmyra, the property I believe you rent from Mr. Bryce."

"Ah, yes, of course." The beautiful teeth gleamed warmth and welcome. "Come on down to the stateroom, gentlemen. I'm sorry I am not properly dressed to receive you." The big brown hands caressed his flanks, the wide mouth turned down in deprecation. "My visitors usually announce themselves on the ship-to-shore. But if you will forgive the informality . . ." Largo allowed the phrase to die on the air and ushered them through a low hatch and down a few aluminum steps into the main cabin. The rubber-lined hatch hissed to behind him.

It was a fine large cabin paneled in mahogany with a deep wine-red carpet and comfortable dark blue leather club chairs. The sun shining through the slats of venetian blinds over the broad square ports added a touch of gay light to an otherwise rather somber and masculine room, its long center table littered with papers and charts, glass-fronted cabinets containing fishing gear and an array of guns and other weapons, and a black rubber underwater diving suit and aqualung suspended, almost like the skeleton in a sorcerer's den, from a rack in one corner. The air-conditioning made the cabin deliciously cool, and Bond felt his damp shirt slowly freeing itself from his skin.

"Please take a chair, gentlemen." Largo carelessly brushed aside the charts and papers on the table as if they were of no importance. "Cigarettes?" He placed a large silver box between them. "And now what can I get you to drink?" He went to the loaded sideboard. "Something cool and not too strong perhaps? A Planter's Punch? Gin and tonic? Or there are various beers. You must have had a hot journey in that open launch. I would have sent my boat for you if only I had known."

They both asked for a plain tonic. Bond said, "I'm very sorry to barge in like this, Mr. Largo. No idea I could have got you on the telephone. We just got in this morning, and as I've only a few days I have to get a move on. The point is, I'm looking for a property down here."

"Oh, yes?" Largo brought the glasses and bottles of tonic to the table and sat down so that they formed a comfortable group. "What a good idea. Wonderful place. I've been here for six months and already I'd like to stay forever. But the prices they're asking—" Largo threw up his hands. "These Bay Street pirates. And the millionaires, they are even worse. But you are wise to come at the end of the season. Perhaps some of the owners are disappointed not to have sold. Perhaps they will not open their mouths so wide."

"That's what I thought." Bond sat comfortably back and lit a cigarette. "Or rather what my lawyer, Mr. Larkin, advised." Leiter shook his head pessimistically. "He had made some inquiries and he frankly advised that real-estate values down here have gone mad." Bond turned politely toward Leiter to bring him into the conversation. "Isn't that so?"

"Daft, Mr. Largo, quite daft. Worse even than Florida. Out of this world. I wouldn't advise any client of mine to invest at these prices."

"Quite so." Largo obviously didn't want to get drawn too deeply into these matters. "You mentioned something about Palmyra. Is there anything I can do to help in that respect?"

Bond said, "I understand you have a lease of the property, Mr. Largo. And there is talk that you may be leaving the house before long. Only gossip, of course. You know what they are in these small islands. But it sounds more or less what I'm looking for and I gather the owner, this Englishman, Bryce, might sell if he got the right price. What I was going to ask you"—Bond looked apologetic—"was whether we might drive out and look the place over. Some time when you weren't there of course. Any time that might suit you."

Largo flashed his teeth warmly. He spread his hands. "But of course, of course, my dear fellow. Whenever you wish. There is no one in residence but my niece and a few servants. And she is out most of the time. Please just call her up on the telephone. I shall tell her that you will be doing so. It is indeed a charming property—so imaginative. A beautiful piece of design. If only all rich men had such good taste."

Bond got to his feet and Leiter followed suit. "Well, that's extraordinarily kind of you, Mr. Largo. And now we'll leave you in peace. Perhaps we may meet again in the town some time. You must come and have lunch. But"—Bond poured admiration and flattery into his voice—"with a yacht like this,

I don't suppose you ever want to come ashore. Must be the only one on this side of the Atlantic. Didn't one used to run between Venice and Trieste? I seem to remember reading about it somewhere."

Largo grinned his pleasure. "Yes, that is right, quite right. They are also on the Italian lakes. For passenger traffic. Now they are buying them in South America. A wonderful design for coastal waters. She only draws four feet when the hydrofoil is operating."

"I suppose accommodation's the problem?"

It is a weakness of all men, though not necessarily of all women, to love their material possessions. Largo said, with a trace of pricked vanity, "No, no. I think you will find that it is not so. You can spare five minutes? We are rather crowded at the moment. You have heard no doubt of our treasure hunt?" He looked sharply at them as a man would who expects ridicule. "But we will not discuss that now. No doubt you do not believe in these things. But my associates in the affair are all on board. With the crew, there are forty of us. You will see that we are not cramped. You would like?" Largo gestured to the door in the rear of the stateroom.

Felix Leiter showed reluctance. "You know, Mr. Bond, that we have that meeting with Mr. Harold Christie at five o'clock?"

Bond waved the objection aside. "Mr. Christie is a charming man. I know he won't mind if we are a few minutes late. I'd love to see over the ship if you're sure you can spare the time, Mr. Largo."

Largo said, "Come. It will not take more than a few minutes. The excellent Mr. Christie is a friend of mine. He will understand." He went to the door and held it open.

Bond had been expecting the politeness. It would interfere with Leiter and his apparatus. He said firmly, "Please go first, Mr. Largo. You will be able to tell us when to duck our heads."

With more affabilities, Largo led the way.

Ships, however modern, are more or less the same—the corridors to port and starboard of the engine room, rows of cabin doors, which Largo explained were occupied, the large communal bathrooms, the galley, where two cheerful-looking Italians in white smocks laughed at Largo's jokes about the

food and seemed pleased with the visitors' interest, the huge
engine room where the chief engineer and his mate, Germans
it seemed, gave enthusiastic information about the powerful
twin Diesels and explained the hydraulics of the hydrofoil de-
pressor—it was all exactly like visiting any other ship and
saying the right things to the crew, using the right superlatives
to the owner.

The short space of afterdeck was occupied by the little two-
seater amphibian, painted dark blue and white to match the
yacht, its wings now folded and its engine cowled against the
sun, a big jolly-boat to hold about twenty men, and an electric
derrick to hoist them in- and outboard. Bond, estimating the
ship's displacement and her freeboard, said casually, "And the
hold? More cabin space?"

"Just storage. And the fuel tanks, of course. She is an
expensive ship to run. We have to carry several tons. The
ballast problem is important with these ships. When her bows
come up, the fuel shifts aft. We have to have big lateral tanks
to correct these things." Talking fluently and expertly, Largo
led them back up the starboard passageway. They were about
to pass the radio room when Bond said, "You said you had
ship-to-shore. What else do you carry? The usual Marconi short
and long wave, I suppose. Could I have a look? Radio has
always fascinated me."

Largo said politely, "Some other time, if you don't mind.
I'm keeping the operator full time on met. reports. They're
rather important to us at the moment."

"Of course."

They climbed up into the enclosed dome of the bridge,
where Largo briefly explained the controls and led them out
on the narrow deck space. "So there you are," said Largo. "The
good ship *Disco Volante*—the Flying Saucer. And she really
does fly, I can assure you. I hope you and Mr. Larkin will
come for a short cruise one of these days. For the present"—
he smiled with a hint of a secret shared—"as you may have
heard, we are rather busy."

"Very exciting, this treasure business. Do you think you've
got a good chance?"

"We like to think so." Largo was deprecating. "I only wish

I could tell you more." He waved an apologetic hand. "Unfortunately, as they say, my lips are sealed. I hope you will understand."

"Yes, of course. You have your shareholders to consider. I only wish I was one so that I could come along. I suppose there's not room for another investor?"

"Alas, no. The issue, as they say, is fully subscribed. It would have been very pleasant to have had you with us." Largo held out a hand. "Well, I see that Mr. Larkin has been looking anxiously at his watch during our brief tour. We must not keep Mr. Christie waiting any longer. It has been a great pleasure to meet you, Mr. Bond. And you, Mr. Larkin."

With a further exchange of courtesies they went down the ladder to the waiting launch and got under way. There was a last wave from Mr. Largo before he vanished through the hatch to the bridge.

They sat in the stern well away from the boatman. Leiter shook his head. "Absolutely negative. Reaction around the engine room and the radio room, but that's normal. It was all normal, damnably normal. What did you make of him and the whole setup?"

"Same as you—damned normal. He looks what he says he is, and behaves that way. Not much crew about, but the ones we saw were either ordinary crew or wonderful actors. Only two small things struck me. There was no way down to the hold that I could see, but of course it could have been a manhole under the passage carpet. But then how do you get the stores he talked of down there? And there's the hell of a lot of space in that hold even if I don't know much about naval architecture. I'll do a check with the oiling wharf through the customs people and see just how much fuel he does carry. Then it's odd that we didn't see any of these shareholders. It was around three o'clock when we went on board and most of them may have been having siestas. But surely not all nineteen of them. What do they do in their cabins all the time? Another small thing. Did you notice that Largo didn't smoke and that there was no trace of tobacco smell anywhere in the ship? That's odd. Around forty men and not one of them is a smoker. If one had anything else to go on one would say that wasn't coincidence but discipline. The real pros don't drink or smoke. But I admit it's a damned long shot. Notice the Decca Navigator and the echo-sounder? Pretty expensive bits of equipment, both of them. Fairly normal on a big yacht, of course, but I'd have expected Largo to point them out when he was showing us the bridge. Rich men are proud of their toys. But that's only clutching at straws. I'd have said the whole outfit's as clean as a whistle if it wasn't for all that missing space we weren't shown. That talk about fuel and ballast sounded a bit glib to me. What do you think?"

"Same as you. There's at least half of that ship we didn't see. But then again there's a perfectly good answer to that. He may have got a stack of secret treasure-hunting gear down there he doesn't want anyone to see. Remember that merchant ship off Gibraltar during the war? The Italian frogmen used it as a base. Big sort of trapdoor affair cut in the hull below the water line. I suppose he hasn't got something like that?"

Bond looked sharply at Leiter. "The *Olterra*. One of the blackest marks against Intelligence during the whole war." He paused. "The *Disco* was anchored in about forty feet of water. Supposing they'd got the bombs buried in the sand below her. Would your Geiger counter have registered?"

"Doubt it. I've got an underwater model and we could go and have a sniff round when it gets dark. But really, James"— Leiter frowned impatiently—"aren't we getting a bit off beam—seeing burglars under the bed? We've got damn-all to go on. Largo's a powerful-looking piratical sort of chap, probably a bit of a crook where women are concerned. But what the hell have we got against him? Have you put a Trace through on him and on these shareholders and the crew members?"

"Yes. Put them all on the wire from Government House, Urgent Rates. We should get an answer by this evening. But look here, Felix." Bond's voice was stubborn. "There's a damned fast ship with a plane and forty men no one knows anything about. There's not another group or even an individual in the area who looks in the least promising. All right, so the outfit looks all right and its story seems to stand up. But just supposing the whole thing was a phony—a damned good one of course, but then so it ought to be with all that's at stake. Take another look at the picture. These so-called shareholders all arrive just in time for June third. On that night the *Disco* goes to sea and stays out till morning. Just supposing she rendezvous'd that plane in shallow water somewhere. Just suppose she picked up the bombs and put them away—in the sand under the ship, if you like. Anyway, somewhere safe and convenient. Just suppose all that and what sort of a picture do you get?"

"A B picture so far as I'm concerned, James." Leiter shrugged resignedly. "But I guess there's just enough to make it a lead." He laughed sardonically. "But I'd rather shoot myself than put it in tonight's report. If we're going to make fools of ourselves, we'd better do it well out of sight and sound of our chiefs. So what's on your mind? What comes next?"

"While you get our communications going, I'm going to check with the oiling wharf. Then we'll call up this Domino girl and try and get ourselves asked for a drink and have a quick look at Largo's shore base—this Palmyra. Then we go to the Casino and look over the whole of Largo's group. And then"—Bond looked stubbornly at Leiter—"I'm going to borrow a good man from the Police Commission to give me a hand, put on an aqualung, and go out and have a sniff round the *Disco* with your other Geiger machine."

Leiter said laconically, "Destry Rides Again! Well, I'll go along with that, James. Just for old times' sake. But don't go and stub your toe on a sea urchin or anything. I see there are free cha-cha lessons in the ballroom of the Royal Bahamian tomorrow. We've got to keep fit for those. I guess there'll be nothing else in this trip for my memory book."

Back in the hotel, a dispatch rider from Government House was waiting for Bond. He saluted smartly, handed over an O.H.M.S. envelope, and got Bond's signed receipt in exchange. It was a cable from the Colonial Office "Personal to the Governor." The text was prefixed PROBOND. The cable read: "YOUR 1107 RECORDS HAVE NOTHING REPEAT NOTHING ON THESE NAMES STOP INFORMATIVELY ALL STATIONS REPORT NEGATIVELY ON OPERATION THUNDERBALL STOP WHAT HAVE YOU QUERY." The message was signed "PRISM," which meant that M had approved it.

Bond handed the cable to Leiter.

Leiter read it. He said, "See what I mean? We're on a bum

steer. This is a thumb-twiddler. See you later in the Pineapple Bar for a dry martini that's half a jumbo olive. I'll go send a postcard to Washington and ask them to send down a couple of WAVES. We're going to have time on our hands."

CHAPTER 14

Sour Martinis

As it turned out, the first half of Bond's program for the evening went by the board. On the telephone Domino Vitali said that it would not be convenient for them to see the house that evening. Her guardian and some of his friends were coming ashore. Yet it was indeed possible that they might meet at the Casino that evening. She would be dining on board and the *Disco* would then sail round and anchor off the Casino. But how would she be able to recognize him in the Casino? She had a very poor memory for faces. Would he perhaps wear a flower in his buttonhole or something?

Bond had laughed. He said that would be all right. He would remember her by her beautiful blue eyes. They were unforgettable. And the blue rinse that matched them. He had put the receiver down halfway through the amused, sexy chuckle. He suddenly wanted to see her again very much.

But the movement of the ship altered his plans for the better. It would be much easier to reconnoiter her in the harbor. It would be a shorter swim and he would be able to go into the water under cover of the harbor police wharf. Equally, with her anchorage empty, it would be all the easier to survey the area where she had been lying. But if Largo moved the yacht about so nonchalantly was it likely the bombs, if there were any, would be hidden at the anchorage? If they were, surely the *Disco* would stand watch over them. Bond decided to put a decision aside until he had more and more expert information about the ship's hull.

He sat in his room and wrote his negative report to M. He read it through. It would be a depressing signal to get. Should he say anything about the wisp of a lead he was working on? No. Not until he had something solid. Wishful intelligence, the desire to please or reassure the recipient, was the most dangerous commodity in the whole realm of secret information. Bond could imagine the reaction in Whitehall where the *Thunderball* war room would be ready, anxious to grasp at straws. M's careful "I think we may conceivably have got a lead in the Bahamas. Absolutely nothing definite, but this particular man doesn't often go wrong on these things. Yes, certainly I'll check back and see if we can get a follow-up." And the buzz would get around: "M's on to something. Agent of his thinks he's got a lead. The Bahamas. Yes, I think we'd better tell the P.M." Bond shuddered. The MOST IMMEDIATES would pour in to him: "Elucidate your 1806." "Flash fullest details." "Premier wants detailed grounds for your 1806." There would be no end to the flood. Leiter would get the same from C.I.A. The whole place would be in an uproar. Then, in answer to Bond's tatty little fragments of gossip and speculation, there would come the blistering: "Surprised you should take this flimsy evidence seriously." "Futurely confine your signals to facts," and, the final degradation, "View speculative nature your 1806 and subsequents comma future signals must repeat must be joint and countersigned by CIA representative."

Bond wiped his forehead. He unlocked the case containing his cipher machine, transposed his text, checked it again, and went off to Police Headquarters, where Leiter was sitting at his keyboard, the sweat of concentration pouring down his neck. Ten minutes later Leiter took off his earphones and handed over to Bond. He mopped his face with an already drenched handkerchief. "First it's sunspots, and I had to swap over to the emergency wavelength. There I found they'd put a baboon on the other end—you know, one of the ones that can write the whole of Shakespeare if you leave him at it long enough." He angrily waved several pages of cipher groups. "Now I've got to unscramble all this. Probably from Accounts about how much extra income tax this sunshine trip will cost me." He sat down at a table and began cranking away at his machine.

Bond put his short message over quickly. He could see it being punched out on the tapes in one of those busy rooms on the eighth floor, going to the supervisor, being marked "Personal for M, copy to OO Section and Records," then another girl hurrying off down the passage with the flimsy yellow forms on a clip file. He queried whether there was anything for him and signed off. He left Leiter and went down to the Commissioner's room.

Harling was sitting at his desk with his coat off, dictating to a police sergeant. He dismissed him, pushed a box of cigarettes over his desk to Bond, and lit one himself. He smiled quizzically. "Any progress?"

Bond told him that the Trace on the Largo group had been negative and that they had called on Largo and gone over the *Disco* with a Geiger counter. This also had been negative. Bond still wasn't satisfied. He told the Commissioner what he wanted to know about the fuel capacity of the *Disco* and the exact location of the fuel tanks. The Commissioner nodded amiably and picked up the telephone. He asked for a Sergeant Molony of the Harbor Police. He cradled the receiver and explained, "We check all fueling. This is a narrow harbor crammed with small craft, deep-sea fishing boats, and so on. Quite a fire hazard if something went wrong. We like to know what everyone is carrying and whereabouts in the ship. Just in case there's some fire-fighting to be done or we want a particular ship to get out of range in a hurry." He went back to the telephone. "Sergeant Molony?" He repeated Bond's questions, listened, said thank-you, and put the receiver down. "She carries a maximum of five hundred gallons of Diesel. Took that amount on on the afternoon of June 2nd. She also carries about forty gallons of lubricating oil and a hundred gallons of drinking water—all carried amidships just forrard of the engine room. That what you want?"

This made nonsense of Largo's talk of lateral tanks and the difficult ballast problem and so forth. Of course he could have wanted to keep some secret treasure-hunting gear out of sight of the visitors, but at least there *was* something on board he wanted to hide, and, for all his show of openness, it was now established that Mr. Largo might be a rich treasure hunter, but he was also an unreliable witness. Now Bond's mind was made up. It was the hull of the ship he wanted to have a look at. Leiter's mention of the *Olterra* had been a long shot, but it just might pay off.

Bond passed on a guarded version of his thoughts to the Commissioner. He told him where the *Disco* would be lying that night. Was there on the force a totally reliable man who could give him a hand with his underwater recce, and was there a sound aqualung, fully charged, available?

Harling gently asked if this was wise. He didn't exactly know the laws of trespass, but these seemed to be good citizens and they were certainly good spenders. Largo was very popular with everyone. Any kind of scandal, particularly if the police were involved, would create the hell of a stink in the Colony.

Bond said firmly, "I'm sorry, Commissioner. I quite see your point. But these risks have to be run and I've got a job to do. Surely the Secretary of State's instructions are sufficient authority," Bond fired his broadside. "I could get specific orders from him, or from the Prime Minister for the matter of that, in about an hour if you feel it's necessary."

The Commissioner shook his head. He smiled. "No need to use the big guns, Commander. Of course you shall have what you want. I was just giving you the local reaction. I'm sure the Governor would have given you the same warning. This is a small puddle here. We're not used to the crash treatment from Whitehall. No doubt we'll get used to it if this flap lasts long enough. Now then. Yes, we've got plenty of what you want. We've got twenty men in the Harbor Salvage Unit. Have to. You'd be surprised how often a small boat gets wrecked in the fairway, just where some cruise ship's going to anchor. And of course there's the occasional body. I'll have Constable Santos assigned to you. Splendid chap. Native of Eleuthera, where he used to win all the swimming prizes. He'll have the gear you want where you want it. Now just give me the details. . . ."

Back in his hotel, Bond took a shower, swallowed a double bourbon old-fashioned, and threw himself down on his bed. He felt absolutely beat—the plane trip, the heat, the nagging sense that he was making a fool of himself in front of the

Commissioner, in front of Leiter, in front of himself, added to the dangers, and probably futile ones at that, of this ugly night swim, had built up tensions that could only be eased by sleep and solitude. He went out like a light—to dream of Domino being pursued by a shark with dazzling white teeth that suddenly became Largo, Largo who turned on him with those huge hands. They were coming closer, they reached slowly for him, they had him by the shoulder. . . . But then the bell rang for the end of the round, and went on ringing.

Bond reached out a drugged hand for the receiver. It was Leiter. He wanted that martini with the jumbo olive. It was nine o'clock. What the hell was Bond doing? Did he want someone to help with the zipper?

The Pineapple Room was paneled in bamboo carefully varnished against termites. Wrought-iron pineapples on the tables and against the wall contained segments of thick red candle, and more light was provided by illuminated aquaria let into the walls and by ceiling lights enclosed in pink glass starfish. The Vinylite banquettes were in ivory white and the barman and the two waiters wore scarlet satin calypso shirts with their black trousers.

Bond joined Leiter at a corner table. They both wore white dinner jackets with their dress trousers. Bond had pointed up his rich, property-seeking status with a wine-red cummerbund. Leiter laughed. "I nearly tied a gold-plated bicycle chain round my waist in case of trouble, but I remembered just in time that I'm a peaceful lawyer. I suppose it's right that you should get the girls on this assignment. I suppose I just stand by and arrange the marriage settlement and later the alimony. Waiter!"

Leiter ordered two dry martinis. "Just watch," he said sourly.

The martinis arrived. Leiter took one look at them and told the waiter to send over the barman. When the barman came, looking resentful, Leiter said, "My friend, I asked for a martini and not a soused olive." He picked the olive out of the glass with the cocktail stick. The glass, that had been three-quarters full, was now half full. Leiter said mildly, "This was being done to me while the only drink you knew was milk. I'd learned the basic economics of your business by the time you'd graduated to Coca-Cola. One bottle of Gordon's gin contains sixteen

true measures—double measures, that is, the only ones I drink.
Cut the gin with three ounces of water and that makes it up to
twenty-two. Have a jigger glass with a big steal in the bottom
and a bottle of these fat olives and you've got around twenty-
eight measures. Bottle of gin here costs only two dollars retail,
let's say around a dollar sixty wholesale. You charge eighty
cents for a martini, a dollar sixty for two. Same price as a
whole bottle of gin. And with your twenty-eight measures to
the bottle, you've still got twenty-six left. That's a clear profit
on one bottle of gin of around twenty-one dollars. Give you
a dollar for the olives and the drop of vermouth and you've
still got twenty dollars in your pocket. Now, my friend, that's
too much profit, and if I could be bothered to take this martini
to the management and then to the Tourist Board, you'd be in
trouble. Be a good chap and mix us two large dry martinis
without olives and with some slices of lemon peel separate.
Okay? Right, then we're friends again."

The barman's face had run through indignation, respect,
and then the sullenness of guilt and fear. Reprieved, but clutching at his scraps of professional dignity, he snapped his fingers
for the waiter to take away the glasses. "Okay, suh. Whatever
you says. But we've got plenty overheads here and the majority
of customers they doan complain."

Leiter said, "Well, here's one who's dry behind the ears.
A good barman should learn to be able to recognize the serious
drinker from the status-seeker who wants just to be seen in
your fine bar."

"Yassuh." The barman moved away with Negro dignity.

Bond said, "You got those figures right, Felix? I always
knew one got clipped, but I thought only about a hundred per
cent—not four or five."

"Young man, since I graduated from Government Service
to Pinkertons, the scales have dropped from my eyes. The
cheating that goes on in hotels and restaurants is more sinful
than all the rest of the sin in the world. Anyone in a tuxedo
before seven in the evening is a crocodile, and if he couldn't
take a good bite at your pocketbook he'd take a good bite at
your ear. The same goes for the rest of the consumer business,
even when it's not wearing a tuxedo. Sometimes it gets me real
mad to have to eat and drink the muck you get and then see

what you're charged for it. Look at our damned lunch today.
Six, seven bucks with fifteen per cent added for what's called
service. And then the waiter hangs about for another fifty cents
for riding up in the elevator with the stuff. Hell"—Leiter ran
an angry hand through his mop of straw hair—"just don't let's
talk about it. I'm fit to bust a gut when I think about it."

The drinks came. They were excellent. Leiter calmed down
and ordered a second round. He said, "Now let's get angry
about something else." He laughed curtly. "Guess I'm just sore
at being back in Government Service again watching all the
taxpayers' money going down the drain on this wild goose
chase. Mark you, James"—there was apology in Leiter's
voice—"I'm not saying this whole operation isn't a true bill,
hell of a——mess in fact, but what riles me is that we should
be a couple of arse-end Charlies stuck down on this sand spit
while the other guys have got the hot spots—you know, places
where something really may be happening—or at least likely
to happen. Tell you the truth, I felt like a damned fool gum-
shoeing around that feller's yacht this afternoon with my little
Geiger toy." He looked keenly at Bond. "You don't find you
grow out of these things? I mean it's all right when there's a
war on. But it seems kinda childish when peace is bustin' out
all over."

Bond said doubtfully, "Of course I know what you mean,
Felix. Perhaps it's just that in England we don't feel quite as
secure as you do in America. The war just doesn't seem to
have ended for us—Berlin, Cyprus, Kenya, Suez, let alone
these jobs with people like SMERSH that I used to get tangled
up in. There always seems to be something boiling up somewhere. Now this damned business. Dare say I'm taking it all
too seriously, but there's something fishy going on around here.
I checked up on that fuel problem and Largo certainly told us
a lie." Bond gave the details of what he had learned at police
headquarters. "I feel I've got to make sure tonight. You realize
there's only about seventy hours to go? If I find anything, I
suggest tomorrow we take a small plane and really run a search
over as much of the area as we can. That plane's a big thing
to hide even under water. You still got your license?"

"Sure, sure." Leiter shrugged his shoulders. "I'll go along
with you. Of course I will. If we find anything, perhaps the

signal I got this evening won't look so damned silly after all."

So this was what had put Leiter into such a vile temper! Bond said, "What was that?"

Leiter took a drink and gazed morosely into his glass. "Well, for my money it's just so much more attitudinizing by those power-struck fatcats at the Pentagon. But that sheaf of stuff I was waving about was a circular to all our men on this job to say that the Army and the Navy and the Air Force are holding themselves ready to give full support to C.I.A. if anything turns up. Think of that, dammit!" Leiter looked angrily at Bond. "Think of the waste of fuel and manpower that must be going on all over the world keeping all these units at readiness! Just to show you, know what I've been allocated as my striking force?" Leiter gave a harsh, derisive laugh. "Half squadron of Super Sabre fighter bombers from Pensacola, and—" Leiter stabbed at Bond's forearm with a hard finger—"and, my friend, the *Manta*! The——*Manta*! Our latest——atomic submarine!" When Bond smiled at all this vehemence, Leiter continued more reasonably: "Mark you, it's not quite so idiotic as it sounds. These Sabres are on anti-submarine sweep duties anyway. Carrying depth charges. They have to be at readiness. And the *Manta* happens to be on some sort of a training cruise in the area, getting ready to go under the South Pole for a change I suppose, or some other damned promotion job to help along the Navy Estimates. But I ask you! Here's all these million dollars' worth of material on instant call from Ensign Leiter, commanding Room 201 in the Royal Bahamian Hotel! Not bad!"

Bond shrugged his shoulders. "Seems to me your President is taking all this a bit more seriously than his man in Nassau. I suppose our Chiefs of Staff have weighed in with our stuff on the other side of the Atlantic. Anyway, no harm in having the big battalions in the offing just in case Nassau Casino happens to be Target No. 1. By the way, what ideas have your people got about these targets? What have you got in this part of the world that fits in with SPECTRE's letter? We've only got the joint rocket base at a place called Northwest Cay at the eastern end of the Grand Bahamas. That's about a hundred and fifty miles north of here. Apparently the gear and prototypes

we and your people have got there would easily be worth
£100,000,000."

"The only possible targets I've been given are Cape Canaveral, the naval base at Pensacola, and, if the party really is
going to take place in this area, Miami for target No. 2, with
Tampa as a possible runner-up. SPECTRE used the words 'a
piece of property belonging to the Western Powers.' That
sounds like some kind of installation to me—something like
the uranium mines in the Congo, for instance. But a rocket
base would fit all right. If we've got to take this thing seriously,
I'd lay odds on Canaveral or this place on Grand Bahama. Only
thing I can't understand, if they've got these bombs, how are
they going to transport them to the target and set them off?"

"A submarine could do it—just lay one of the bombs off-
shore through a torpedo tube. Or a sailing dinghy, for the matter
of that. Apparently exploding these things is no problem so
long as they recovered all the parts from the plane. Apparently
you'd just have to insert some kind of fuse thing in the right
place between the T.N.T. and the plutonium, and screw the
impact fuse off the nose and fit a time fuse that would give
you time to get a hundred miles away." Bond added casually,
"Have to have an expert who knows the drill of course, but the
trip would be no problem for the *Disco,* for instance. She could
lay the bomb off Grand Bahama at midnight and be back at
anchor off Palmyra by breakfast time." He smiled. "See what
I mean? It all adds up."

"Nuts," said Leiter succinctly. "You'll have to do better
than that if you want my blood pressure to go up. Anyway,
let's get the hell out of here and go have ourselves some eggs
and bacon in one of those clip joints on Bay Street. It'll cost
us twenty dollars plus tax, but the *Manta* probably burns that
every time her screws turn full circle. Then we'll go along to
the Casino and see if Mr. Fuchs or Signor Pontecorvo is sitting
beside Largo at the blackjack table."

CHAPTER 15

Cardboard Hero

The Nassau Casino is the only legal casino on British soil anywhere in the world. How this is justified under the laws of the Commonwealth no one can quite figure. It is leased each year to a Canadian gambling syndicate and their operating profits in the smart winter season are estimated to average around $100,000. The only games played are roulette, with two zeroes instead of one, which increases the take to the house from the European 3.6 to a handsome 5.4; blackjack, or 21, on which the house makes between 6 and 7 per cent; and one table of *chemin de fer,* whose cagnotte yields a modest 5 per cent. The operation is run as a club in a handsome private house on West Bay Street and there is a pleasant dance and supper room with a three-piece combo that plays old favorites in strict time, and a lounge bar. It is a well-run, elegant place that deserves its profit.

The Governor's A.D.C. had presented Bond and Leiter with membership cards, and after they had had coffee and a stinger at the bar they separated and went to the tables.

Largo was playing *chemin de fer*. He had a fat pile of hundred-dollar plaques in front of him and half a dozen of the big yellow thousand-dollar biscuits. Domino Vitali sat behind him chain-smoking and watching the play. Bond observed the game from a distance. Largo was playing expansively, bancoing whenever he could and letting his own banks run. He

was winning steadily, but with excellent manners, and by the
way people joked with him and applauded his coups he was
obviously a favorite in the Casino. Domino, in black with a
square-cut neckline and with one large diamond on a thin chain
at her throat, was looking morose and bored. The woman on
Largo's right, having bancoed him three times and lost, got up
and left the table. Bond went quickly across the room and slid
into the empty place. It was a bank of eight hundred dollars—
the round sum being due to Largo making up the cagnotte after
each play.

It is good for the banker when he has got past the third
banco. It often means the bank is going to run. Bond knew
this perfectly well. He was also painfully aware that his total
capital was only one thousand dollars. But the fact that everyone
was so nervous of Largo's luck made him bold. And, after all,
the table has no memory. Luck, he told himself, is strictly for
the birds. He said, "Banco."

"Ah, my good friend Mr. Bond." Largo held out a hand.
"Now we have the big money coming to the table. Perhaps I
should pass the bank. The English know how to play at railway
trains. But still"—he smiled charmingly—"if I have to lose
I would certainly like to lose to Mr. Bond."

The big brown hand gave the shoe a soft slap. Largo eased
out the pink tongue of playing card and moved it across the
baize to Bond. He took one for himself and then pressed out
one more for each of them. Bond picked up his first card and
flicked it face up into the middle of the table. It was a nine,
the nine of diamonds. Bond glanced sideways at Largo. He
said, "That is always a good start—so good that I will also
face my second card." He casually flicked it out to join the
nine. It turned over in mid-air and fell besides the nine. It was
a glorious ten, the ten of spades. Unless Largo's two cards also
added up to nine or nineteen, Bond had won.

Largo laughed, but the laugh had a hard edge to it. "You
certainly make me try," he said gaily. He threw his cards to
follow Bond's. They were the eight of hearts and the king of
clubs. Largo had lost by a pip—two naturals, but one just
better than the other, the cruelest way to lose. Largo laughed
hugely. "Somebody had to be second," he said to the table at
large. "What did I say? The English can pull what they like
out of the shoe."

The croupier pushed the chips across to Bond. Bond made a small pile of them. He gestured at the heap in front of Largo: "So, it seems, can the Italians. I told you this afternoon we should go into partnership."

Largo laughed delightedly. "Well, let's just try once again. Put in what you have won and I will banco it in partnership with Mr. Snow on your right. Yes, Mr. Snow?"

Mr. Snow, a tough-looking European who, Bond remembered, was one of the shareholders, agreed. Bond put in the eight hundred and they each put in four against him. Bond won again, this time with a six against a five for the table—once more by one point.

Largo shook his head mournfully. "Now indeed we have seen the writing on the wall. Mr. Snow, you will have to continue alone. This Mr. Bond has green fingers against me, I surrender."

Now Largo was smiling only with his mouth. Mr. Snow suivied and pushed forward sixteen hundred dollars to cover Bond's stake. Bond thought: I have made sixteen hundred dollars in two coups, over five hundred pounds. And it would be fun to pass the bank and for the bank to go down on the next hand. He withdrew his stake and said, *"La main passe."* There was a buzz of comment. Largo said dramatically, "Don't do it to me! Don't tell me the bank's going to go down on the next hand! If it does I shoot myself. Okay, okay, I will buy Mr. Bond's bank and we will see." He threw some plaques out on to the table—sixteen hundred dollars' worth.

And Bond heard his own voice say banco! He was bancoing his own bank—telling Largo that he had done it to him once, then twice, and now he was going to do it, inevitably, again!

Largo turned round to face Bond. Smiling with his mouth, he narrowed his eyes and looked carefully, with a new curiosity, at Bond's face. He said quietly, "But you are hunting me, my dear fellow. You are pursuing me. What is this? Vendetta?"

Bond thought: I will see if an association of words does something to him. He said, "When I came to the table I saw a spectre." He said the word casually, with no hint at double meaning.

The smile came off Largo's face as if he had been slapped. It was at once switched on again, but now the whole face was tense, strained, and the eyes had gone watchful and very hard.

His tongue came out and touched his lips. "Really? What do you mean?"

Bond said lightly, "The spectre of defeat. I thought your luck was on the turn. Perhaps I was wrong." He gestured at the shoe. "Let's see."

The table had gone quiet. The players and spectators felt that a tension had come between these two men. Suddenly there was the smell of enmity where before there had been only jokes. A glove had been thrown down, by the Englishman. Was it about the girl? Probably. The crowd licked its lips.

Largo laughed sharply. He stitched gaiety and bravado back on his face. "Aha!" His voice was boisterous again. "My friend wishes to put the evil eye upon my cards. We have a way to deal with that where I come from." He lifted a hand, and with only the first and little fingers outstretched in a fork, he prodded once, like a snake striking toward Bond's face. To the crowd it was a playful piece of theater, but Bond, within the strong aura of the man's animal magnetism, felt the ill temper, the malevolence behind the old Mafia gesture.

Bond laughed good-naturedly. "That certainly put the hex on me. But what did it do to the cards? Come on, your spectre against my spectre!"

Again the look of doubt came over Largo's face. Why again the use of this word? He gave the shoe a hefty slap. "All right, my friend. We are wrestling the best of three falls. Here comes the third."

Quickly his first two fingers licked out the four cards. The table had hushed. Bond faced his pair inside his hand. He had a total of five—a ten of clubs and a five of hearts. Five is a marginal number. One can either draw or not. Bond folded the cards face down on the table. He said, with the confident look of a man who has a six or a seven, "No card, thank you."

Largo's eyes narrowed as he tried to read Bond's face. He turned up his cards, flicked them into the middle of the table with a gesture of disgust. He also had a count of five. Now what was he to do? Draw or not draw? He looked again at the quiet smile of confidence on Bond's face—and drew. It was a nine, the nine of spades. By drawing another card instead of standing on his five and equaling Bond, he had drawn and now had a four to Bond's five.

Impassively Bond turned up his cards. He said, "I'm afraid you should have killed the evil eye in the pack, not in me."

There was a buzz of comment round the table. "But if the Italian had stood on his five..." "I always draw on a five." "I never do." "It was bad luck." "No, it was bad play."

Now it was an effort for Largo to keep the snarl off his face. But he managed it, the forced smile lost its twist, the balled fists relaxed. He took a deep breath and held out his hand to Bond. Bond took it, folding his thumb inside his palm just in case Largo might give him a bone-crusher with his vast machine tool of a hand. But it was a firm grasp and no more. Largo said, "Now I must wait for the shoe to come round again. You have taken all my winnings. I have a hard evening's work ahead of me just when I was going to take my niece for a drink and a dance." He turned to Domino. "My dear, I don't think you know Mr. Bond, except on the telephone. I'm afraid he has upset my plans. You must find someone else to squire you."

Bond said, "How do you do. Didn't we meet in the tobacconist's this morning?"

The girl screwed up her eyes. She said indifferently, "Yes? It is possible. I have such a bad memory for faces."

Bond said, "Well, could I give you a drink? I can just afford even a Nassau drink now, thanks to the generosity of Mr. Largo. And I have finished here. This sort of thing can't last. I mustn't press my luck."

The girl got up. She said ungraciously, "If you have nothing better to do." She turned to Largo: "Emilio, perhaps if I take this Mr. Bond away, your luck will turn again. I will be in the supper room having caviar and champagne. We must try and get as much of your funds as we can back in the family."

Largo laughed. His spirits had returned. He said, "You see, Mr. Bond, you are out of the frying pan into the fire. In Dominetta's hands you may not fare so well as in mine. See you later, my dear fellow. I must now get back to the salt mines where you have consigned me."

Bond said, "Well, thanks for the game. I will order champagne and caviar for three. My spectre also deserves his reward." Wondering again whether the shadow that flickered in Largo's eyes at the word had more significance than Italian superstition, he got up and followed the girl between the crowded tables to the supper room.

Domino made for a shadowed table in the farthest corner of the room. Walking behind her, Bond had noticed for the first time she had the smallest trace of a limp. He found it endearing, a touch of childish sweetness beneath the authority and blatant sex appeal of a girl to whom he had been inclined to award that highest, but toughest, French title—a *courtisane de marque*.

When the Clicquot rosé and fifty dollars' worth of Beluga caviar came—anything less, he had commented to her, would be no more than a spoonful—he asked her about the limp. "Did you hurt yourself swimming today?"

She looked at him gravely. "No. I have one leg an inch shorter than the other. Does it displease you?"

"No. It's pretty. It makes you something of a child."

"Instead of a hard old kept woman. Yes?" Her eyes challenged him.

"Is that how you see yourself?"

"It's rather obvious isn't it? Anyway, it's what everyone in Nassau thinks." She looked him squarely in the eyes, but with a touch of pleading.

"Nobody's told me that. Anyway, I make up my own mind about men and women. What's the good of other people's opinions? Animals don't consult each other about other animals. They look and sniff and feel. In love and hate, and everything in between, those are the only tests that matter. But people are unsure of their own instincts. They want reassurance. So they ask someone else whether they should like a particular person or not. And as the world loves bad news, they nearly always get a bad answer—or at least a qualified one. Would you like to know what I think of you?"

She smiled. "Every woman likes to hear about herself. Tell me, but make it sound true, otherwise I shall stop listening."

"I think you're a young girl, younger than you pretend to be, younger than you dress. I think you were carefully brought up, in a red-carpet sort of way, and then the red carpet was suddenly jerked away from under your feet and you were thrown more or less into the street. So you picked yourself up and started to work your own way back to the red carpet you had got used to. You were probably fairly ruthless about it. You had to be. You only had a woman's weapons and you probably used them pretty coolly. I expect you used your body. It would be a wonderful asset. But in using it to get what you wanted, your sensibilities had to be put aside. I don't expect they're very far underground. They certainly haven't atrophied. They've just lost their voice because you wouldn't listen to them. You couldn't afford to listen to them if you were to get back on that red carpet and have the things you wanted. And now you've got the things." Bond touched the hand that lay on the banquette between them. "And perhaps you've almost had enough of them." He laughed. "But I mustn't get too serious. Now about the smaller things. You know all about them, but just for the record, you're beautiful, sexy, provocative, independent, self-willed, quick-tempered, and cruel."

She looked at him thoughtfully. "There's nothing very clever about all that. I told you most of it. You know something about Italian women. But why do you say I'm cruel?"

"If I was gambling and I took a knock like Largo did and I had my woman, a woman, sitting near me watching, and she didn't give me one word of comfort or encouragement I would say she was being cruel. Men don't like failing in front of their women."

She said impatiently, "I've had to sit there too often and watch him show off. I wanted you to win. I cannot pretend. You didn't mention my only virtue. It's honesty. I love to the hilt and I hate to the hilt. At the present time, with Emilio, I am halfway. Where we were lovers, we are now good friends who understand each other. When I told you he was my guardian, I was telling a white lie. I am his kept woman. I am a bird in a gilded cage. I am fed up with my cage and tired of my bargain." She looked at Bond defensively. "Yes, it is cruel for Emilio. But it is also human. You can buy the outside of the body, but you cannot buy what is inside—what people call the heart and the soul. But Emilio knows that. He wants women for use. Not for love. He has had thousands in this way. He knows where we both stand. He is realistic. But it is becoming more difficult to keep to my bargain—to, to, let's call it sing for my supper."

She stopped abruptly. She said, "Give me some more champagne. All this silly talking has made me thirsty. And I would like a packet of Players"—she laughed "—Please, as they say in the advertisements. I am fed up with just smoking smoke. I need my Hero."

Bond bought a packet from the cigarette girl. He said, "What's that about a hero?"

She had entirely changed. Her bitterness had gone, and the lines of strain on her face. She had softened. She was suddenly a girl out for the evening. "Ah, you don't know! My one true love! The man of my dreams. The sailor on the front of the packet of Players. You have never thought about him as I have." She came closer to him on the banquette and held the packet under his eyes. "You don't understand the romance of this wonderful picture—one of the great masterpieces of the world. This man"—she pointed—"was the first man I ever sinned with. I took him into the woods, I loved him in the dormitory, I spent nearly all my pocket money on him. In exchange he introduced me to the great world outside the Cheltenham Ladies College. He grew me up. He put me at ease with boys my own age. He kept me company when I was lonely or afraid of being young. He encouraged me, gave me assurance. Have you never thought of the romance behind this picture? You see nothing, yet the whole of England is there! Listen." She took his arm eagerly. "This is the story of Hero, the name on his cap badge. At first he was a young man, a powder monkey or whatever they called it, in that sailing ship behind his right ear. It was a hard time for him. Weevils in the biscuits, hit with marlinspikes and ropes' ends and things, sent up aloft to the top of all that rigging where the flag flies. But he persevered. He began to grow a mustache. He was fair-haired and rather too pretty." She giggled. "He may even have had to fight for his virture or whatever men call it, among all those hammocks. But you can see from his face—that line of concentration between his eyes—and from his fine head, that he was a man to get on." She paused and swallowed a glass of champagne. The dimples were now deep holes in her cheeks. "Are you listening to me? You are not bored having to listen about my hero?"

"I'm only jealous. Go on."

"So he went all over the world—to India, China, Japan,

America. He had many girls and many fights with cutlasses and fists. He wrote home regularly—to his mother and to a married sister who lived at Dover. They wanted him to come home and meet a nice girl and get married. But he wouldn't. You see, he was keeping himself for a dream girl who looked rather like me. And then"—she laughed—"the first steamships came in and he was transferred to an ironclad—that's the picture of it on the right. And by now he was a bosun, whatever that is, and very important. And he saved up from his pay and instead of going out fighting and having girls he grew that lovely beard, to make himself look older and more important, and he set to with a needle and colored threads to make that picture of himself. You can see how well he did it—his first windjammer and his last ironclad with the lifebuoy as a frame. He only finished it when he decided to leave the Navy. He didn't really like steamships. In the prime of life, don't you agree? And even then he ran out of gold thread to finish the rope around the lifebuoy, so he just had to tail it off. There, you can see on the right where the rope crosses the blue line. So he came back home on a beautiful golden evening after a wonderful life in the Navy and it was so sad and beautiful and romantic that he decided he would put the beautiful evening into another picture. So he bought a pub at Bristol with his savings and in the mornings before the pub opened he worked away until he had finished and there you can see the little sailing ship that brought him home from Suez with his duffel bag full of silks and seashells and souvenirs carved out of wood. And that's the Needles Lighthouse beckoning him in to harbor on that beautiful calm evening. Mark you"—she frowned—"I don't like that sort of bonnet thing he's wearing for a hat, and I'd have liked him to have put 'H.M.S.' before the 'Hero,' but you can see that would have made it lopsided and he wouldn't have been able to get all the 'Hero' in. But you must admit it's the most terrifically romantic picture. I cut it off my first packet, when I smoked one in the lavatory and felt terribly sick, and kept it until it fell to pieces. Then I cut off a fresh one. I carried him with me always until things went wrong and I had to go back to Italy. Then I couldn't afford Players. They're too expensive in Italy and I had to smoke things called Nazionales."

Bond wanted to keep her mood. He said, "But what happened to the Hero's pictures? How did the cigarette people get hold of them?"

"Oh, well, you see one day a man with a stovepipe hat and a frock coat came into the Hero's pub with two small boys. Here." She held the packet sideways. "Those are the ones, 'John Player & Sons.' You see, it says that their Successors run the business now. Well they had one of the first motor cars, a Rolls Royce, and it had broken down outside the Hero's pub. The man in the stovepipe hat didn't drink, of course—those sort of people didn't, not the respectable merchants who lived near Bristol. So he asked for ginger beer and bread and cheese while his chauffeur mended the car. And the hero got it for them. And Mr. John Player and the boys all admired the two wonderful tapestry pictures hanging on the wall of the pub. Now this Mr. Player was in the tobacco and snuff business and cigarettes had just been invented and he wanted to start making them. But he couldn't for the life of him know what to call them or what sort of a picture to put on the packet. And he suddenly had a wonderful idea. When he got back to the factory he talked to his manager and the manager came along to the pub and saw the Hero and offered him a hundred pounds to let his two pictures be copied for the cigarette packet. And the Hero didn't mind and anyway he wanted just exactly a hundred pounds to get married on." She paused. Her eyes were far away. "She was very nice, by the way, only thirty and a good plain cook and her young body kept him warm in bed until he died many years later. And she bore him two children, a boy and a girl. And the boy went into the Navy like his father. Well, anyway, Mr. Player wanted to have the Hero in the lifebuoy on one side of the packet and the beautiful evening on the other. But the manager pointed out that that would leave no room for all this"—she turned over the packet—"about 'Rich, Cool,' and 'Navy Cut Tobacco' and that extraordinary trademark of a doll's house swimming in chocolate fudge with Nottingham Castle written underneath. So then Mr. Player said, 'Well then, we'll put one on top of the other.' And that's just exactly what they did and I must say I think it fits in very well, don't you? Though I expect the Hero was pretty annoyed at the mermaid being blanked out."

"The mermaid?"

"Oh, yes. Underneath the bottom corner of the lifebuoy where it dips into the sea, the Hero had put a tiny mermaid combing her hair with one hand and beckoning him home with the other. That was supposed to be the woman he was going to find and marry. But you can see there wasn't room and anyway her breasts were showing and Mr. Player, who was a very strong Quaker, didn't think that was quite proper. But he made it up to the Hero in the end."

"Oh, how did he do that?"

"Well you see the cigarettes were a great success. It was really the picture that did it. People decided that anything with a wonderful picture like that on the outside must be good and Mr. Player made a fortune and I expect his Successors did too. So when the Hero was getting old and hadn't got long to live, Mr. Player had a copy of the lifebuoy picture drawn by the finest artist of the day. It was just the same as the Hero's except that it wasn't in color and it showed him very much older, and he promised the Hero that this picture too would always be on his cigarette packets, only on the inside bit. Here." She pushed out the cardboard container. "You see how old he looks? And one other thing, if you look closely, the flags on the two ships are flying at half mast. Rather sweet of Mr. Player, don't you think, to ask the artist for that. It meant that the Hero's first and last ship were remembering him. And Mr. Player and his two sons came and presented it to him just before he died. It must have made it much easier for him, don't you think?"

"It certainly must. Mr. Player must have been a very thoughtful man."

The girl was slowly returning from her dreamland. She said in a different, rather prim voice, "Well, thank you anyway for having listened to the story. I know it's all a fairy tale. At least I suppose it is. But children are stupid in that way. They like to have something to keep under the pillow until they're quite grown up—a rag doll or a small toy or something. I know that boys are just the same. My brother hung on to a little metal charm his nanny had given him until he was nineteen. Then he lost it. I shall never forget the scenes he made. Even though he was in the Air Force by then and it was the middle of the war. He said it brought him luck." She shrugged her shoulders.

There was sarcasm in her voice as she said, "He needn't have worried. He did all right. He was much older than me, but I adored him. I still do. Girls always love crooks, particularly if they're their brother. He did so well that he might have done something for me. But he never did. He said that life was every man for himself. He said that his grandfather had been so famous as a poacher and a smuggler in the Dolomites that his was the finest tombstone among all the Petacchi graves in the graveyard at Bolzano. My brother said he was going to have a finer one still, and by making money the same way."

Bond held his cigarette steady. He took a long draw at it and let the smoke out with a quiet hiss. "Is your family name Petacchi, then?"

"Oh, yes. Vitali is only a stage name. It sounded better so I changed it. Nobody knows the other. I've almost forgotten it myself. I've called myself Vitali since I came back to Italy. I wanted to change everything."

"What happened to your brother? What was his first name?"

"Giuseppe. He went wrong in various ways. But he was a wonderful flyer. Last time I heard of him he'd been given some high-up job in Paris. Perhaps that'll make him settle down. I pray every night that it will. He's all I've got. I love him in spite of everything. You understand that?"

Bond stabbed out his cigarette in the ashtray. He called for the bill. He said, "Yes, I understand that."

CHAPTER 16

Swimming the Gantlet

The dark water below the police wharf sucked and kissed at the rusty iron stanchions. In the latticed shadows cast through the ironwork by the three-quarter moon, Constable Santos heaved the single aqualung cylinder up onto Bond's back and Bond secured the webbing at his waist so that it would not snarl the strap of Leiter's second Geiger counter, the underwater model. He fitted the rubber mouthpiece between his teeth and adjusted the valve release until the air supply was just right. He turned off the supply and took out the mouthpiece. The music of the steel band in the Junkanoo night club tripped gaily out over the water. It sounded like a giant spider dancing on a tenor xylophone.

Santos was a huge colored man, naked except for his swimming trunks, with pectoral muscles the size of dinner plates. Bond said, "What should I expect to see at this time of night? Any big fish about?"

Santos grinned. "Usual harbor stuff, sah. Some barracuda perhaps. Mebbe a shark. But they's lazy an overfed with the refuse an muck from de drains. Dey won't trouble you—less you bleedin' that is. They'll be night-crawlin' things on the bottom—lobster, crab, mebbe a small pus-feller or two. The bottom's mostly seagrass on bits o' iron from wrecks an plenty of bottle and suchlike. Mucky, if you get me, sah. But the water's clear and you'll be hokay with this moon and the lights

153

from the *Disco* to guide you. Tek you bout twelve, fifteen minute, I'da say. Funny ting. I been lookin' for an hour and dere's no watchman on deck an no one in the wheelhouse. An the bit o' breeze should hide you bubbles. Coulda give you an oxygen rebreather, but ah doan like dem tings. Them dangerous."

"All right, let's go then. See you in about half an hour." Bond felt for the knife at his waist, shifted the webbing, and put the mouthpiece between his teeth. He turned on the air and, his fins slapping on the muddy sand, walked down and into the water. There he bent down, spat into his mask to prevent it steaming up, washed it out, and adjusted it. Then he walked slowly on, getting used to the breathing. By the end of the wharf he was up to his ears. He quietly submerged and launched himself forward into an easy leg crawl, his hands along his flanks.

The mud shelved steeply and Bond kept on going down, until, at about forty feet, he was only a few inches above the bottom. He glanced at the big luminous figures on the dial of his watch—12:10. He untensed himself and put his legs into an easy, relaxed rhythm.

Through the roof of small waves the pale moonlight flickered on the gray bottom, and the refuse—motor tires, cans, bottles—cast black shadows. A small octopus, feeling his shock wave, turned from dark brown to pale gray and squeezed itself softly back into the mouth of the oil-drum that was its home. Sea flowers, the gelatinous polyps that grow out of the sand at night, whisked down their holes as Bond's black shadow touched them. Other tiny night things puffed thin jets of silt out of their small volcanoes in the mud as they felt the tremor of Bond's passage, and an occasional hermit crab snapped itself back into its borrowed shell. It was like traveling across a moon landscape, on and under which many mysterious creatures lived minute lives. Bond watched it all, carefully, as if he had been an underwater naturalist. He knew that was the way to keep nerves steady under the sea—to focus the whole attention on the people who lived there and not try to probe the sinister gray walls of mist for imaginary monsters.

The rhythm of his steady progress soon became automatic,

and while Bond, keeping the moon at his right shoulder, held to his course, his mind reached back to Domino. So she was the sister of the man who probably highjacked the plane! Probably even Largo, if Largo was in fact involved in the plot, didn't know this. So what did the relationship amount to? Coincidence. It could be nothing else. Her whole manner was so entirely innocent. And yet it was one more thin straw to add to the meager pile that seemed in some indeterminate way to be adding up to Largo's involvement. And Largo's reaction at the word "spectre." That could be put down to Italian superstition—or it could not. Bond had a deadly feeling that all these tiny scraps amounted to the tip of an iceberg—a few feet of ice pinnacle, with, below, a thousand tons of the stuff. Should he report? Or shouldn't he? Bond's mind boiled with indecision. How to put it? How to grade the intelligence so that it would reflect his doubts? How much to say and how much to leave out?

The extrasensory antennae of the human body, the senses left over from the jungle life of millions of years ago, sharpen unconsciously when man knows that he is on the edge of danger. Bond's mind was concentrating on something far away from his present risks, but beneath his conscious thoughts his senses were questing for enemies. Now suddenly the alarm was sounded by a hidden nerve—Danger! Danger! Danger!

Bond's body tensed. His hand went to his knife and his head swiveled sharply to the right—not to the left or behind him. His senses told him to look to the right.

A big barracuda, if it is twenty pounds or over, is the most fearsome fish in the sea. Clean and straight and malevolent, it is all hostile weapon, from the long snarling mouth in the cruel jaw that can open like a rattlesnake's to an angle of ninety degrees, along the blue and silver steel of the body to the lazy power of the tail fin that helps to make this fish one of the five fastest sprinters in the sea. This one, moving parallel with Bond, ten yards away just inside the wall of gray mist that was the edge of visibility, was showing its danger signals. The broad lateral stripes showed vividly—the angry hunting sign— the gold and black tiger's eye was on him, watchful, incurious, and the long mouth was open half an inch so that the moonlight glittered on the sharpest row of teeth in the ocean—teeth that don't bite at the flesh, teeth that tear out a chunk and swallow and then hit and scythe again.

Bond's stomach crawled with the ants of fear and his skin tightened at his groin. Cautiously he glanced at his watch. About three more minutes to go before he was due to come up with the *Disco*. He made a sudden turn and attacked fast toward the great fish, flashing his knife in fast offensive lunges. The giant barracuda gave a couple of lazy wags of its tail and when Bond turned back on his course it also turned and resumed its indolent, sneering cruise, weighing him up, choosing which bit—the shoulder, the buttock, the foot—to take first.

Bond tried to recall what he knew about big predator fish, what he had experienced with them before. The first rule was not to panic, to be unafraid. Fear communicates itself to fish as it does to dogs and horses. Establish a quiet pattern of behavior and stick to it. Don't show confusion or act chaotically. In the sea, untidiness, ragged behavior, mean that the possible victim is out of control, vulnerable. So keep to a rhythm. A thrashing fish is everyone's prey. A crab or a shell thrown upside down by a wave is offering its underside to a hundred enemies. A fish on its side is a dead fish. Bond trudged rhythmically on, exuding immunity.

Now the pale moonscape changed. A meadow of soft seagrass showed up ahead. In the deep, slow currents it waved languidly, like deep fur. The hypnotic motion made Bond feel slightly seasick. Dotted sparsely in the grass were the big black footballs of dead sponges growing out of the sand like giant puffballs—Nassau's only export until a fungus had got at them and had killed the sponge crop as surely as myxomatosis has killed rabbits. Bond's black shadow flickered across the breathering lawn like a clumsy bat. To the right of his shadow, the thin black lance cast by the barracuda moved with quiet precision.

A dense mass of silvery small fry showed up ahead, suspended in midstream as if they had been bottled in aspic. When the two parallel bodies approached, the mass divided sharply, leaving wide channels for the two enemies, and then closing behind them into the phalanx they adopted for an illusory protection. Through the cloud of fish Bond watched the barracuda.

It moved majestically on, ignoring the food around it as a fox creeping up on the chicken run will ignore the rabbits in the warren. Bond sealed himself in the armor of his rhythm, transmitting to the barracuda that he was a bigger, a more dangerous fish, that the barracuda must not be misled by the whiteness of the flesh.

Amongst the waving grass, the black barb of the anchor looked like another enemy. The trailing chain rose from the bottom and disappeared into the upper mists. Bond followed it up, forgetting the barracuda in his relief at hitting the target and in the excitement of what he might find.

Now he swam very slowly, watching the white explosion of the moon on the surface contract and define itself. Once he looked down. There was no sign of the barracuda. Perhaps the anchor and chain had seemed inimical. The long hull of the ship grew out of the upper mists and took shape, a great Zeppelin in the water. The folded mechanism of the hydrofoil looked ungainly, as if it did not belong. Bond clung for a moment to its starboard flange to get his bearings. Far down to his left, the big twin screws, bright in the moonlight, hung suspended, motionless but somehow charged with thrashing speed. Bond moved slowly along the hull toward them, staring upward for what he sought. He drew in his breath. Yes, it was there, the ridge of a wide hatch below the water line. Bond groped over it, measuring. About twelve feet square, divided down the center. Bond paused for a moment, wondering what was inside the closed doors. He pressed the switch of the Geiger counter and held the machine against the steel plates. He watched the dial of the meter on his left wrist. It trembled to show the machine was alive, but it registered only the fraction Leiter had told him to expect from the hull. Bond switched the thing off. So much for that. Now for home.

The clang beside his ear and the sharp impact against his left shoulder were simultaneous. Automatically, Bond sprang back from the hull. Below him the bright needle of the spear wavered slowly down into the depths. Bond whirled. The man, his black rubber suit glinting like armor in the moonlight, was pedaling furiously in the water while he thrust another spear down the barrel of the CO_2 gun. Bond hurled himself toward him, flailing at the water with his fins. The man pulled back the loading lever and leveled the gun. Bond knew he couldn't make it. He was six strokes away. He stopped suddenly, ducked his head, and jackknifed down. He felt the small shock wave of the silent explosion of gas and something hit his foot. Now! He soared up below the man and scythed upward with his knife. The blade went in. He felt the black rubber against his hand. Then the butt of the gun hit him behind the ear and a white hand came down and scrabbled at his airpipe. Bond slashed wildly with the knife, his hand moving with terrifying slowness through the water. The point ripped something. The hand let go of the mask, but now Bond couldn't see. Again the butt of the gun crashed down on his head. Now the water was full of black smoke, heavy, stringy stuff that clung to the glass of his mask. Bond backed painfully, slowly away, clawing at the glass. At last it cleared. The black smoke was coming out of the man, out of his stomach. But the gun was coming up again slowly, agonizingly, as if it weighed a ton, and the bright sting of the spear showed at its mouth. Now the webbed feet were hardly stirring, but the man was sinking slowly down to Bond's level. Suspended straight in the water, he looked like one of those little celluloid figures in a Ptolemy jar that rise and fall gracefully with pressure on the rubber top to the jar. Bond couldn't get his limbs to obey. They felt like lead. He shook his head to clear it, but still his hands and flippers moved only half consciously, all speed gone. Now he could see the bared teeth round the other man's rubber mouthpiece. The gun was at his head, at his throat, at his heart. Bond's hands crept up his chest to protect him while his flippers moved sluggishly, like broken wings, below him.

And then, suddenly, the man was hurled toward Bond as if he had been kicked in the back. His arms spread in a curious gesture of embrace for Bond and the gun tumbled slowly away between them and disappeared. A puff of black blood spread out into the sea from behind the man's back and his hands wavered out and up in vague surrender while his head twisted on his shoulders to see what had done this to him.

And now, a few yards behind the man, shreds of black rubber hanging from its jaws, Bond saw the barracuda. It was lying broadside on, seven or eight feet of silver and blue torpedo, and round its jaws there was a thin mist of blood, the taste in the water that had triggered its attack.

Now the great tiger's eye looked coldly at Bond and then downward at the slowly sinking man. It gave a horrible yawning gulp to rid itself of the shreds of rubber, turned lazily three-quarters on, quivered in all its length, and dived like a bolt of white light. It hit the man on the right shoulder with wide-open jaws, shook him once, furiously, like a dog with a rat, and then backed away. Bond felt the vomit rising in his gorge like molten lava. He swallowed it down and slowly, as if in a dream, began swimming with languid, sleepy strokes away from the scene.

Bond had not gone many yards when something hit the surface to his left and the moonlight glinted on a silvery kind of egg that turned lazily over and over as it went down. It meant nothing to Bond, but two strokes later, he received a violent blow in the stomach that knocked him sideways. It also knocked sense into him, and he began to move fast through the water, at the same time planing downward toward the bottom. More buffets hit him in quick succession, but the grenades were bracketing the blood patch near the ship's hull and the shock waves of the explosions became less.

The bottom showed up—the friendly waving fur, the great black toadstools of the dead sponges and the darting shoals of small fish fleeing with Bond from the explosions. Now Bond swam with all his strength. At any moment a boat would be got over the side and another diver would go down. With any luck he would find no traces of Bond's visit and conclude that the underwater sentry had been killed by shark or barracuda. It would be interesting to see what Largo would report to the harbor police. Difficult to explain the necessity for an armed underwater sentry for a pleasure yacht in a peaceful harbor!

Bond trudged on across the shifting seagrass. His head ached furiously. Gingerly he put up a hand and felt the two great bruises. The skin felt intact. But for the cushion of water, the two blows with the butt of the gun would have knocked him out. As it was, he still felt half stunned and when he came to the end of the seagrass and to the soft white moon landscape with its occasional little volcano puffs from the sea worms he felt as if he was on the edge of delirium. Wild commotion at the edge of his field of vision shocked him out of the semitrance. A giant fish, the barracuda, was passing him. It seemed to have gone mad. It was snaking wildly along, biting at its tail, its long body curling and snapping back in a jackknife motion, its mouth opening wide and shutting again in spasms. Bond watched it hurtle away into the gray mist. He felt somehow sorry to see the wonderful king of the sea reduced to this hideous jiggling automaton. There was something obscene about it, like the blind weaving of a punchy boxer before he finally crashes to the canvas. One of the explosions must have crushed a nerve center, wrecked some delicate balance mechanism in the fish's brain. It wouldn't last long. A greater predator than itself, a shark, would note the signs, the loss of symmetry that is suicide in the sea. He would follow for a while until the spasms slackened. Then the shark would make a short jabbing run. The barracuda would react sluggishly and that would be the end—in three great grunting bites, the head first and then the still jerking body. And the shark would cruise quietly on, its sickle mouth trailing morsels for the black and yellow pilot fish below his jaws and perhaps for the remora or two, the parasites that travel with the great host, that pick the shark's teeth when it is sleeping and the jaws are relaxed.

And now there were the gray-slimed motor tires, the bottles, the cans, and the scaffolding of the wharf. Bond slid over the shelving sand and knelt in the shallows, his head down, not capable of carrying the heavy aqualung up the beach, an exhausted animal ready to drop.

CHAPTER 17

The Red-Eye Catacomb

Bond, putting on his clothes, dodged the comments of Constable Santos. It seemed there had been sort of underwater explosions, with eruptions on the surface, on the starboard side of the yacht. Several men had appeared on deck and there had been some kind of commotion. A boat had been lowered on the port side, out of sight of the shore. Bond said he knew nothing of these things. He had cracked his head against the side of the ship. Silly thing to do. He had seen what he had wanted to see and had then swum back. Entirely successful. The Constable had been a great help. Thank you very much and good night. Bond would be seeing the Commissioner in the morning.

Bond walked with careful steadiness up the side street to where he had parked Leiter's Ford. He got to the hotel and telephoned Leiter's room and together they drove to police headquarters. Bond described what had happened and what he had discovered. Now he didn't care what the consequences might be. He was going to make a report. It was eight a.m. in London and there were under forty hours to go to zero hour. All these straws were adding up to half a haystack. His suspicions were boiling like a pressure cooker. He couldn't sit on the lid any longer.

Leiter said decisively, "You do just that. And I'll file a copy to C.I.A. and endorse it. What's more, I'm going to call up the *Manta* and tell her to get the hell over here."

"You are?" Bond was amazed at this change of tune.
"What's got into you all of a sudden?"

"Well, I was sculling around the Casino taking a good look
at anyone I thought might be a shareholder or a treasure hunter.
They were mostly in groups, standing around trying to put up
the front of having a good time—sunshine holiday and all that.
They weren't succeeding. Largo was doing all the work, being
gay and boyish. The others looked like private dicks or the rest
of the Torrio gang just after the St. Valentine Day massacre.
Never seen such a bunch of thugs in my life—dressed up in
tuxedos and smoking cigars and drinking champagne and all
that—just a glass or two to show the Christmas spirit. Orders,
I suppose. But all of them with that smell one gets to know
in the Service, or in Pinkertons for the matter of that. You
know, careful, cold-fish, thinking-of-something-else kinda
look the pros have. Well, none of the faces meant anything to
me until I came across a little guy with a furrowed brow and
a big egghead with pebble glasses who looked like a Mormon
who's got into a whorehouse by mistake. He was peering about
nervously and every time one of these other guys spoke to him
he blushed and said what a wonderful place it was and he was
having a swell time. I got close enough to hear him say the
same thing to two different guys. Rest of the time he just
mooned around, sort of helpless and almost sucking a corner
of his handkerchief, if you get me. Well that face meant something to me. I knew I'd seen it before somewhere. You know
how it is. So after puzzling for a bit I went to the reception
and told one of the guys behind the desk in a cheery fashion
that I thought I'd located an old classmate who'd migrated to
Europe, but I couldn't for the life of me remember his name.
Very embarrassing as he seemed to recognize me. Would the
guy help? So he came along and I pointed this feller out and
he went back to his desk and went through the membership
cards and came up with the one I wanted. Seemed he was a
man called Traut, Emil Traut. Swiss passport. One of Mr.
Largo's group from the yacht." Leiter paused. "Well, I guess
it was the Swiss passport that did it." He turned to Bond.
"Remember a fellow called Kotze, East German physicist?
Came over to the West about five years ago and sang all he

knew to the Joint Scientific Intelligence boys? Then he disappeared, thanks to a fat payment for the info, and went to ground in Switzerland. Well, James. Take my word for it. That's the same guy. The file went through my hands when I was still with C.I.A. doing desk work in Washington. All came back to me. It was one hell of a scoop at the time. Only saw his mug on the file, but there's absolutely no doubt about it. That man's Kotze. And now what the hell is a top physicist doing on board the *Disco*? Fits, doesn't it?"

They had come to police headquarters. Lights burned only on the ground floor. Bond waited until they had reported to the duty sergeant and had gone up to their room before he answered. He stood in the middle of the room and looked at Leiter. He said, "That's the clincher, Felix. So now what do we do?"

"With what you got this evening, I'd pull the whole lot in on suspicion. No question at all."

"Suspicion of what? Largo would reach for his lawyer and they'd be out in five minutes. Democratic processes of the law and so forth. And what single fact have we got that Largo couldn't dodge? All right, so Traut is Kotze. We're hunting for treasure, gentlemen, we need an expert mineralogist. This man offered his services. Said his name was Traut. No doubt he's still worried about the Russians getting after him. Next question? Yes, we've got an underwater compartment on the *Disco*. We're going to hunt treasure through it. Inspect it? Well, if you must. There you are gentlemen—underwater gear, skids, perhaps even a small bathyscaphe. Underwater sentry? Of course. People have spent six months trying to find out what we're after, how we're going to get it. We're professionals, gentlemen. We like to keep our secrets. And anyway, what was this Mr. Bond, this rich gentleman looking for a property in Nassau, doing underneath my ship in the middle of the night? Petacchi? Never heard of him. Don't care what Miss Vitali's family name was. Always known her as Vitali..." Bond made a throwaway gesture with one hand. "See what I mean? This treasure-hunting cover is perfect. It explains everything. And what are we left with? Largo pulls himself up to his full height and says, 'Thanks gentlemen. So I may go now? And so I shall, within the hour. I shall find another base for my work and you will be hearing from my lawyers forthwith—wrongful detention and trespass. And good luck to your tourist trade, gentlemen.'" Bond smiled grimly. "See what I mean?"

Leiter said impatiently, "So what do we do? Limpet mine? Send her to the bottom—in error, so to speak?"

"No. We're going to wait." At the expression on Leiter's face, Bond held up a hand. "We're going to send our report, in careful, guarded terms so we don't get an airborne division landing on Windsor Field. And we're going to say the *Manta* is all we need. And so it is. With her, we can keep tabs on the *Disco* just as we please. And we'll stay under cover, keep a hidden watch on the yacht and see what happens. At present we're not suspected. Largo's plan, if there is one, that is, and don't forget this treasure-hunting business still covers everything perfectly well, is going along all right. All he's got to do now is collect the bombs and make for Target No. 1 ready for zero hour in around thirty hours' time. We can do absolutely nothing to him until he's got one or both of those bombs on board or we catch him at their hiding place. Now, that can't be far away. Nor can the Vindicator, if she's hereabouts. So tomorrow we take that amphibian they've got for us and hunt the area inside a radius of a hundred miles. We'll hunt the seas and not the land. She must be in shoal water somewhere and damned well hidden. With this calm weather, we should be able to locate her—if she's here. Now, come on! Let's get those reports off and get some sleep. And say we're out of communication for ten hours. And disconnect your telephone when you get back to your room. However careful we are, this signal is going to set the Potomac on fire as well as the Thames."

Six hours later, in the crystal light of early morning, they were out at Windsor Field and the ground crew was hauling the little Grumman Amphibian out of the hangar with a jeep. They had climbed on board and Leiter was gunning the engines when a uniformed motorcycle dispatch rider came driving uncertainly toward them across the tarmac.

Bond said, "Get going! Quick! Here comes paper work."

Leiter released the brakes and taxied fast toward the single north-south runway. The radio crackled angrily. Leiter took a careful look over the sky. It was clear. He slowly pushed down on the joystick and the little plane snarled its way faster and faster down the concrete and, with a final bump, soared off over the low bush. The radio still crackled. Leiter reached up and switched it off.

Bond sat with the Admiralty chart on his lap. They were flying north. They had decided to start with the Grand Bahama group and have a first look at the possible area of Target No. 1. They flew at a thousand feet. Below them the Berry Islands were a necklace of brown spits set in cream and emerald and turquoise. "See what I mean?" said Bond. "You can see anything big through that water down to fifty feet. Anything as big as the Vindicator would have been spotted anywhere on any of the air routes. So I've marked off the areas where there's the minimum traffic. They'd have ditched somewhere well out of the way. Assuming, and it's the hell of an assumption, that, when the *Disco* made off to the southeast on the night of the third, it was a ruse, it'll be reasonable to hunt to the north and the west. She was away eight hours. Two of those would have been at anchor doing the salvage work. That leaves six hours' sailing at around thirty knots. Cut an hour off for laying the false trail, and that leaves five. I've marked off an area from the Grand Bahamas down to south of the Bimini group. That fits—if anything fits."

"Did you get on the Commissioner?"

"Yes. He's going to have a couple of good men with day-and-night glasses keeping an eye on the *Disco*. If she moves from her Palmyra anchorage where she's due back at midday, and if we're not back in time, he'll have her shadowed by one of the Bahama Airways charter planes. I got him quite worried with just one or two bits of information. He wanted to go to the Governor with the story. I said not yet. He's a good man. Just doesn't want too much responsibility without someone else's okay. I used the P.M.'s name to keep him quiet until we get back. He'll play all right. When do you think the *Manta* could be here?"

"S'evening, I'd say." Leiter's voice was uneasy. "I must have been drunk last night to have sent for her. Christ, we're creating one hell of a flap, James. It doesn't look too good in the cold light of dawn. Anyway, what the hell? There's Grand Bahama coming up dead ahead. Want me to give the rocket base a buzz? Prohibited flying area, but we might as well go

in up to our ears while we're about it. Just listen to the bawling
out we'll be getting in just a minute or two." He reached up
and switched on the radio.

They flew eastward along the fifty miles of beautiful coast
toward what looked like a small city of aluminum hutments
among which red and white and silver structures rose like small
skyscrapers above the low roofs. "That's it," said Leiter. "See
the yellow warning balloons at the corners of the base? Warning
to aircraft and fishermen. There's a flight test on this morning.
Better get out to sea a bit and keep south. If it's a full test,
they'll be firing toward Ascension Island—about five thousand
miles east. Off the African coast. Don't want to get an Atlas
missile up our backsides. Look over there to the left—sticking
up like a pencil beside that red and white gantry! Atlas or a
Titan—intercontinental. Or might be a prototype Polaris. The
other two gantries'll be for Matador and Snark and perhaps
your Thunderbird. That big gun thing, like a howitzer, that's
the camera tracker. The two saucer-shaped reflectors are the
radar screen. Golly! One of them's turning away toward us!
We're going to get hell in a minute. That strip of concrete
down the middle of the island. That's the skid strip for bringing
in missiles that are recallable. Can't see the central control for
telemetering and guidance and destruction of the things if they
go mad. That'll be underground—one of those squat blockhouse things. Some brass hat'll be sitting down there with his
staff getting all set for the count-down or whatever's going to
happen and telling someone to do something about that goddamn little plane that's fouling up the works."

Above their heads the radio crackled. A metallic voice said,
"N/AKOI, N/AKOI. You're in a prohibited area. Can you hear
me. Change course southwards immediately. N/AKOI. This
is Grand Bahama Rocket Base. Keep clear. Keep clear."

Leiter said, "Oh, hell! No use interfering with world progress. Anyway, we've seen all we want. No good getting on
the Windsor Field report to add to our troubles." He banked
the little plane sharply. "But you see what I mean? If that little
heap of iron-mongery isn't worth a quarter of a billion dollars
my name's P. Rick. And it's just about a hundred miles from
Nassau. Perfect for the *Disco*."

The radio started again: "N/AKOI, N/AKOI. You will be

reported for entering a prohibited area and for failing to ac-knowledge. Keep flying south and watch out for sudden tur-bulence. Over." The radio went silent.

Leiter said, "That means they're going to fire a test. Keep an eye on them and let me know when. I'll cut down the revs. No harm in watching ten million dollars of the taxpayer's money being blown off. Look! The radar scanner's turned back to the east. They'll be sweating it out in that blockhouse all right. I've seen 'em at it. Lights'll be blinking all over the big board way down underground. The Kibitzers'll be at their per-iscopes. Voices'll come down over the P.A. system—'Beacon contact . . . Warning balloons up . . . Telemeter contact . . . Tank pressure okay . . . Gyros okay . . . Rocket-tank pressure cor-rect . . . Rocket clear . . . Recorders alive . . . Lights all green . . . Ten, nine, eight, seven, six . . . Fire!' "

Despite Leiter's graphic count-down, nothing happened. Then, through his glasses, Bond saw a wisp of steam coming from the base of the rocket. Then a great cloud of steam and smoke and a flash of bright light that turned red. Breathlessly, for there was something terrible in the sight, Bond gave the blow-by-blow to Leiter. "It's edging up off the pad. There's a jet of flame. It seems to be sitting on it. Now it's going up like a lift. Now it's off! God, it's going fast! Now there's nothing but a spark of fire in the sky. Now it's gone. Whew!" Bond mopped his brow. "Remember that Moonraker job I was on a few years back? Interesting to see what the people out front saw."

"Yeah. You were lucky to get out of that deep fry." Leiter brushed aside Bond's reminiscences. "Now then, next stop those spits in the ocean north of Bimini and then a good run down the Bimini Group. Around seventy miles southwest. Keep an eye out. If we miss those dots, we'll end up in the grounds of the Fountain Blue in Miami."

A quarter of an hour later, the tiny necklet of cays showed up. They were barely above the water line. There was much shoal. It looked an ideal hiding-place for the plane. They came down to a hundred feet and slowly cruised in a zigzag down the group. The water was so clear that Bond could see big fish meandering around the dark clumps of coral and seaweed in the brilliant sand. A big diamond-shaped sting ray cowered and buried itself in the sand as the black shadow of the plane pursued and shot over it. There was nothing else and no possibility of concealment. The green shoal waters were as clean and innocent as if they had been open desert. The plane flew on south to North Bimini. Here there were a few houses and some small fishing hotels. Expensive-looking deep-sea fishing craft were out, their tall rods streaming. Gay people in the well-decks waved to the little plane. A girl, sunbathing naked on the roof of a smart cabin cruiser, hastily snatched at a towel. "Authentic blonde!" commented Leiter. They flew on south to the Cat Cays that trail away south from the Biminis. Here there was still, an occasional fishing craft. Leiter groaned. "What the hell's the good of this? These fishermen would have found it by now if it was here." Bond told him to keep on south. Thirty miles farther south there were little unnamed specks on the Admiralty chart. Soon the dark blue water began to shoal again to green. They passed over three sharks circling aimlessly. Then there was nothing—just dazzling sand under the glassy surface, and occasional patches of coral.

They went on carefully down to where the water turned again to blue. Leiter said dully, "Well, that's that. Fifty miles on there's Andros. Too many people there. Someone would have heard the plane—if there was a plane." He looked at his watch. "Eleven-thirty. What next, Hawkshaw? I've only got fuel for another two hours' flying."

Something was itching deep down in Bond's mind. Something, some small detail, had raised a tiny question mark. What was it? Those sharks! In about forty feet of water! Circling on the surface! What were they doing there? Three of them. There must be something—something dead that had brought them to that particular patch of sand and coral. Bond said urgently, "Just go back up once more, Felix. Over the shoals. There's something—"

The little plane made a tight turn. Felix cut down the revs and just kept flying speed about fifty feet above the surface. Bond opened the door and craned out, his glasses at short focus. Yes, there were the sharks, two on the surface with their dorsals out, and one deep down. It was nosing at something. It had its teeth into something and was pulling at it. Among the dark and pale patches, a thin straight line showed on the bottom.

Bond shouted, "Get back over again!" The plane zoomed round and back. Christ! Why did they have to go so fast? But now Bond had seen another straight line on the bottom, leading off at ninety degrees from the first. He flopped back into his seat and banged the door shut. He said quietly, "Put her down over those sharks, Felix. I think this is it."

Leiter took a quick glance at Bond's face. He said, "Christ!" Then, "Well, I hope I can make it. Damned difficult to get a true horizon. This water's like glass." He pulled away, curved back, and slowly put the nose down. There was a slight jerk and then the hiss of the water under the skids. Leiter cut his engines and the plane came to a quick stop, rocking in the water about ten yards from where Bond wanted. The two sharks on the surface paid no attention. They completed their circle and came slowly back. They passed so close to the plane that Bond could see the incurious, pink button eyes. He peered down through the small ripples cast by the two dorsal fins. Yes! Those "rocks" on the bottom were bogus. They were painted patches. So were the areas of "sand." Now Bond could clearly see the straight edges of the giant tarpaulin. The third shark had nosed back a big section. Now it was shoveling with its flat head trying to get underneath.

Bond sat back. He turned to Leiter. He nodded. "That's it, all right. Big camouflaged tarpaulin over her. Take a look."

While Leiter leaned across Bond and stared down, Bond's mind was racing furiously. Get the Police Commissioner on the police wavelength and report? Get signals sent off to London? No! If the radio operator on the *Disco* was doing his job, he would be keeping watch on the police frequency. So go on down and have a look. See if the bombs were still there. Bring up a piece of evidence. The sharks? Kill one and the others would go for the corpse.

Leiter sat back. His face was shining with excitement. "Well, I'll be goddamned! Boy oh boy!" He clapped Bond on the back. "We've found it! We've found the goddam plane. Whaddya know? Jesus Kerist!"

Bond had taken out the Walther PPK. He checked to see there was a round in the chamber, rested it on his left forearm, and waited for the two sharks to come round again. The first was the bigger, a hammerhead, nearly twelve feet long. Its hideously distorted head moved slowly from side to side as it nuzzled through the water, watching what went on below, waiting for a sign of meat. Bond aimed for the base of the dorsal fin that cut through the water like a dark sail. It was fully erect, a sign of tension and awareness in the big fish. Just below it was the spine, unassailable except with a nickel-plated bullet. He pulled the trigger. There was a *phut* as the bullet hit the surface just behind the dorsal. The boom of the heavy gun rolled away over the sea. The shark paid no attention. Bond fired again. The water foamed as the fish reared itself above the surface, dived shallowly, and came up thrashing sideways like a broken snake. It was a brief flurry. The bullet must have severed the spinal cord. Now the great brown shape began moving sluggishly in circles that grew ever wider. The hideous snout came briefly out of the water to show the sickle mouth gasping. For a moment it rolled over on its back, its stomach white to the sun. Then it righted itself and, dead probably, continued its mechanical, disjointed swim.

The following shark had watched all this. Now it approached cautiously. It made a short snapping run and swerved away. Feeling safe, it darted in again, seemed to nuzzle at the dying fish, and then lifted its snout above the surface and came down with all its force, scything into the flank of the hammerhead. It got hold, but the flesh was tough. It shook its great brown head like a dog, worrying at the mouthful, and then tore itself away. A cloud of blood poured over the sea. Now the other shark appeared from below and both fish, in a frenzy, tore and tore again at the still moving hulk whose nervous system refused to die.

The dreadful feast moved away on the current and was soon only a distant splashing on the surface of the quiet sea.

Bond handed Leiter the gun. "I'll get on down. May be rather a long job. They've got enough to keep them busy for half an hour, but if they come back, wing one of them. And if for any reason you want me back on the surface, fire straight down at the water and go on firing. The shock wave should just about reach me."

Bond began to struggle out of his clothes and, with Leiter's help, into his aqualung. It was a cramped, difficult business. It would be still worse getting back into the plane and it occurred to Bond that he would have to jettison the underwater gear. Leiter said angrily, "I wish to God I could get down there with you. Trouble with this damned hook, it just won't swim like a hand. Have to think up some rubber webbing gadget. Never occurred to me before."

Bond said, "You'll have to keep steam up on this crate. We've already drifted a hundred yards. Get her back up, like a good chap. I don't know who I'm going to find sharing the wreck with me. It's been here a good five days and other visitors may have moved in first."

Leiter pressed the starter and taxied back into position. He said, "You know the design of the Vindicator? You know where to look for the bombs and these detonator things the pilot has charge of?"

"Yes. Full briefing in London. Well, so long. Tell Mother I died game!" Bond scrambled onto the edge of the cockpit and jumped.

He got his head under and swam leisurely down through the brilliant water. Now he could see that there were swarms of fish over the whole area below him—bill fish, small barracuda, jacks of various types—the carnivores. They parted grudgingly to make room for their big, pale competitor. Bond touched down and made for the edge of the tarpaulin that had been dislodged by the shark. He pulled out a couple of the long corkscrew skewers that secured it to the sand, switched on his waterproof torch and, his other hand on his knife, slipped under the edge.

He had been expecting it, but the foulness of the water made him retch. He clamped his lips more tightly round the mouth-piece and squirmed on to where the bulk of the plane raised the tarpaulin into a domed tent. He stood up. His torch glittered on the underside of a polished wing and then, below it, on something that lay under a scrabbling mass of crabs, langoustes, sea caterpillars and starfish. This also Bond had been prepared for. He knelt down to his grisly work.

It didn't take long. He unclipped the gold identification disk and unlatched the gold wristwatch from the horrible wrists and noted the gaping wound under the chin that could not have been caused by sea creatures. He turned his torch on the gold disk. It said, "Giuseppe Petacchi. No. 15932." He strapped the two bits of evidence to his own wrists and went on toward the fuselage that loomed in the darkness like a huge silver submarine. He inspected the exterior, noted the rent where the hull had been broken on impact, and then climbed up through the open safety hatch into the interior.

Inside, Bond's torch shone everywhere into red eyes that glowed like rubies in the darkness, and there was a soft movement and scuttling. He sprayed the light up and down the fuselage. Everywhere there were octopuses, small ones, but perhaps a hundred of them, weaving on the tips of their tentacles, sliding softly away into protecting shadows, changing their camouflage nervously from brown to a pale phosphorescence that gleamed palely in the patches of darkness. The whole fuselage seemed to be crawling with them, evilly, horribly, and as Bond shone his torch on the roof the sight was even worse. There, bumping softly in the slight current, hung the corpse of a crew member. In decomposition, it had risen up from the floor, and octopuses, hanging from it like bats, now let go their hold and shot, jet-propelled, to and fro inside the plane—dreadful, glinting, red-eyed comets that slapped themselves into dark corners and stealthily squeezed themselves into cracks and under seats.

Bond closed his mind to the disgusting nightmare and, weaving his torch in front of him, proceeded with his search.

He found the red-striped cyanide canister and tucked it into his belt. He counted the corpses, noted the open hatch to the bomb bay, and verified that the bombs had gone. He looked in the open container under the pilot's seat and searched in alternative places for the vital fuses for the bombs. But they also had gone. Finally, having a dozen times had to slash away groping tentacles from his naked legs, he felt his nerve was quickly seeping away. There was much he should have taken with him, the identification disks of the crew, the pulp of the log book that showed nothing but routine flight details and no hint of emergency readings from the instrument panel, but he couldn't stand another second of the squirming, red-eyed catacomb. He slid out through the escape hatch and swam almost hysterically toward the thin line of light that was the edge of the tarpaulin. Desperately, he scrabbled his way under it, snagged the cylinder on his back in the folds, and had to back under again to free himself. And then he was out in the beautiful crystal water and soaring up to the surface. At twenty feet the pain in his ears reminded him to stop and decompress. Impatiently, staring up at the sweet hull of the seaplane above him, he waited until the pain had subsided. Then he was up and clinging to a float and tearing at his equipment to get rid of it and its contamination. He let it all go and watched it tumbling slowly down toward the sand. He rinsed his mouth out with the sweetness of pure salt water and swam to within reach of Leiter's outstretched hand.

CHAPTER 18

How to Eat a Girl

As they approached Nassau on their way back, Bond asked Leiter to take a look at the *Disco* lying off Palmyra. She was there all right, just where she had been the day before. The only difference, which had little meaning, was that she had only her bow anchor out. There was no movement on board. Bond was thinking that she looked beautiful and quite harmless lying there reflecting her elegant lines in the mirror of the sea, when Leiter said excitedly, "Say, James, take a look at the beach place. The boathouse alongside the creek. See those double tracks leading up out of the water? Up to the door of the boathouse. They look odd to me. They're deep. What could have made them?"

Bond focused his glasses. The tracks ran parallel. Something, something heavy, had been hauled between the boathouse and the sea. But it couldn't be, surely it couldn't! He said tensely, "Let's get away quick, Felix." Then as they zoomed off overland: "I'm damned if I can think of anything that could have made those. And dammit, if it was what it might have been, they'd have swept off those tracks pretty quick."

Leiter said laconically, "People make mistakes. We'll have to give that place the going-over. Ought to have done it before. Nice-looking dump. I think I'll take Mr. Largo up on his invitation and get out there on behalf of my esteemed client, Mr. Rockefeller Bond."

It was one o'clock by the time they got back to Windsor Field. For half an hour the control tower had been searching for them on the radio. Now they had to face the commandant of the field and, providentially as it happened, the Governor's A.D.C., who gave the Governor's blanket authorization for the string of their misdemeanors and then handed Bond a thick envelope which contained signals for both of them.

The contents began with the expected rockets for breaking communication and demands for further news ("That they'll get!" commented Leiter as they raced toward Nassau in the comfortable back of the Governor's Humber Snipe saloon.) E.T.A. for the *Manta* was five o'clock that evening. Inquiries through Interpol and the Italian police confirmed that Giuseppe Petacchi was in fact the brother of Dominetta Vitali, whose personal history as given to Bond stood up in all other respects. The same sources confirmed that Emilio Largo was a big-time adventurer and suspected crook though technically his dossier was clean. The source of his wealth was unknown but did not stem from funds held in Italy. The *Disco* had been paid for in Swiss francs. The constructors confirmed the existence of the underwater compartment. It contained an electric hoist and provision for launching small underwater craft and releasing skin divers. In Largo's specifications, this modification to the hull had been given as a requirement for underwater research. Further inquiry into the "shareholders" had yielded no further facts—with the significant exception that most of their backgrounds and professions dated back no further than six years. This suggested the possibility that their identities might be of recent fabrication and, at any rate in theory, this would equate with possible membership of SPECTRE, if such a body did in fact exist. Kotze had left Switzerland for an unknown destination four weeks previously. Latest photographs of the man were on the midday Pan American plane. Nevertheless the *Thunderball* war room had to accept the solidity of Largo's cover unless further evidence came to hand, and the present intention was to continue the world-wide search while allotting priority to the Bahamas area. In view of this priority, and the extremely urgent time factor, Brigadier Fairchild, C.B.,

D.S.O., British Military Attaché in Washington, with Rear Admiral Carlson, U.S.N. Ret., until recently Secretary to the U.S. Chiefs of Staff Committee, would be arriving at 1900 E.S.T. by the President's Boeing 707 "Columbine" to take joint command of further operations. The full cooperation of Messrs. Bond and Leiter was requested and, until the arrival of above-named officers, full reports every hour on the hour were to be radioed to London, copy to Washington, under joint signature.

Leiter and Bond looked at each other in silence. Finally Leiter said, "James, I propose we disregard the last bit and take formal note of the remainder. We've already missed four hours and I don't propose we spend the rest of the day sweating it out in our radio room. There's just too much to do. Tell you what. I'll do the stint of telling them the latest and then I'll say we're going off the air in view of the new emergency. I then propose to go and look over Palmyra on your behalf, sticking to our cover story. And I propose to have a damned good look at the boathouse and see what those tracks mean. Right? Then, at five, we'll rendezvous with the *Manta* and prepare to intercept the *Disco* if and when she sails. As for the Big Brass in the President's Special, well they can just play pinochle in Government House until tomorrow morning. Tonight's the night and we just can't waste it on the 'After you Alphonse' routine. Okay?"

Bond reflected. They were coming into the outskirts of Nassau, through the shanty-town slums tucked away behind the millionaire façade along the waterfront. He had disobeyed many orders in his life, but this was to disobey the Prime Minister of England and the President of the United States— a mighty left and right. But things were moving a damned sight too fast. M had given him this territory and, right or wrong, M would back him up, as he always backed up his staff, even if it meant M's own head on a charger. Bond said, "I agree, Felix. With the *Manta* we can manage this on our own. The vital thing is to find out when those bombs go on board the *Disco*. I've got an idea for that. May work, may not. It means giving the Vitali girl a rough time, but I'll try and handle that side. Drop me at the hotel and I'll get cracking. Meet you here again around four-thirty. I'll call up Harling and see if he's got anything new on the *Disco* and ask him to pass the word upstairs to you if anything's cooking. You've got all that straight about the plane? Okay. I'll hang on to Petacchi's identification disk for the time being. Be seeing you."

Bond almost ran through the lobby of the hotel. When he picked up his key at the reception desk they gave him a telephone message. He read it going up in the lift. It was from Domino: "Please telephone quickly."

In his room, Bond first ordered a club sandwich and a double bourbon on the rocks and then called the Police Commissioner. The *Disco* had moved to the oiling wharf at first light and had filled her tanks. Then she had moved back to her anchorage off Palmyra. Half an hour ago, at one-thirty precisely, the seaplane had been lowered over the side and, with Largo and one other on board, had taken off eastward. When the Commissioner had heard this on the walkie-talkie from his watchers he had got on to the control tower at Windsor Field and had asked for the plane to be radar-tracked. But she had flown low, at about three hundred feet, and they had lost her among the islands about fifty miles to the southeast. Nothing else had come up except that the harbor authorities had been alerted to expect an American submarine, the *Manta*, the nuclear-powered one, at around five in the evening. That was all. What did Bond know?

Bond said carefully that it was too early to tell. It looked as if the operation was hotting up. Could the watchers be asked to rush the news back as soon as the seaplane was sighted coming back to the *Disco*? This was vital. Would the Commissioner please pass on his news to Felix Leiter, who was on his way to the radio room at that moment? And could Bond be lent a car—anything—to drive himself? Yes, a Land Rover would be fine. Anything with four wheels.

Then Bond got on to Domino out at Palmyra. She sounded eager for his voice. "Where have you been all morning, James?" It was the first time she had used his Christian name. "I want you to come swimming this afternoon. I have been told to pack and come on board this evening. Emilio says they are going after the treasure tonight. Isn't it nice of him to take me? But it's a dead secret, so don't tell anyone, will you. But he is vague about when we will be back. He said something about

Miami. I thought"—she hesitated—"I thought you might have gone back to New York by the time we get back. I have seen so little of you. You left so suddenly last night. What was it?"

"I suddenly got a headache. Touch of the sun, I suppose. It had been quite a day. I didn't want to go. And I'd love to come for a swim. Where?"

She gave him careful directions. It was a beach a mile farther along the coast from Palmyra. There was a side road and a thatched hut. He couldn't miss it. The beach was sort of better than Palmyra's. The skin-diving was more fun. And of course there weren't so many people. It belonged to some Swedish millionaire who had gone away. When could he get there? Half an hour would be all right. They would have more time. On the reef, that is.

Bond's drink came and the sandwich. He sat and consumed them, looking at the wall, feeling excited about the girl, but knowing what he was going to do to her life that afternoon. It was going to be a bad business—when it could have been so good. He remembered her as he had first seen her, the ridiculous straw hat tilted down over the nose, the pale blue ribbons flying as she sped up Bay Street. Oh, well . . .

Bond rolled his swimming trunks into a towel, put on a dark blue sea-island cotton shirt over his slacks, and slung Leiter's Geiger counter over his shoulder. He glanced at himself in the mirror. He looked like any other tourist with a camera. He felt in his trousers pocket to make sure he had the identification bracelet and went out of the room and down in the lift.

The Land Rover had Dunlopillo cushions, but the ripple-edged tarmac and the pitted bends of Nassau's coastal road were tough on the springs and the quivering afternoon sun was a killer. By the time Bond found the sandy track leading off into the casuarinas and had parked the car on the edge of the beach, all he wanted to do was get into the sea and stay in it. The beach hut was a Robinson Crusoe affair of plaited bamboo and screwpine with a palm thatch whose wide eaves threw black shadows. Inside were two changing rooms labeled HIS and HERS. HERS contained a small pile of soft clothes and the white doeskin sandals. Bond changed and walked out again into the sun. The small beach was a dazzling half-moon of white sand enclosed on both sides by rocky points. There was no sign of the girl. The beach shelved quickly through green to blue under the water. Bond took a few steps through the shallows and dived through the blood-warm upper water down into the cool depths. He kept down there as long as possible, feeling the wonderful cold caress on his skin and through his hair. Then he surfaced and crawled lazily out to sea, expecting to see the girl skin-diving around one of the headlands. But there was no sign of her, and after ten minutes Bond turned back to the shore, chose a patch of firm sand, and lay down on his stomach, his face cradled in his arms.

Minutes later, something made Bond open his eyes. Coming toward him across the middle of the quiet bay was a thin trail of bubbles. When it passed over the dark blue into the green Bond could see the yellow single cylinder of the aqualung tank and the glint of a mask with a fan of dark hair streaming out behind. The girl beached herself in the shallows. She raised herself on one elbow and lifted the mask. She said severely, "Don't lie there dreaming. Come and rescue me."

Bond got to his feet and walked the few steps to where she lay. He said, "You oughtn't to aqualung by yourself. What's happened? Has a shark been lunching off you?"

"Don't make silly jokes. I've got some sea-egg spines in my foot. You'll have to get them out somehow. First of all get this aqualung off me. It hurts too much to stand on my foot with all this weight." She reached for the buckle at her stomach and released the catch. "Now just lift it off."

Bond did as he was told and carried the cylinder up into the shade of the trees. Now she was sitting in the shallow water, inspecting the sole of her right foot. She said, "There are only two of them. They're going to be difficult."

Bond came and knelt beside her. The two black spots, close together, were almost under the curl of the middle toes. He got up and held out a hand. "Come on. We'll get into the shade. This is going to take time. Don't put your foot down or you'll push them in further. I'll carry you."

She laughed up at him. "My hero! All right. But don't drop me." She held up both arms. Bond reached down and put one arm under her knees and another under her armpits. Her arms closed round his neck. Bond picked her up easily. He stood for a moment in the lapping water and looked down into her upturned face. The bright eyes said yes. He bent his head and kissed her hard on the half-open, waiting mouth.

The soft lips held his and drew slowly away. She said rather breathlessly, "You shouldn't take your reward in advance."

"That was only on account." Bond closed his hand firmly over her right breast and walked out of the water and up the beach into the shade of the casuarinas. He laid her gently down in the soft sand. She put her hands behind her head to keep the sand out of her straggling hair and lay waiting, her eyes half hidden behind the dark mesh of her eyelashes.

The mounded V of the bikini looked up at Bond and the proud breasts in the tight cups were two more eyes. Bond felt his control going. He said roughly, "Turn over."

She did as she was told. Bond knelt down and picked up her right foot. It felt small and soft, like a captured bird, in his hand. He wiped away the specks of sand and uncurled the toes. The small pink pads were like the buds of some multiple flower. Holding them back, he bent and put his lips to where the broken ends of the black spines showed. He sucked hard for about a minute. A small piece of grit from one of the spines came into his mouth and he spat it out. He said, "This is going to be a long business unless I hurt a bit. Otherwise it'll take all day and I can't waste too much time over just one foot. Ready?"

He saw the muscles of her behind clench to take the pain. She said dreamily, "Yes."

Bond sunk his teeth into the flesh round the spines, bit as softly as he could, and sucked hard. The foot struggled to get away. Bond paused to spit out some fragments. The marks of his teeth showed white and there were pinpoints of blood at the two tiny holes. He licked them away. There was almost no black left under the skin. He said, "This is the first time I've eaten a woman. They're rather good."

She squirmed impatiently but said nothing.

Bond knew how much it would be hurting. He said, "It's all right, Domino. You're doing fine. Last mouthful." He gave the sole of her foot a reassuring kiss and then, as tenderly as he could, put his teeth and lips back to work.

A minute or two later and he spat out the last section of spine. He told her it was over and gently laid the foot down. He said, "Now you mustn't get sand into it. Come on, I'll give you another lift into the hut and you can put your sandals on."

She rolled over. Her black eyelashes were wet with the tears of small pain. She wiped a hand over them. She said, looking seriously up at him, "Do you know, you're the first man who's ever made me cry." She held up her arms and now there was complete surrender.

Bond bent and picked her up. This time he didn't kiss the waiting mouth. He carried her to the door of the hut. HIS or HERS? He carried her into HIS. He reached out a hand for his shirt and shorts and threw them down to make a scrap of a bed. He put her down softly so that she was standing on his shirt. She kept her arms round his neck while he undid the single button of the brassière and then the tapes of the taut slip. He stepped out of his bathing trunks and kicked them away.

CHAPTER 19

When the Kissing Stopped

Bond leaned on one elbow and looked down at the beautiful drowned face. There was a dew of sweat below the eyes and at the temples. A pulse beat fast at the base of the neck. The lines of authority had been sponged away by the love-making and the face had a soft, sweet, bruised look. The wet eyelashes parted and the tawny eyes, big and faraway, looked up with remote curiosity into Bond's. They focused lazily and examined him as if they were seeing him for the first time.

Bond said, "I'm sorry. I shouldn't have done that."

The words amused her. The dimples at each side of the mouth deepened into clefts. She said, "You talk like a girl who has had it for the first time. Now you are frightened that you will have a baby. You will have to tell your mother."

Bond leaned down and kissed her. He kissed the two corners of her mouth and then the parted lips. He said, "Come and swim. Then I must talk to you." He got to his feet and held out his hands. Reluctantly she took them. He pulled her up and against him. Her body flirted with his, knowing it was safe. She smiled impishly up at him and became more wanton. Bond crushed her fiercely to him, to stop her and because he knew they had only a few more minutes of happiness. He said, "Stop it, Domino. And come on. We don't need any clothes. The sand won't hurt your foot. I was only pretending."

She said, "So was I when I came out of the sea. The spines didn't hurt all that much. And I could have cured them if I'd wanted to. Like the fishermen do. You know how?"

Bond laughed. "Yes I do. Now, into the sea." He kissed her once and stood back and looked at her body to remember how it had been. Then he turned abruptly and ran to the sea and dived deeply down.

When he got back to shore she was already out and dressing. Bond dried himself. He answered her laughing remarks through the partition with monosyllables. Finally she accepted the change in him. She said, "What is the matter with you, James? Is anything wrong?"

"Yes, darling." Pulling on his trousers, Bond heard the rattle of the little gold chain against the coins in his pocket. He said, "Come outside. I've got to talk to you."

Sentimentally, Bond chose a patch of sand on the other side of the hut from where they had been before. She came out and stood in front of him. She examined his face carefully, trying to read it. Bond avoided her eyes. He sat with his arms around his knees and looked out to sea. She sat down beside him, but not close. She said, "You are going to hurt me. Is it that you too are going away? Be quick. Do it cleanly and I will not cry."

Bond said, "I'm afraid it's worse than that, Domino. It's not about me. It's about your brother."

Bond sensed the stiffening of her body. She said in a low, tense voice, "Go on. Tell me."

Bond took the bracelet out of his pocket and silently handed it to her.

She took it. She hardly gave it a glance. She turned a little away from Bond. "So he is dead. What happened to him?"

"It is a bad story, and a very big one. It involves your friend Largo. It is a very great conspiracy. I am here to find out things for my government. I am really a kind of policeman. I am telling you this and I will tell you the rest because hundreds and perhaps thousands of people will die unless you help to prevent it. That is why I had to show you that bracelet and hurt you so that you would believe me. I am breaking my oath in doing this. Whatever happens, whatever you decide to do, I trust you not to tell what I am going to say."

"So that is why you made love to me—to make me do what you want. And now you blackmail me with the death of my brother." The words came out between her teeth. Now in a soft, deadly whisper, she said, "I hate you, I hate you, I hate you."

Bond said coldly, in a matter-of-fact voice, "Your brother was killed by Largo, or on his orders. I came here to tell you that. But then"—he hesitated—"you were there and I love you and want you. When what happened began to happen I should have had strength to stop it. I hadn't. I knew it was then or perhaps never. Knowing what I knew, it was a dreadful thing to have done. But you looked so beautiful and happy. I wanted to put off hurting you. That is my only excuse." Bond paused. "Now listen to what I have to tell you. Try and forget about your hate for me. In a moment you will realize that we are nothing in all this. This is a thing by itself." Bond didn't wait for her to comment. He began from the beginning and went slowly, minutely, through the whole case, omitting only the advent of the *Manta,* the one factor that could now be of help to Largo and perhaps alter his plans. He ended, "So you see, there is nothing we can do until those weapons are actually on board the *Disco*. Until that moment comes, Largo has a perfect alibi with his treasure-hunt story. There is nothing to link him with the crashed plane or with SPECTRE. If we interfere with him now, this moment, arrest the ship on some excuse, put a watch on her, prevent her sailing, there will only be a delay in the SPECTRE plan. Only Largo and his men know where the bombs are hidden. If the plane has gone for them, it will be keeping contact with the *Disco* by radio. If there's any hitch, the plane can leave the bombs at the hiding place or at another, dump them in shallow water anywhere, and return for them when the trouble has blown over. Even the *Disco* could be taken off the job and some other ship or plane used any time in the future. SPECTRE headquarters, wherever they are, will inform the Prime Minister that there has been a change of plan, or they can say nothing at all. Then, perhaps weeks from now, they will send another communication. And this time there will perhaps be only twenty-four hours' notice for the money to be dropped. The terms will be tougher. And we shall have to accept them. So long as those bombs are still lost to us, the threat is there. You see that?"

"Yes. So what is to be done?" The voice was harsh. The girl's eyes glittered fiercely as they looked at and through Bond toward some distant target—not, he thought, at Largo the great conspirator, but at Largo who had had her brother killed.

"We have got to know when those bombs are on board the *Disco*. That is all that matters. Then we can act with all our weight. And we have one great factor on our side. We are pretty sure that Largo feels secure. He still believes that the wonderful plan, and it is wonderful, is going exactly as it was meant to do. That is our strength and our only strength. You see that?"

"And how are you to know when the bombs come on board the yacht?"

"You must tell us."

"Yes." The monosyllable was dull, indifferent. "But how am I to know? And how am I to tell you? This man is no fool. He is only foolish in wanting his mistress"—she spat the word out—"when so much else is at stake." She paused. "These people have chosen badly. Largo cannot live without a woman within reach. They should have known that."

"When did Largo tell you to come back on board?"

"Five. The boat is coming to fetch me at Palmyra."

Bond looked at his watch. "It is now four. I have this Geiger counter. It is simple to use. It will tell at once if the bombs are on board. I want you to take it with you. If it says there is a bomb on board, I want you to show a light at your porthole—switch the lights on in your cabin several times, anything like that. We have men watching the ship. They will be told to report. Then get rid of the Geiger counter. Drop it overboard."

She said scornfully, "That is a silly plan. It is the sort of melodramatic nonsense people write about in thrillers. In real life people don't go into their cabins and switch on their lights in daylight. No. If the bombs are there, I will come up on deck—show myself to your men. That is natural behavior. If they are not there, I will stay in my cabin."

"All right. Have it your own way. But will you do this?"

"Of course. If I can prevent myself killing Largo when I see him. But on condition that when you get him you will see that he is killed." She was entirely serious. She looked at him with matter-of-fact eyes as if he were a travel agent and she were reserving a seat on a train.

"I doubt if that will happen. I should say that every man on board will get a life sentence in prison."

She considered this. "Yes. That will do. That is worse than being killed. Now show me how this machine works." She got to her feet and took a couple of steps up the beach. She seemed to remember something. She looked down at the bracelet in her hand. She turned and walked down to the edge of the sea and stood for a moment looking out across the quiet water. She said some words that Bond couldn't hear. Then she leaned back and with all her strength threw the gold chain far out over the shoal into the dark blue. The chain twinkled briefly in the strong sun and there was a small splash. She watched the ripples widen and, when the smashed mirror was whole again, turned and walked back up the sand, her small limp leaving footmarks of uneven depth.

Bond showed her the working of the machine. He eliminated the wristwatch indicator and told her to depend entirely on the telltale clicking. "Anywhere in the ship should be all right," he explained. "But better near the hold if you can get there. Say you want to take a photograph from the well deck aft or something. This thing's made up to look like a Rolleiflex. It's got all the Rolleiflex lenses and gadgets on the front, lever to press and all. It just hasn't got a film. You could say that you'd decided to take some farewell pictures of Nassau and the yacht, couldn't you?"

"Yes." The girl, who had been listening attentively, now seemed distracted. Tentatively she put out a hand and touched Bond's arm. She let the hand fall. She looked up at him and then swiftly away. She said shyly, "What I said, what I said about hating you. That is not true. I didn't understand. How could I—all this terrible story? I still can't quite believe it, believe that Largo has anything to do with it. We had a sort of an affair in Capri. He is an attractive man. Everyone else wanted him. It was a challenge to take him from all these other smart women. Then he explained about the yacht and this wonderful trip looking for treasure. It was like a fairy tale. Of course I agreed to come. Who wouldn't have? In exchange, I was quite ready to do what I had to do." She looked briefly at him and away. "I am sorry. But that is how it is. When we got to Nassau and he kept me ashore, away from the yacht, I was surprised but I was not offended. The islands are beautiful. There was enough for me to do. But what you have told me explains many small things. I was never allowed in the radio room. The crew were silent and unfriendly—they treated me like someone who was not wanted on board, and they were on curious terms with Largo, more like equals than paid men. And they were tough men and better educated than sailors usually are. So it all fits. I can even remember that, for a whole week before last Thursday, Largo was terribly nervous and irritable. We were already getting tired of each other. I put it down to that. I was even making plans for flying home by myself. But he has been better the last few days and when he told me to be packed and ready to come on board this evening, I thought I might just as well do as he said. And of course I was very excited over this treasure hunt. I wanted to see what it was all about. But then"—she looked out to sea—"there was you. And this afternoon, after what happened, I had decided to tell Largo I would not go. I would stay here and see where you went and go with you." For the first time she looked him full in the face and held his eyes. "Would you have let me do that?"

Bond reached out and put his hand against her cheek. "Of course I would."

"But what happens now? When shall I see you again?"

This was the question Bond had dreaded. By sending her back on board, and with the Geiger counter, he was putting her in double danger. She could be found out by Largo, in which case her death would be immediate. If it came to a chase, which seemed almost certain, the *Manta* would sink the *Disco* by gunfire or torpedo, probably without warning. Bond had added up these factors and had closed his mind to them. He kept it closed. He said, "As soon as this is over. I shall look for you wherever you are. But now you are going to be in danger. You know this. Do you want to go on with it?"

She looked at her watch. She said, "It is half past four. I must go. Do not come with me to the car. Kiss me once and stay here. Do not worry about what you want done. I will do it well. It is either that or a stiletto in the back for this man." She held out her arms. "Come."

Minutes later Bond heard the engine of the MG come to life. He waited until the sound had receded in the distance down the Western Coast Road; then he went to the Land Rover and climbed in and followed.

A mile down the coast, at the two white obelisks that marked the entrance to Palmyra, dust still hung in the driveway. Bond sneered at his impulse to drive in after her and stop her from going out to the yacht. What in hell was he thinking of? He drove on fast down the road to Old Fort Point, where the police watchers were housed in the garage of a deserted villa. They were there, one man reading a paperback in a canvas chair while the other sat before tripod binoculars that were trained on the *Disco* through a gap in the blinds of a side window. The khaki walkie-talkie set was beside them on the floor. Bond gave them the new briefing and got on the radio to the Police Commissioner and confirmed it to him. The Commissioner passed two messages to him from Leiter. One was to the effect that the visit to Palmyra had been negative except that a servant had said the girl's baggage had gone on board the *Disco* that afternoon. The boathouse was completely innocent. It contained a glass-bottomed boat and pedallo. The pedallo would have made the tracks they had seen from the air. The second message said that the *Manta* was expected in twenty minutes. Would Bond meet Leiter at the Prince George Wharf, where she would dock.

The *Manta*, coming with infinite caution up-channel, had none of the greyhound elegance of the conventional submarine. She was blunt and thick and ugly. The bulbous metal cucumber, her rounded nose shrouded with tarpaulin to hide the secrets of her radar scanner from the Nassavians, held no suggestion of her speed, which Leiter said was around forty knots submerged. "But they won't tell you that, James. That's Classified.

I guess we're going to find that even the paper in the can is Classified when we go aboard. Watch out for these Navy guys. Nowadays they're so tight-lipped they think even a belch is a security risk."

"What else do you know about her?"

"Well, we won't tell this to the captain, but of course in C.I.A. we had to be taught the basic things about these atom subs, so we could brief agents on what to look for and recognize clues in their reports. She's one of the George Washington Class, about four thousand tons, crew of around a hundred, cost about a hundred million dollars. Range, anything you want until the chow runs out or until the nuclear reactor needs topping up—say every hundred thousand miles or so. If she has the same armament as the George Washington, she'll have sixteen vertical launching tubes, two banks of eight, for the Polaris solid-fuel missile. These have a range of around twelve hundred miles. The crews call the tubes the 'Sherwood Forest' because they're painted green and the missile compartment looks like rows of great big tree trunks. These Polaris jobs are fired from way down below the surface. The sub stops and holds dead steady. They have the ship's exact position at all times through radio fixes and star sights through a tricky affair called a star-tracker periscope. All this dope is fed into the missiles automatically. Then the chief gunner presses a button and a missile shoots up through the water by compressed air. When it breaks surface the solid-fuel rockets ignite and take the missile the rest of the way. Hell of a weapon, really, when you come to think of it. Imagine these damned things shooting up out of the sea anywhere in the world and blowing some capital city to smith-ereens. We've got six of them already and we're going to have more. Good deterrent when you come to think of it. You don't know where they are or when. Not like bomber bases and firing pads and so on you can track down and put out of action with your first rocket wave."

Bond commented drily, "They'll find some way of spotting them. And presumably an atomic depth charge set deep would send a shock wave through hundreds of miles of water and blow anything to pieces over a huge area. But has she got anything smaller than these missiles? If we're going to do a job on the *Disco* what are we going to use?"

"She's got six torpedo tubes up front and I dare say she's got some smaller stuff—machine guns and so forth. The trouble's going to be to get the commander to fire them. He's not going to like firing on an unarmed civilian yacht on the orders of a couple of plainclothes guys, and one of them a Limey at that. Hope his orders from the Navy Department are as solid as mine and yours."

The huge submarine bumped gently against the wharf. Lines were thrown and an aluminum gangplank was run ashore. There was a ragged cheer from the crowd of watchers being held back by a cordon of police. Leiter said, "Well, here we go. And to one hell of a bad start. Not a hat between us to salute the quarter deck with. You curtsy, I'll bow."

CHAPTER 20

Time for Decision

The interior of the submarine was incredibly roomy, and it was stairs and not a ladder that led down into the interior. There was no clutter, and the sparkling paintwork was in two-tone green. Powerlines painted in vivid colors provided a cheerful contrast to the almost hospital décor. Preceded by the officer of the watch, a young man of about twenty-eight, they went down two decks. The air (70° with 46% humidity, explained the officer) was beautifully cool. At the bottom of the stairs he turned left and knocked on a door that said *"Commander P. Pedersen, U.S.N."*

The captain looked about forty. He had a square, rather Scandinavian face with a black crew-cut just going gray. He had shrewd, humorous eyes but a dangerous mouth and jaw. He was sitting behind a neatly stacked metal desk smoking a pipe. There was an empty coffee cup in front of him and a signal pad on which he had just been writing. He got up and shook hands, waved them to two chairs in front of his desk, and said to the officer of the watch, "Coffee, please, Stanton. And have this sent, would you?" He tore the top sheet off the signal pad and handed it across. "Most Immediate."

He sat down. "Well, gentlemen. Welcome aboard. Commander Bond, it's a pleasure to have a member of the Royal

Navy visit the ship. Ever been in subs before?"

"I have," said Bond, "but only as a supercargo. I was in Intelligence—R.N.V.R. Special Branch. Strictly a chocolate sailor."

The captain laughed. "That's good! And you, Mr. Leiter?"

"No, Captain. But I used to have one of my own. You operated it with a sort of rubber bulb and tube. Trouble was they'd never let me have enough depth of water in the bath to see what she could really do."

"Sounds rather like the Navy Department. They'll never let me try this ship full out. Except once on trials. Every time you want to get going, the needle comes across a damn red line some interfering so-and-so has painted on the dial. Well gentlemen"—the captain looked at Leiter—"what's the score? Haven't had such a flood of Top Secret Most Immediates since Korea. I don't mind telling you, the last one was from the Chief of the Navy, Personal. Said I was to consider myself under your orders, or, on your death or incapacity, under Commander Bond's, until Admiral Carlson arrives at 1900 this evening. So what? What's cooking? All I know is that all signals have been prefixed Operation Thunderball. What is this operation?"

Bond had greatly taken to Commander Pedersen. He liked his ease and humor and, in general—the old Navy phrase came back to him—the cut of his jib. Now he watched the stolid good-humored face as Leiter told his story down to the departure of Largo's amphibian at one-thirty and the instructions Bond had given to Domino Vitali.

In the background to Leiter's voice there was a medley of soft noises—the high, constant whine of a generator overlaid by the muted background of canned music—the Ink Spots singing, "I love coffee, I love tea." Occasionally the P.A. system above the captain's desk crackled and sang with operational double-talk—"Roberts to Chief of the Boat"—"Chief Engineer wants Oppenshaw"—"Team Blue to Compartment F"—and from somewhere came the suck and gurgle of a pump-like apparatus that sounded punctually every two minutes. It was like being inside the simple brain of a robot that worked by hydraulics and electrical impulses with a few promptings from its human masters.

After ten minutes, Commander Pedersen sat back. He reached for his pipe and began filling it absent-mindedly. He said, "Well, that's one hell of a story." He smiled. "And strangely enough, even if I hadn't had these signals from the Navy Department, I'd believe it. Always did think something like this would happen one of these days. Hell! I have to carry these missiles around, and I'm in command of a nuclear ship. But that doesn't mean I'm not terrified by the whole business. Got a wife and two children, and that doesn't help either. These atomic weapons are just too damned dangerous. Why, any one of these little sandy cays around here could hold the whole of the United States to ransom—just with one of my missiles trained on Miami. And here am I, fellow called Peter Pedersen, age thirty-eight, maybe sane or maybe not, toting around sixteen of the things—enough to damn near wipe out England. However"—he put his hands down on the desk in front of him—"that's all by the way. Now we've got just one small piece of the problem on our hands—small, but as big as the world. So what are we to do? As I see it, the idea of you gentlemen is that this man Largo will be coming back any minute now in his plane after picking up the bombs from where he hid them. If he's got the bombs, and on what you've told me I'll go along with the probability that he has, this girl will give us the tip-off. Then we close in and arrest his ship or blow it out of the water. Right? But supposing he hasn't got the bombs on board, or for one reason or another we don't get the tip-off, what do we do then?"

Bond said quietly, "We follow him, sit close on his tail, until the time limit, that's about twenty-four hours from now, is up. That's all we can do without causing one hell of a legal stink. When the time limit's up, we can hand the whole problem back to our governments and they can decide what to do with the *Disco* and the sunken plane and all the rest. By that time, some little man in a speedboat we've never heard of may have left one of the bombs off the coast of America and Miami may have gone up in the air. Or there may be a big bang somewhere else in the world. There's been plenty of time to take those bombs off the plane and get them thousands of miles from here. Well, that'll be too bad and we'll have muffed it. But at this moment we're in the position of a detective watching a man he thinks is going to commit a murder. Doesn't even know for sure whether he's got a gun on him or not. There's nothing the detective can do but follow the man and wait until he actually pulls the gun out of his pocket and points it. Then, and only then, the detective can shoot the man or arrest him." Bond turned to Leiter. "Isn't that about it, Felix?"

"That's how it figures. And Captain, Commander Bond here and I are damn sure Largo's our man and that he'll be sailing for his target in no time at all. That's why we agreed to panic and ask you along. One gets you a hundred he'll be placing that bomb at night and tonight's the last night he's got. By the way, Captain, have you got steam up, or whatever the atom boys call it?"

"I have, and we can be under way in just about five minutes." The captain shook his head. "But there's one bit of bad news for you, gentlemen. I just can't figure how we're going to keep track of the *Disco*."

"How's that? You've got the speed, haven't you?" Leiter caught himself pointing his steel hook threateningly at the captain, and hastily brought it down again to his lap.

The captain smiled. "Guess so. Guess we could give her a good race on a straight course, but you gentlemen don't seem to have figured on the navigational hazards in this part of the ocean." He pointed at the British Admiralty chart on the wall. "Take a look at that. Ever seen a chart with so many figures on it? Looks like a spilled ants' nest. Those are soundings, gentlemen, and I can tell you that unless the *Disco* sticks to one of the deep-water channels—Tongue of the Ocean, Northwest Providence Channel, or the Northeast—we've had it, as Commander Bond would say. All the rest of that area"—he waved a hand—"may look the same blue color on a map, but after your trip in that Grumman Goose you know darned well it isn't the same blue color. Darned near the whole of that area is banks and shoal with only around three to ten fathoms over it. If I was quite crazy and looking for a nice cosy job ashore, I'd take the ship along surfaced in ten fathoms—if I could bribe the navigator and seal off the echo-sounder from crew members. But even if we got a long spell of ten fathoms on the chart, you got to remember that's an old chart, dates back to the days of sail, and these banks have been shifting for more than fifty years since it was drawn up. Then there's the tides that set directly onto and off the banks, and the coral nigger-heads that won't show up on the echo-sounder until you hear the echo of them smashing up the hull or the screw." The captain turned back to his desk. "No, gentlemen. This Italian vessel was darned well chosen. With that hydrofoil device of hers, she probably doesn't draw more than a fathom. If she chooses to keep to the shallows, we just haven't got a chance. And that's flat." The captain looked from one to another of them. "Want me to call up the Navy Department and have Fort Lauderdale take over with those fighter bombers you've got on call—get them to do a shadowing job?"

The two men looked at each other. Bond said, "She won't be showing lights. They'll have the hell of a job picking her up at night. What do you say, Felix? Maybe we'd better call them out even if it's only to keep some sort of a watch off the American coast. Then, if the Captain's willing, we'll take the Northwest Channel—if the *Disco* sails, that is—and bank on the Bahamas Rocket Station being Target No. 1."

Felix Leiter ran his left hand through the mop of straw-colored hair. "Goddammit," he said angrily. "Hell, yes, I suppose so. We're looking fools enough already bringing the *Manta* on stage. What's a squadron of planes? Sure. We've just *got* to back our hunch that it's Largo and the *Disco*. Come on, let's get together with the Captain and whip off a signal that doesn't look too damned silly—copy to C.I.A. and to your Chief. How do you want it to go?"

"Admiralty for M, prefixed Operation Thunderball." Bond wiped a hand down over his face. "God, this is going to put the cat among the pigeons." He looked up at the big metal wall clock. "Six. That'll be midnight in London. Popular time to get a signal like this."

The P.A. system in the ceiling spoke more clearly. "Watch Officer to Captain. Police officer with urgent message for Commander Bond." The captain pressed a switch and spoke into a desk microphone. "Bring him below. Prepare to cast off lines. All hands prepare for sailing." The captain waited for the acknowledgment and released the switch. The captain smiled across at them. He said to Bond, "What's the name of that girl? Domino? Well, Domino, say the good word."

The door opened. A police corporal, his hat off, crashed to attention on the steel flooring and extended a stiff arm. Bond took the buff O.H.M.S. envelope and slit it open. He ran his eyes down the penciled message signed by the Police Commissioner. Unemotionally he read out:

"PLANE RETURNED 1730 HOISTED INBOARD, DISCO SAILED AT 1755, FULL SPEED, COURSE NORTHWEST STOP GIRL DID NOT REPEAT NOT REAPPEAR ON DECK AFTER BOARDING.

Bond borrowed a signal blank from the captain and wrote:

MANTA WILL ENDEAVOR SHADOW VIA NORTHWEST PROVIDENCE CHANNEL STOP FIGHTER BOMBER SQUADRON FROM FORT LAUDERDALE WILL BE ASKED THROUGH NAVY DEPARTMENT TO COOPERATE WITHIN RADIUS OF TWO HUNDRED MILES OFF FLORIDA COAST STOP MANTA WILL KEEP CONTACT THROUGH WINDSOR FIELD AIR CONTROL STOP NAVY DEPARTMENT AND ADMIRALTY BEING INFORMED STOP PLEASE INFORM GOVERNOR ALSO ADMIRAL CARLSON AND BRIGADIER FAIRCHILD ON ARRIVAL.

Bond signed the message and passed it to the captain, who also signed, as did Leiter. Bond put the message in an envelope and gave it to the corporal, who wheeled smartly and clanked out in his heavy boots.

When the door was shut, the captain pressed down the switch on the intercom. He gave orders to sail, surfaced, course due north, at ten knots. Then he switched off. In the short silence, there was a flurry of background noise, piping of bosuns' whistles, a thin mechanical whine, and the sound of running feet. The submarine trembled slightly. The captain said quietly, "Well, gentlemen, that's that. I'd like to have the goose a bit less wild and a bit more solid. But I'll be glad to chase her for you. Now then, that signal."

With only half his mind on the wording of the signal, Bond sat and worried about the significance of the Commissioner's

message and about Domino. It looked bad. It looked as if either
the plane had not brought back the two bombs, or one of them,
in which case the mobilization of the *Manta* and of the fighter
bombers was a pretty meaningless precaution, hardly justified
by the evidence. It could easily be that the crashed Vindicator
and the missing bombs were the work of some entirely different
group and that, while they chased the *Disco,* the field was
being left clear for SPECTRE. But Bond's instincts refused to
allow him to accept this possibility. As cover, the whole
Disco-Largo set-up was one hundred per cent watertight. It
could not be faulted in any respect. That in itself was enough
to arouse Bond's suspicions. A plot of this magnitude and
audacity would only have been conceived under faultless cover
and down to the smallest detail. Largo could have just set off
on his treasure hunt, and everything, down to the last-minute
plane recce of the treasure location, to see if there were any
fishing boats about for instance, fitted in with that possibility.
Or he could be sailing to lay the bomb, adjust the time fuse
for perhaps a few hours after the deadline to allow time for its
recovery or destruction if England and America at the last
moment agreed to pay the ransom, and get far enough away
from the danger area to avoid the explosion and establish an
alibi. But where was the bomb? Had it arrived on board in the
plane and had Domino for some reason been unable to go up
on deck to make her signal? Or was it going to be picked up
en route to the target area? The westerly course from Nassau,
heading perhaps for the Northwest Light, through the Berry
Island Channel, fitted both possibilities. The sunken plane lay
westward, south of the Biminis, and so did Miami and other
possible targets on the American coast. Or, after passing
through the channel, about fifty miles west of Nassau, the
Disco could veer sharply northward and, after another fifty
miles of sailing through shoal water that would discourage
pursuit, get back into the Northwest Providence Channel and
make straight for the Grand Bahamas and the missile station.

Bond, fretted with indecision and the fear that he and Leiter
were making majestic fools of themselves, forced himself to
face one certainty—he and Leiter and the *Manta* were engaged
on a crazy gamble. If the bomb was on board, if the *Disco*

veered north for the Grand Bahamas and the missile station, then, by racing up the Northwest Channel, the *Manta* might intercept her in time.

But if this gamble came off, with all its possibilities of error, why hadn't Domino made her signal? What had happened to her?

CHAPTER 21

Very Softly, Very Slowly

The *Disco*, a dark torpedo leaving a deep, briefly creaming wake, hurtled across the indigo mirror of the sea. In the big stateroom there was silence save for the dull boom of the engines and the soft tinkle of a glass on the sideboard. Although, as a precaution, the storm shutters were battened down over the portholes, the only light inside came from a single port navigation lantern hung from the roof. The dim red light only just illuminated the faces of the twenty men sitting round the long table, and the red-and-black-shadowed features, contorting with the slight sway of the top light, gave the scene the appearance of a conspiracy in hell.

At the top of the table Largo, his face, though the cabin was air-conditioned, shining with sweat, began to speak. His voice was tense and hoarse with strain. "I have to report that we are in a state of emergency. Half an hour ago, No. 17 found Miss Vitali in the well deck. She was standing fiddling with a camera. When No. 17 came upon her she lifted the camera and pretended to take a photograph of Palmyra, although the safety cap was over the lens. No. 17 was suspicious. He reported to me. I went below and took her to her cabin. She struggled with me. Her whole attitude aroused my suspicions. I was forced to subdue her by drastic measures. I took the camera and examined it." Largo paused. He said quietly, "The camera was a fake. It concealed a Geiger counter. The counter

was, very naturally, registering over 500 milliroentgens. I
brought her back to consciousness and questioned her. She
refused to talk. In due course I shall force her to do so and
then she will be eliminated. It was time to sail. I again rendered
her unconscious and roped her securely to her bunk. I have
now summoned this meeting to acquaint you of this occurrence,
which I have already reported to No. 2."

Largo was silent. A threatening, exasperated growl came
from round the table. No. 14, one of the Germans, said through
his teeth, "And what, Mister No. 1, did No. 2 have to say
about this?"

"He said we were to carry on. He said the whole world is
full of Geiger counters looking for us. The secret services of
the whole world have been mobilized against us. Some busy-
body in Nassau, the police probably, was perhaps ordered to
have a radiation search made of all ships in harbor. Perhaps
Miss Vitali was bribed to bring the counter on board. But No.
2 said that once we have placed the weapon in the target area
there will be nothing to fear. I have had the radio operator
listening for unusual traffic between Nassau and the Coast. The
density is quite normal. If we were suspected, Nassau would
be deluged with wireless traffic from London and Washington.
But all is quiet. So the operation will proceed as planned. When
we are well away from the area, we will dispose of the lead
casing of the weapon. The lead casing will contain Miss Vitali."

No. 14 persisted: "But you will first obtain the truth from
this woman? It is not pleasant for our future plans to think that
we may be under suspicion."

"Interrogation will begin as soon as the meeting is over. If
you want my opinion, those two men who came on board
yesterday—this Bond and the man Larkin—may be involved.
They may be secret agents. The so-called Larkin had a camera.
I did not look at it closely, but it was similar to that in the
possession of Miss Vitali. I blame myself for not having been
more careful with these two men. But their story was con-
vincing. On our return to Nassau tomorrow morning. we shall
have to be circumspect. Miss Vitali will have fallen overboard.
I will work out the details of the story. There will be an inquest.
This will be irritating but nothing more. Our witnesses will be
unshakable. It will be wise to use the coins as additional alibi

for our whereabouts tonight. No. 5, is the state of erosion of the coins satisfactory?"

No. 5, Kotze the physicist, said judiciously, "It is no more than adequate. But they will pass examination, a cursory examination. They are authentic doubloons and Reals of the early seventeenth century. Sea water has no great effect on gold and silver. I have used a little acid to pit them. They will of course have to be handed to the coroner and declared as treasure trove. It would need a far greater expert than he or the court to pass judgment on them. There will be no compulsion to reveal the location of the treasure. We could perhaps give the depth of water—ten fathoms let us say, and an unspecified reef. I see no means by which our story could be upset. There is often very deep water outside reefs. Miss Vitali could have had trouble with her aqualung and could have been seen disappearing over the deep shelf where our echo-sounder gave the depth as a hundred fathoms. We did our best to dissuade her from taking part in the search. But she was an expert swimmer. The romance of the occasion was too much for her." No. 5 opened his hands. "There are often accidents of this nature. Many lives are lost in this way every year. A thorough search was instituted, but there were shark. The treasure hunt was broken off and we immediately returned to Nassau to report the tragedy." No. 5 shook his head decisively. "I see no reason to be dismayed by this occurrence. But I am in favor of a most rigorous interrogation." No. 5 turned his head politely in Largo's direction. "There are certain uses of electricity of which I have knowledge. The human body cannot resist them. If I can be of any service . . . ?"

Largo's voice was equally polite. They might have been discussing remedies for a seasick passenger. "Thank you. I have means of persuasion that I have found satisfactory in the past. But I shall certainly call upon you if the case is an obstinate one." Largo looked down the table into the shadowed, ruby faces. "And now we will quickly run through the final details." He glanced down at his watch. "It is midnight. There will be two hours' moonlight starting at three a.m. The first light of dawn will be shortly after five a.m. We thus have two hours for the operation. Our course will bring us in towards West End from the south. This is a normal entry to the islands, and even if our further progress toward the target area is noted by the missile-station radar it will only be assumed that we are a yacht that has strayed slightly off course. We shall anchor at exactly three a.m. and the swimming party will leave for the half-mile swim to the laying point. The fifteen of you who will be taking part in this swim will, as arranged, swim in arrow formation, the Chariot and the sled with the missile in the center. Formation must be strictly kept to avoid straying. The blue torch on my back should be an adequate beacon, but if any man gets lost, he returns to the ship. Is that understood? The first duty of the escort will be to watch for shark and barracuda. I will again remind you that the range of your guns is not much more than twenty feet and that fish must be hit in or behind the head. Any man who is about to fire must warn his neighbor, who will then stand by to give additional fire if required. However, one hit should be sufficient to kill if the curare is, as we have been informed, not affected by the passage through sea water. Above all"—Largo put his hands decisively down on the table before him—"do not forget to remove the small protective sheath from the barb before firing." Largo raised his hands. "You will forgive me for repeating these points. We have had many exercises in similar conditions and I have confidence that all will be well. But the underwater terrain will be unfamiliar and the effect of the dexedrine pills—they will be issued to the swimming party after this meeting—will be to sensitize the nervous system as well as provide the extra stamina and en-couragement. So we must all be prepared for the unexpected and know how to handle it. Are there any further questions?"

During the planning stages, months before in Paris, Blofeld had warned Largo that if trouble was caused by any members of his team it was to be expected from the two Russians, the ex-members of SMERSH, No. 10 and No. 11. "Conspiracy," Blo-feld had said, "is their life blood. Hand in hand with conspiracy walks suspicion. These two men will always be wondering if they are not the object of some subsidiary plot—to give them the most dangerous work, to make them fall-guys for the police, to kill them and steal their share of the profits. They will be inclined to inform against their colleagues and always to have reservations about the plans that are agreed upon. For them, the obvious plan, the right way to do a thing, will have been chosen for some ulterior reason which is being kept hidden from them. They will need constant reassurance that nothing is being kept hidden from them, but, once they have accepted their orders, they will carry them out meticulously and without regard for their personal safety. Such men, apart from their special talents, are worth having. But you will please remember what I have said and, should there be trouble, should they try and sow mistrust within the team, you must act quickly and with utter ruthlessness. The maggots of mistrust and disloyalty must not be allowed to get a hold in your team. They are the enemies within that can destroy even the most meticulous planning."

Now No. 10, a once-famous SMERSH terrorist called Strelik, began talking. He was sitting two places away from Largo, on his left. He did not address Largo, but the meeting. He said, "Comrades, I am thinking of the interesting matters recounted by No. 1, and I am telling myself that everything has been excellently arranged. I am also thinking that this operation will be a very fine one and that it will certainly not be necessary to explode the second weapon on Target No. 2. I have some documentations on these islands and I am learning from the *Yachtsman's*" (No. 10 had trouble with the word) "*Guide to the Bahamas* that there is a big new hotel within a few miles of our target site, also a scattered township. I am therefore estimating that the explosion of Weapon No. 1 will destroy perhaps two thousand persons. Two thousand persons is not very many in my country and their death, compared with the devastation of this important missile station, would not, in the Soviet Union, be considered of great importance. I am thinking that it will be otherwise in the West and that the destruction of these people and the rescuing of the survivors will be considered a grave matter that will act decisively towards immediate agreement with our terms and the saving of Target No. 2 from destruction. This being so, Comrades"—the dull, flat voice gained a trace of animation—"I am saying to myself that within as little as twenty-four hours our labors will have been completed and the great prize will be within our grasp. Now Comrades"—the red and black shadows turned the taut little smile into a dark grimace—"with so much money so near at hand, a most unworthy thought has come into my mind." (Largo put his hand in his coat pocket and put up the safe on the little Colt .25). "And I would not be performing my duty to my Russian comrade, No. 11, nor to the other members of our team, if I did not share this thought with you, at the same time requesting forbearance for what may be unfounded suspicions."

The meeting was very quiet, ominously so. These men had all been secret agents or conspirators. They recognized the smell of insurrection, the shadow of approaching disloyalty. What did No. 10 know? What was he going to divulge? Each man got ready to decide very quickly which way to jump when the cat was let out of the bag. Largo slipped the gun out of his pocket and held it along his thigh.

"There will come a moment," continued No. 10, watching the faces of the men opposite for a quick gauge of their re-actions, "very shortly, when fifteen of us, leaving five members and six sub-agents on board this ship, will be out there"—he waved a hand at the cabin wall—"in the darkness, at least half an hour's swim from this ship. At that moment, Comrades"—the voice became sly—"what a thing it would be if those remaining on board were to sail the ship away and leave us in the water." There was a shifting and muttering round the table. No. 10 held up a hand. "Ridiculous I am thinking, and so no doubt are you, Comrades. But we are men of a feather. We recognize the unworthy urges that can come upon even the best of friends and comrades when fortunes are at stake. And Com-rades, with fifteen of us gone, how much more of a fortune would there be for those remaining, with their story for No. 2 of a great fight with sharks in which we all succumbed?"

Largo said softly, "And what is it you propose, No. 10?"

For the first time, No. 10 looked to his right. He could not see the expression in Largo's eye. He spoke at the great red and black mass of his face. The tone of his voice was obstinate. He said, "I am proposing that one member of each national group should stay on board to safeguard the interests of the other members of his national group. That would reduce the swimming party to ten. In this way those who are undertaking this dangerous work would go about it with more enthusiasm knowing that no such happening as I have mentioned could come about."

Largo's voice was polite, unemotional. He said, "I have

one very short and simple answer to your suggestion, No. 10."
The light glittered redly on the metal thumb that protruded from
the big hand. The three bullets pumped so quickly into the face
of the Russian that the three explosions, the three bright flashes,
were almost one. No. 10 put up two feeble hands, palms forward, as if to catch any further bullets, gave a jerk forward
with his stomach at the edge of the table, and then crashed
heavily backward, in a splinter of chair wood, onto the floor.

Largo put the muzzle of the gun up to his nose and delicately
sniffed at it, moving it to and fro under the nostrils as if it was
some delicious phial of perfume. In the silence, he looked
slowly down one rank of faces and up the other. Finally he
said softly, "The meeting is now at an end. Will all members
please return to their cabins and look for a last time to their
equipment. Food will be ready from now on in the galley. One
drink of alcohol will also be available for those who want it.
I will detail two crew members to look after the late No. 10.
Thank you."

When Largo was alone he got to his feet, stretched, and
gave a great cavernous yawn. Then he turned to the sideboard,
opened a drawer and took out a box of Corona cigars. He chose
one and, with a gesture of distaste, lit it. He then took the
closed red rubber container that held the ice cubes and walked
out of the door and along to the cabin of Domino Vitali.

He closed the door and locked it. Here also, a red riding
light hung from the ceiling. Under it, on the double bunk, the
girl lay offered like a starfish, her ankles and wrists strapped
to the four corners of the ironwork below the mattress. Largo
put the icebox down on the chest of drawers and balanced the
cigar carefully beside it so that the glowing tip would not spoil
the varnish.

The girl watched him, her eyes glittering red points in the
semi-darkness.

Largo said, "My dear, I have had great enjoyment out of
your body, much pleasure. In return, unless you tell me who
gave you that machine to bring on board, I shall be forced to
cause you great pain. It will be caused with these two simple
instruments," he held up the cigar and blew on the tip until it
glowed brightly, "this for heat, and these ice cubes for cold.
Applied scientifically, as I shall apply them, they will have the

inevitable effect of causing your voice, when it has stopped screaming, to speak, and speak the truth. Now then. Which is it to be?"

The girl's voice was deadly with hate. She said, "You killed my brother and you will now kill me. Go on and enjoy yourself. You are already a piece of death yourself. When the rest of it comes, very soon, I pray God you will suffer a million times more than both of us."

Largo's laugh was a short, harsh bark. He walked over to the edge of the bunk. He said, "Very well, my dear. We must see what we can do with you, very softly and very, very slowly."

He bent down and hooked his fingers in the neckline of her shirt and the join of the brassière. Very slowly, but with great force, he tore downward, the whole length of her. Then he threw aside the torn halves of material and exposed the whole gleaming length of her body. He examined it carefully and reflectively and then went to the chest of drawers and took the cigar and the bowl of ice cubes and came back and made himself comfortable on the edge of the bunk.

Then he took a puff at the cigar, knocked the ash off onto the floor, and leaned forward.

CHAPTER 22

The Shadower

In the attack center of the *Manta* it was very quiet. Commander Pedersen, standing behind the man at the echo-sounder, occasionally made a comment over his shoulder to Bond and Leiter, who had been given canvas-backed chairs well away from the depth and speed gauges, which had been hooded so that they could be read only by the navigating team. These three men sat side by side on red leather, foam-cushioned, aluminum seats, handling the rudder and the forward and aft diving planes as if they were pilots in an airliner. Now the captain left the echo-sounder and came over to Bond and Leiter. He smiled cheerfully. "Thirty fathoms and the nearest cay is a mile to westwards. Now we've got a clear course all the way to Grand Bahama. And we're making good speed. If we keep it up, we've got about four hours' sailing. Be off Grand Bahama about an hour before first light. How about some food and a bit of sleep? There won't be anything on the radar for an hour—these Berry Islands'll fill the screen until we're clear of them. Then'll come the big question. When we clear them, shall we see that one of the smallest of the cays has broken loose and is sailing fast northwards on a parallel course to ours? If we see that on the screen, it'll be the *Disco*. If she's there, we'll submerge. You'll hear the alarm bells. But you can just roll over and have a bit more sleep. Nothing can happen until it's certain that she's in the target area. Then we'll

209

have to think again." The captain made for the stairway. "Mind if I lead the way? Watch your head on the pipes. This is the one part of the ship where there isn't much clearance."

They followed him down and along a passage to the mess hall, a well-lighted dining room finished in cream with pastel pink and green panels. They took their places at the head of one of the Formica-top tables away from the other officers and men, who looked curiously at the two civilians. The captain waved a hand at the walls of the room. "Bit of a change from the old battleship gray. You'd be surprised how many eggheads are involved in the design of these ships. Have to be, if you want to keep your crew happy when the ship's submerged for a month or more at a time. The trick-cyclists said we couldn't have just one color, must have contrast everywhere or the men's eyes get sort of depressed. This hall's used for movies, closed-circuit television, cribbage tournaments, bingo, God knows what—anything to keep the men off duty from getting bored. And you notice there's no smell of cooking or engine smells. Electrostatic precipitators all over the ship that filter them off." A steward came with menus. "Now then, let's get down to it. I'm having the baked Virginia ham with red-eye gravy, apple pie with ice cream, and iced coffee. And steward, don't go too easy on that red-eye." He turned to Bond. "Getting out of harbor always gives me an appetite. You know, it isn't the sea the captain hates, it's the land."

Bond ordered poached eggs with rye toast and coffee. He was grateful for the captain's cheerful talk, but he himself had no appetite. There was a gnawing tension inside him which would be released only when the *Disco* was picked up on the radar and there would be a prospect of action. And lurking behind his concern about the whole operation was worry about the girl. Had he been right to trust her with so much of the truth? Had she betrayed him? Had she been caught? Was she alive? He drank down a glass of iced water, and listened to the captain explaining how the ice cubes and the water were distilled from the sea.

Finally Bond became impatient with the cheerful, even tone of the conversation. He said, "Forgive me, Captain, but could I interrupt for a moment and clear my mind about what we're going to do if we're right about the *Disco* and if we come up with her off the Grand Bahama? I can't quite figure what the next step ought to be. I've got my own ideas, but were you thinking we'd try and go alongside and board her, or just blow her out of the water?"

The captain's gray eyes were quizzical. He said, "I was kind of leaving all that to you fellers. The Navy Department says that I'm under your orders. I'm just the chauffeur. Supposing you tell me what you have in mind and I'll be glad to go along with anything you suggest so long as it doesn't endanger my ship"—he smiled—"too much, that is. In the last resort, if the Navy Department means what it says, and from your account of this operation it does, the safety of the ship will also have to go by the board. As I told you aloft in the attack center, I got acknowledgment of our signal and full approval for our proposed course of action. That's all the clearance I need. Now then, you tell me."

The food came. Bond pecked at his eggs and pushed them away. He lit a cigarette. He said, looking at Felix Leiter, "Well, I don't know what you've worked out, Felix, but this is how I see the picture we may find around four o'clock in the morning, on the assumption, that is, that the *Disco* has been sailing north in shoal water under cover of the Berry Islands and that she'll then make for the Grand Bahama shore somewhere off the site of the missile station. Well now, on that assumption, I've had a good look at the charts and it seems to me that, if she's going to lay that bomb as close to the target as she can, she'll heave to and anchor about a mile off-shore in about ten fathoms and get the bomb another half-mile or so closer to the target, lay it in twelve feet of water or so, switch on the time mechanism, and get the hell away. That's how I'd go about it. She'd be away by first light and there's plenty of yacht traffic around West End from what I can gather from the pilot. She'd show up on the station radar, of course, but she'd be just another yacht. Assuming the bomb's set for the twelve hours Largo's got before the time limit expires, he could be back in Nassau or twice as far away if he wanted in the time he's got. For my money, he'll go back to Nassau with his treasure-hunting story and wait for the next lot of orders from SPECTRE." Bond paused. He avoided Leiter's eyes. "That is, unless he's managed to get information out of the girl."

Leiter said stanchly, "Hell, I don't believe that girl would talk. She's a tough cookie. And supposing she did? He's only got to drop her overboard with some lead round her neck and say her aqualung failed on the treasure hunt, or some spiel of that sort. He'd go back to Nassau all right. That man's cover's as solid as J. P. Morgan and Company."

The captain interrupted. "Leaving all that aside, Commander Bond, and sticking to the operational angles, how do you suggest he's going to get that bomb out of the ship and right into the target area? I agree that according to the charts he can't get much closer in the yacht, and if he did he might be in trouble with the waterfront guard at the missile station. I see from my dope on the place that they've got some kind of a guard boat for chasing away fishermen and suchlike when they're going to do a practice shoot."

Bond said decisively, "I'm sure that's the real purpose of the underwater compartment in the *Disco*. They've got one of those underwater sleds in there, and probably an electric torpedo to haul it. They'll load the bomb on the sled and take it in with a team of underwater swimmers, lay it, and come back to the ship. Otherwise, why have all that underwater gear?"

The captain said slowly, "You may be right, Commander. It makes sense. But so what do you want me to do about it?"

Bond looked the captain in the eye. "There's only one moment to nail these people. If we show our hand too soon, the *Disco* can get the hell away—only a few hundred yards maybe, and dump the bombs in a hundred fathoms. The only time to get them, and the bomb, the first bomb anyway, is when that team has left the ship and is on its way to the laying point. We've got to get their underwater team with our underwater team. The second bomb, if it's aboard, doesn't matter. We can sink the ship with the second bomb inside her."

The captain looked down at his plate. He arranged the knife and fork tidily together, straightened the dessert spoon, and took the remains of his iced coffee and swirled the fragments of ice round so that they tinkled. He put the glass back on the table and looked up, first at Leiter then at Bond. He said thoughtfully, "I guess what you say makes sense, Commander. We have plenty of oxygen rebreathers on board. We also have ten of the finest swimmers in the nuclear flotilla. But they'll

only have knives to fight with. I'll have to ask for volunteers."
He paused. "Who's going to lead them?"

Bond said, "I'll do that. Skin-diving happens to be one of
my hobbies. And I know what fish to look out for and which
ones not to mind about. I'll brief your men about those things."

Felix Leiter interrupted. He said obstinately, "And don't
think you're going to leave me behind eating Virginia ham. I
put an extra foot-flipper on this"—he held up the shining
hook—"and I'll race you over half a mile any day, gammy leg
and all. You'd be surprised the things one gets around to im-
provise when someone chews off one of your arms. Compen-
sation it's called by the medics, in case you hadn't heard about
it."

The captain smiled. He got to his feet. "Okay, okay. I'll
leave you two heroes to fight it out while I have a word to the
men over the speaker system. Then we'll have to get together
with the charts and see that the gear's okay and suchlike. You
fellers aren't going to get any sleep after all. I'll have a ration
of battle pills issued to you. You're going to need them." He
raised a hand and went off down the mess hall.

Leiter turned to Bond. "You goddamn shyster. Thought you
were going to leave your old pal behind, didn't you? God, the
treachery of you Limeys! Perfidious Albion is right, all right."

Bond laughed. "How the hell was I to know you'd been in
the hands of rehabilitators and therapists and so on? I never
knew you took life so seriously. I suppose you've even found
some way of petting with that damned meathook of yours."

Leiter said darkly, "You'd be surprised. Get a girl round
the arm with this and you'd be amazed the effect it has on their
good resolutions. Now then, let's get down to cases. What sort
of formation are we going to swim in? Can we get some of
those knives made into lances? How are we going to recognize
our side from theirs underwater, and in semi-darkness at that?
We've got to make this operation pretty solid. That Pedersen's
a good guy. We don't want to get some of his men killed
through some damn silly mistake of ours."

The voice of the captain sounded over the communication
system. "Now hear this. This is your Captain speaking. It is
possible that we may encounter hazards in the course of this
operation. I will tell you how this may come about. This ship

has been chosen by the Navy Department for an exercise that is tantamount to an operation of war. I will tell you the story, which will remain classified top secret until further orders. This is what has happened..."

Bond, asleep in one of the duty officers' bunks, was awakened by the alarm bell. The iron voice of the P.A. system said: "Diving stations. Diving stations," and almost at once his bunk tilted slightly and the distant whine of the engines altered pitch. Bond smiled grimly to himself. He slipped off the bunk and went along and up to the attack center. Felix Leiter was already there. The captain turned away from the plot. His face was tense. He said, "It looks as if you were right, gentlemen. We've got her, all right. About five miles ahead and two points to starboard. She's doing around thirty knots. No other ship could be holding that speed, or would be likely to. And she's showing no lights. Here, care to have a look through the scope? She's raising quite a wake and kicking up plenty of phosphorescence. No moon yet, but you'll see the white blur when your eyes get used to the dark."

Bond bent to the rubber eye sockets. In a minute he had her, a white scut on the horizon of the soft, feathery swell. He stood back. "What's her course?"

"Same as ours—western end of Grand Bahama. We'll go deeper now and put on a bit of speed. We've got her on the Sonar as well, so we shan't lose her. We'll get up parallel and close in a bit later. The met. report gives a light westerly breeze in the early hours. That'd be a help. Don't want it too calm when we unload the swimming party. The surface'll boil quite a bit as each man goes out. Here." He turned to a powerful-looking man in white ducks. "This is Petty Officer Fallon. He's in command of the swimming party, under your and Mr. Leiter's orders, of course. All the top swimmers volunteered. He's chosen nine of them. I've taken them off all duties. Maybe you gentlemen would like to get acquainted with your team. You'll want to discuss your routines. I guess discipline'll have to be pretty tight—recognition signals and so forth. Okay? The sergeant at arms is looking after the weapons." He smiled. "He's rustled up a dozen flick knives. Had some difficulty persuading the men to give them up, but he's done it. He's barbed them and sharpened them down almost to needles, then fitted them into the tops of broom handles. Guess he'll make you sign an indent for the brooms or he'll have the supply officer on top of him when we get out of this. All right then. Be seeing you. Ask for anything you want." He turned back to the plot.

Bond and Leiter followed Petty Officer Fallon along the lower deck to the engine room and then to the engine-repair shop. On their way they passed through the reactor room. The reactor, the equivalent of a controlled atomic bomb, was an obscene knee-level bulge rising out of the thickly leaded deck. As they passed it, Leiter whispered to Bond, "Liquid sodium Submarine Intermediate Reactor Mark B." He grinned sourly and crossed himself.

Bond gave the thing a sideways kick with his shoe. "Steam-age stuff. Our Navy's got the Mark C."

The repair shop, a long low room equipped with various forms of precision machinery, presented a curious sight. At one end were grouped the nine swimmers clad only in bathing trunks, their fine bodies glowing with sunburn. At the other, two men in gray overalls, drab figures of the machine age, were working in semi-darkness with only pinpoints of bright light cast on the whirring lathes from which the knife blades threw small fountains of blue and orange sparks. Some of the swimmers already had their spears. After the introductions, Bond took one and examined it. It was a deadly weapon, the blade, sharpened to a stiletto and notched near the top into a barb, firmly wired into the top of a long stout stave. Bond thumbed the needle-sharp steel and touched the tip. Even a shark's skin would not stand up to that. But what would the enemy have? CO_2 guns for a certainty. Bond looked the smiling bronzed young men over. There were going to be casualties— perhaps many. Everything must be done to effect surprise. But those golden skins and his own and Leiter's paler skins would show at twenty feet in the moonlight—all right for the guns, but well out of range of the spears. Bond turned to Petty Officer Fallon: "I suppose you don't have rubber suits on board?"

"Why sure, Commander. Have to, for escape in cold waters." He smiled. "We're not always sailing among the palm trees."

"We'll all need them. And could you get white or yellow numbers, big ones, painted on their backs? Then we'll know more or less who's who."

"Sure, sure." He called to his men. "Hey, Fonda and Johnson. Go along to the Quartermaster and draw rubber suits for the whole team. Bracken, get a pail of rubber solution paint from Stores. Paint numbers on the backs of the suits. A foot deep. From one to twelve. Get going."

Later, with the gleaming black suits hanging like giant bat skins along the wall, Bond called the team together. "Men, we're going to have one hell of an underwater battle. There'll be casualties. Anyone care to change his mind?" The faces grinned back at him. "All right, then. Now, we'll be swimming at around ten feet for a quarter, perhaps half a mile. It'll be pretty light. The moon'll be up and the bottom's white sand with some seagrass. We'll take it easy and go in triangle formation with me, No. 1, leading followed by Mr. Leiter here as No. 2, and Petty Officer Fallon as No. 3. Then we broaden out behind like a wedge of geese. All you have to do is follow the number in front of you and no one'll get lost. Watch out for isolated niggerheads. As far as I can gather from the chart there's no true reef, only broken clumps. It'll be getting on for early feeding time for the fish, so watch out for anything big. But leave it alone unless it gets too inquisitive. Then three of you take it on with the spears. But don't forget that it's most unlikely any fish will attack us. Close together we'll look like one hell of a big black fish to anyone else and I guess we'll be given a wide berth. Watch out for sea eggs on the coral and mind the tips of your spears. Hold them right up near the blade. Above all, keep quiet. We must try and get surprise on our side. The enemy's got CO_2 guns, range above twenty feet. But they're slow things to reload. If one's aimed at you, try and give a small target. Keep flat in the water. Don't put your feet down and give him a full-length target. As soon as he's fired, go for him like hell with your spear right out. One jab of those things in almost any part of the head or body and your man's had it. Wounded men will have to look after themselves. We can't spare stretcher bearers. If you're wounded, back out of the fight and get away to a coral clump and rest on it. Or make for the shore and shallow water. If you've got a spear in you, don't try and pull it out. Just hold it in the wound until someone gets to you. Petty Officer Fallon will have one of the ship's signal flares. He'll release that to the surface as soon as our attack begins and your captain will at once surface and put out an escape dinghy with an armed party and the ship's surgeon. Now then, any questions?"

"What do we do as soon as we get out of the sub, sir?"

"Try and not make any fuss on the surface. Get down quickly to ten feet and take your place in the formation. We're likely to get help from a light breeze, but we're bound to create turbulence on the surface. Keep it down as much as you can."

"What about signals underwater, sir? Suppose a mask goes wrong or something."

"Thumbs down for any kind of emergency. Arm held straight out for a big fish. Thumbs up means 'I understand' or 'Coming to help you.' That's all you'll need." Bond smiled. "If the feet go up, that's the signal that you've had it."

The men laughed various kinds of laugh.

There came the sudden voice of the P.A. system. "Swimming party to the escape hatch. I repeat, swimming party to the escape hatch. Don equipment, Don equipment. Commander Bond to the attack center, please."

The whine of the engines died to a moan and then was silent. There was a slight bump as the *Manta* hit bottom.

CHAPTER 23

Naked Warfare

Bond shot upward out of the escape hatch in a blast of compressed air. Far above him the surface of the sea was a glittering plate of quicksilver bubbling and swirling with the small waves that Bond was glad to see had materialized. The balloon of air rushed on past him and he watched it hit the silver ceiling like a small bomb. There was a sharp pain in his ears. To get decompression he fought with his fins and slowed down until he hung suspended ten feet below the surface. Below him the long black shape of the *Manta* looked sinister and dangerous. He thought of the electric light blazing inside her and a hundred men going about their business. It gave him a creepy feeling. Now there came a great explosion from the escape hatch as if the *Manta* was firing at Bond, and the black projectile of Leiter shot up at him through the burst of silver air bubbles. Bond moved out of his path and swam on up to the surface. Cautiously he looked above the small flurry of the waves. The *Disco*, still blacked out, lay stopped less than a mile away to his left. There were no signs of activity on board. A mile to the north lay the long dark outline of Grand Bahama edged with the white of sand and small waves. There were small patches of broken white on the coral and niggerheads in the intervening water. Above the island, on top of the tall rocket gantries that showed as indistinct black skeletons, the red aircraft warning lights winked on and off. Bond got his bearings and quietly jackknifed his body down below the surface. He stopped at about ten feet and, keeping his body pointed like a compass needle along the course he would have to follow, lay, paddling softly with his fins to keep position, and waited for the rest of his team.

Ten minutes before, Commander Pedersen's stolid calm had given way to controlled excitement. "By gum, it's working out like you said it would!" he had said wonderingly when Bond came into the attack center. "They hove to just about ten minutes ago, and since then the Sonar keeps on picking up odd noises, underwater noises, just what one would expect if they were getting things mobilized in that underwater compartment of theirs. Nothing else to go on, but it's quite enough. I guess you and the boys had better get going. As soon as you're out of the way, I'm going to float up a surface antenna and get a signal off to Navy Department, give them a Sitrep and have the missile station warned to stand by to evacuate if things go wrong. Then I'm going to come up to twenty feet or so and have two tubes loaded and keep a periscope watch. I'm issuing Petty Officer Fallon with a second flare. I've told him to keep out of trouble as much as he can and be ready to let off the second flare if it looks as if things are going really bad for our side. Unlikely, but I can't take chances with things as they are. If that second flare comes up, I'm going to close in. Knock a piece or two off the *Disco* with the four-inch and then board her. Then I'm going to be rough as hell until that bomb's been recovered and rendered safe." The captain shook his head doubtfully. He ran his hand over the black iron filings of his crew-cut. "This is one hell of a situation, Commander. We'll just have to play it by ear." He held out his hand. "Well. You'd better get going. Good luck. I hope my boys'll be a credit to the ship."

Bond felt a tap on his shoulder. It was Leiter. He grinned through his mask and jerked up a thumb. Bond took a quick look behind him. The man lay spread out in a rough wedge, their fins and hands working slowly as they marked time in the water. Bond nodded and got going, moving forward with a slow, even trudge, one hand at his side and the other holding his spear up the shaft against his chest. Behind him, the black

wedge fanned out into formation and cruised forward like some
giant delta-winged stingray on the prowl.

It was hot and sticky inside the black suit and the recircu-
lating oxygen coming through the mouthpiece tasted of rubber,
but Bond forgot the discomfort as he concentrated on keeping
an even pace and a dead steady course on a prominent niggerhead with waves washing its head that he had chosen as a
fix for his first contact with the shoal waters.

Far below, where the dancing moon shadows could not
penetrate, the bottom was even white sand with an occasional
dark patch that would be seagrass. All around there was nothing
but the great pale luminous hall of the sea at night, a vast lonely
mist through which, against his will and his intelligence, Bond
expected at any moment the dark torpedo of a great fish to
materialize, its eyes and senses questing toward the rippling
shape of the black intruder. But there was nothing, and nothing
came, and gradually the patches of seagrass became more distinct and ripples showed on the sandy bottom as it shelved
slowly up from fifty to forty and then to thirty feet.

To reassure himself that all was well, Bond took a quick
glance over his shoulder. Yes, they were all there, the oval
panes of eleven gleaming masks with the fluttering fins kicking
up behind them and the glint of the moonlight on the blades
of the spears. Bond thought: By God, if only we can achieve
surprise! What a terrifying ambush to meet coming at you
through the shadows and shapes of the reef! His heart lifted
momentarily at the thought, only to be checked by the deep
gnawing of his hidden fears about the girl. Supposing she was
part of the enemy team! Supposing he came face to face with
her. Would he bring himself to do it—with the spear? But the
whole idea was ridiculous. She was on board, safe. He would
be seeing her again soon, as soon as this work was done.

A small coral clump showed up below and refocused his
mind. Now he gazed watchfully ahead. There were more
clumps, the ink splashes of sea eggs, crowds of small glittering
reef fish, a small forest of sea fans that beckoned and waved
with the ebb and flow like the hair of drowned women. Bond
slowed and felt Leiter or Fallon bump into his fins. He made
the slowing signal with his free hand. Now he crept carefully
forward, looking for the silvery wash of the waves against the

top of his navigation mark. Yes, it was there, away to the left.
He was a good twenty feet off course. He swerved toward it,
gave the halt signal, and came slowly up under its protection.
With infinite caution he raised his head through the sucking
waves. He glanced first toward the *Disco*. Yes, she was still
there, showing more plainly with the moon now full on her.
No sign of life. Bond inched his gaze slowly across the intervening sea. Nothing. A flurry of wavelets down the mirrored
pathway of the moon. Now Bond slid round to the other side
of the coral head. Nothing but the broken waters of the shoal
and, five or six hundred yards away, the clear coastline and
the beach. Bond searched the clear channels for unusual tur-
bulence in the water, for shapes, for anything moving. What
was that? A hundred yards away, on the edge of a big patch,
almost a lagoon of clear water among the coral, a head, a pale
head with the glitter of a mask across it, had broken the surface
for an instant, taken a quick look around, and immediately
submerged.

Bond held his breath. He could feel his thrilled heart hammering against the inside of his rubber suit. Feeling stifled, he
took the breathing tube from between his teeth and let his breath
burst out of him. He quickly gulped in some mouthfuls of fresh
air, got a good fix on the position, crammed the tube roughly
between his lips and slid back and down.

Behind, the masks gazed blankly at him, waiting for a signal. Bond jerked up his thumb several times. Through the near
masks he could see the answering flash of teeth. Bond shifted
his grasp on the spear down to an attacking position and surged
forward over the low coral.

Now it was only a question of speed and careful navigation
among the occasional higher outcrops. Fish squirted out of his
path and all the reef seemed to waken with the shock wave of
the twelve hastening bodies. Fifty yards on, Bond signaled to
slow, to fan out in the attacking line. Then he crept on again,
his eyes, aching and bloodshot with the strain, boring ahead
through the jagged shapes among the pale mist. Yes! There
was the glitter of white flesh, and there and there. Bond's arm
made the hurling signal for the attack. He plunged forward,
his spear held in front of him like a lance.

Bond's group came in from the flank. It was a mistake, as Bond quickly saw, for the SPECTRE team was still moving forward and at a speed that surprised Bond until he saw the small whirring propellers on the backs of the enemy. Largo's men were wearing compressed-air speed packs, bulky cylinders strapped between the twin cylinders of their aqualungs, that operated small screws. Combined with the trudge of the fins, this gave them at least double normal swimming speed in open water, but here, among the broken coral, and slowed by the maneuvering of the sled preceded by the electric Chariot, the team was perhaps only a knot faster than Bond's group, now thrashing their way forward to an interception point that was rapidly escaping them. And there were a hell of a lot of the enemy. Bond stopped counting after twelve. And most of them carried CO_2 guns with extra spears in quivers strapped to their legs. The odds were bad. If only he could get within spear range before the alarm was given!

Thirty yards, twenty. Bond glanced behind him. There were six of his men almost at arm's length; the rest straggled out in a crooked line. Still the masks of Largo's men pointed forward. Still they hadn't seen the black shapes making for them through the coral. But now, when Bond was level with Largo's rear guard, the moon threw his shadow forward across a pale patch of sand and one man, then another, glanced quickly round. Bond got a foot against a lump of coral and, with this to give him impetus, flung himself forward. The man had no time to defend himself. Bond's spear caught him in the side and hurled him against the next man in line. Bond thrust and wrenched sickeningly. The man dropped his gun and bent double, clutching his side. Bond bored on into the mass of naked men now scattering in all directions, with their jet packs accelerated. Another man went down in front of him, clawing at his face. A chance thrust of Bond's had smashed the glass of his mask. He threshed his way up toward the surface, kicking Bond in the face as he went. A spear ripped into the rubber protecting Bond's stomach and Bond felt pain and wetness that might be blood or sea water. He dodged another flash of metal and a gun butt hit him hard on the head, but with most of its force spent against the cushion of water. It knocked him silly and

he clung for a moment to a niggerhead to get his bearings while
the black tide of his men swept past him and individual fights
filled the water with black puffs of blood.

The battleground had now shifted to a wide expanse of clear
water fringed with broken coral. On the far side of this, Bond
saw the grounded sled laden with something long and bulky
with a rubber covering, the silver torpedo of the Chariot, and
a close group of men that included the unmistakable, oversize
figure of Largo. Bond melted back among the coral clumps,
got close down to the sand, and began to swim cautiously round
the flank of the big clear pool. Almost immediately he had to
stop. A squat figure was cowering in the shadows. His gun
was raised and he was taking careful aim. It was at Leiter, in
difficulties with one of Largo's men who had him by the throat
while Leiter, the swim fin on his hook gone, clawed with the
hook at the man's back. Bond gave two hard kicks of his
flippers and hurled his spear from six feet. The light wood of
the handle had no momentum, but the blade cut into the man's
arm just as the bubbles of gas burst from the muzzle of the
gun. His shot went wide, but he flashed round and thrust at
Bond with the empty gun. Out of the corner of his eye Bond
saw his spear floating slowly up toward the surface. He dived
for the man's legs in a clumsy rugby tackle and clawed them
off the ground. Then, as the gun muzzle hit him on the temple,
he reached a desperate hand for the enemy's mask and ripped
it off his face. That was enough. Bond swam aside and watched
the man, blinded by the salt water, groping his way up toward
the surface. Bond felt a nudge at his arm. It was Leiter, clutching at his oxygen tube. His face inside the mask was contorted.
He made a feeble gesture upward. Bond got the message. He
seized Leiter round the waist and leaped for the surface fifteen
feet up. As they broke through the silver ceiling, Leiter tore
the broken tube from his mouth and gulped frantically for air.
Bond held him through the paroxysm and then guided him to
a clump of shallow coral, and, when Leiter pushed him angrily
away and told him to get the hell back under and leave him
alone, he put up a thumb and dived down again.

Now he kept well in the forest of coral and began again his
stalk of Largo. Occasionally he caught glimpses of individual
battles and once he passed under a man, one of his men from

the *Manta*, staring down at him from the surface. But the face under the water, framed in its streaming hair, had no mask or oxygen tube, and the mouth gaped hideously in death. On the bottom, among the coral clumps, there were bits of wrack from the tide of battle—an oxygen pack, strips of black rubber, a complete aqualung and several spears from the CO_2 guns. Bond picked up two of them. Now he was on the edge of the open lagoon of battle water. The sled, with its obscene rubber sausage, was still there, guarded by two of Largo's men with their guns at the ready. But there was no sign of Largo. Bond peered into the misty wall through which the moonlight, paler now, filtered down onto the ripples in the sand, their pretty patterns scuffed and churned by the feet of the combatants. Where the sand had been disturbed, reef fish were swarming to pick up minute fragments of algae and other fodder, like seagulls and rooks when the plow has passed. There was nothing else to be seen and there was no way for Bond to guess how the battle, dispersed into a dozen separate running fights, was going. What was happening on the surface? When Bond had taken Leiter up, the sea had been lit by the red flare. How soon would the rescue dinghy from the *Manta* be on the scene? Ought he to stay where he was and watch over the bomb?

With frightening suddenness, the decision was made for him. Out of the mists to Bond's right the gleaming torpedo shape of the electric Chariot shot into the arena. Largo sat astride it in the saddle. He was bent down behind the small perspex shield to get extra speed and his left hand held two of the *Manta* spears pointing forward while he controlled the single joystick with his right. As he appeared, the two guards dropped their guns on the sand and held up the coupling of the sled. Largo slowed down and drifted up to them. One man caught the rudder and wrestled to pull the Chariot backward toward the couplings. They were going to get out! Largo was going to take the bomb back out through the reef and drop it in deep water or bury it! The same thing would be done with the second bomb in the *Disco*. With the evidence gone, Largo would say that he had been ambushed by rival treasure hunters. How was he to know they came from a United States submarine? His men had fought back with their shark guns, but only because they had been attacked first. Once again the treasure-hunt cover would hide everything!

The men were still wrestling with the coupling. Largo was looking back anxiously. Bond measured the distance and flung himself forward with a great kick against the coral.

Largo turned in time to fling up an arm and parry Bond's stab with his right-hand spear and Bond's stab with the left rattled harmlessly off the aqualung cylinders on Largo's back. Bond drove on head first, his hands outstretched for the air tube in Largo's mouth. Largo's hands flashed to protect himself, dropping his two spears and jerking back the joystick he had been holding in his right. The Chariot surged forward away from the two guards and shot obliquely upward toward the surface while the two bodies clung and struggled on its back.

It was impossible to fight scientifically. Both men tore vaguely at each other while their teeth clenched desperately on the rubber mouthpieces that were their lifelines, but Largo had a firm grip on the Chariot between his knees while Bond had to use one hand to hang on to Largo's equipment to prevent himself from being thrown. Again and again Largo's elbow crashed into Bond's face while Bond dodged from side to side to take the blows on the mouth and not on the precious glass of his mask. At the same time Bond hammered with his free hand at his only target, Largo's kidneys, beneath the brown square of flesh that was all he could reach.

The Chariot broke surface fifty yards down the wide channel leading to the open sea and tore crazily on, its nose, tilted by Bond's weight over the tail, sticking at forty-five degrees out of the water. Now Bond was half in the wash, and it would only be minutes before Largo managed to twist and get both hands to him. Bond made up his mind. He let go of Largo's aqualung and, clutching the stern of the torpedo between his legs, slid back until he felt the top of the rudder at his back. Now, if he could avoid the screw! He reached one hand down between his legs, got a firm grip on the rudder, and heaved himself backward and off the machine. Now his face, inches away from the whirring propeller, was buffeted by the turbulence, but he dragged hard downward and felt the stern coming with him. Soon the damned thing would be almost upright. Bond wrenched the blade of the rudder sideways in a right-angled turn and then, his arms almost torn out of their sockets by the strain, let go. Above and in front of him, as the torpedo veered right-handed, Largo's body, thrown by the sharp turn and the change of balance, crashed into the water, twisted quickly over and faced downward, the mask searching for Bond.

Bond was beat, utterly defeated by exhaustion. Now there was nothing for him but to get away and somehow stay alive. The bomb was immobilized, the Chariot gone, careering in circles over the sea. Largo was finished. Bond summoned the remains of his strength and sluggishly dived down toward his last hope, a refuge among the coral.

Almost lazily, Largo, his strength unimpaired, came down after him, swimming in a giant, easy crawl. Bond swerved in among the coral heads. A white sand passage showed up and he followed it; then there was a fork. Bond, trusting to the small extra protection of his rubber suit, followed the narrower lane between the sharp clumps. But now a black shadow was above him, following him. Largo had not bothered to get into the channel. He was swimming above the coral, looking down, watching Bond, biding his time. Bond looked up. There was a gleam of teeth round the mouthpiece. Largo knew he had got him. Bond flexed his fingers to get more life into them. How could he hope to defeat those great hands, those hands that were machine tools?

And now the narrrow passage was widening. There was the glint of a sandy channel ahead. There was no room for Bond to turn round. He could only swim on into the open trap. Bond stopped and stood. It was the only thing to do. Largo had him like a rat in a trap. But at least Largo would have to come in and get him. Bond looked upward. Yes, the great gleaming body, followed by its string of silver bubbles, was forging carefully on into the open water. Now, swiftly, like a pale seal, he dived down to the firm sand and stood facing Bond. Slowly he advanced between the walls of coral, the big hands held forward for the first hold. At ten paces he stopped. His eyes swiveled sideways to a coral clump. His right hand shot out at something and gave a quick yank. When the hand pulled back, it was writhing, writhing with eight more fingers. Largo held the baby octopus in front of him like a small, waving flower. His teeth drew away from the rubber mouthpiece and the clefts of a smile appeared in his cheeks. He put up one hand and significantly tapped his mask. Bond bent down and picked up a rock covered with seaweed. Largo was being melodramatic. A rock in Largo's mask would be more efficient than having an octopus slapped across his. Bond wasn't worried by the octopus. Only a day before he had been in company with a hundred of them. It was Largo's longer reach that worried him.

Largo took a pace forward and then another. Bond crouched, backing carefully, so as not to cut his rubber skin, into the narrow passage. Largo came on, slowly, deliberately. In two more paces he would attack.

Bond caught a glint of movement out in the open behind Largo. Someone to the rescue? But the glint was white, not black. It was one of theirs!

Largo leaped forward.

Bond kicked off the coral and dived down for Largo's groin, the jagged rock in his hand. But Largo was ready. His knee came up hard against Bond's head and at the same time his right hand came swiftly down and clamped the small octopus across Bond's mask. Then from above, both his hands came down and got Bond by the neck, lifted him up like a child, and held him at arm's length, pressing.

Bond could see nothing. Vaguely he felt the slimy tentacles groping over his face, getting a grip on the mouthpiece between his teeth, pulling. But the blood was roaring in his head and he knew he was gone.

Slowly he sank to his knees. But how, why was he sinking? What had happened to the hands at his throat? His eyes, squeezed tight in agony, opened and there was light. The octopus, now at his chest, let go and shot away among the coral. In front of him Largo, Largo with a spear sticking horribly through his neck, lay kicking feebly on the sand. Behind him and looking down at the body stood a small, pale figure fitting another spear into an underwater gun. The long hair flowed round her head like a veil in the luminous sea.

Bond got slowly to his feet. He took a step forward. Suddenly he felt his knees beginning to give. A wave of blackness began to creep up over his vision. He leaned against the coral, his mouth slackening round the oxygen tube. Water seeped into his mouth. No! He said to himself. No! Don't let that happen!

A hand took one of his. But Domino's eyes behind her mask were somewhere else. They were blank, lost. She was ill! What was the matter with her? Bond was suddenly awake again. His eyes took in the blood patches on her bathing dress, the angry red marks on her body between the scraps of bikini. They would both die, standing there, unless he did something about it. Slowly his leaden legs began to stir the black fins. They were moving up. It wasn't so difficult after all. And now, vaguely, her own fins were helping.

The two bodies reached the surface together and lay, face downward, in the shallow troughs of the waves.

The oyster light of dawn slowly turned pink. It was going to be a beautiful day.

CHAPTER 24

"Take It Easy, Mr. Bond"

Felix Leiter came into the white, antiseptic room and closed the door conspiratorially behind him. He came and stood beside the bed where Bond lay on the edge of drugged sleep. "How's it going, feller?"

"Not bad. Just doped."

"Doctor said I wasn't to see you. But I thought you might care to hear the score. Okay?"

"Sure." Bond struggled to concentrate. He didn't really care. All he could think about was the girl.

"Well, I'll make it quick. Doctor's just doing his rounds and I'll get hell if he finds me here. They've recovered both bombs, and Kotze—the physicist chap—is singing like a bird. Seems SPECTRE's a bunch of really big-time hoodlums—ex-operators of SMERSH, the Mafia, the Gestapo—all the big outfits. Headquarters in Paris. Top man's called Blofeld, but the bastard got away—or anyway they haven't caught up with him yet, according to C.I.A. Probably Largo's radio silence warned him. Must be quite a Mister Genius. Kotze says SPECTRE's banked millions of dollars since they got going five or six years ago. This job was going to be the final haul. You were right about Miami. It *was* going to be Target No. 2. Same sort of operation. They were going to plant the second bomb in the yacht basin."

Bond smiled weakly. "So now everybody's happy."

"Oh, sure. Except me. Haven't been able to get away from my damned radio until now. Valves were almost blowing. And there's a pile of cipher stuff from M just longing for you to get around to it. Thank God the top brass from C.I.A. and a team from your outfit are flying in this evening to take charge. Then we can hand over and watch our two Governments getting snarled up over the epilogue—what to tell the public, what to do with these SPECTRE guys, whether to make you a lord or a duke, how to persuade me to run for President—tricky little details like that. And then we'll damned well get away and have ourselves a ball some place. Maybe you'd care to take that girl along? Hell, she's the one that rates the medals! The guts! They cottoned onto her Geiger counter. God knows what that bastard Largo did to her. But she didn't sing—not a damned word! Then, when the team was under way, she somehow got herself out of the cabin porthole, with her gun and aqualung, and went to get him. Got him, and saved your life into the bargain! I swear I'll never call a girl a 'frail' again—not an Italian girl, anyway." Leiter cocked an ear. He moved swiftly to the door. "Hell, there's that damned medic gum-shoeing down the corridor! Be seeing you, James." He quickly turned the door handle, listened for a moment, and slipped out of the room.

Feebly, desperately, Bond called, "Wait! Felix! Felix!" But the door had closed. Bond sank back and lay staring at the ceiling. Slowly anger boiled up inside him—and panic. Why in hell didn't someone tell him about the girl? What the hell did he care about all the rest? Was she all right? Where was she? Was she . . .

The door opened. Bond jerked himself upright. He shouted furiously at the white-coated figure, "The girl. How is she? Quick! Tell me!"

Dr. Stengel, the fashionable doctor of Nassau, was not only fashionable but a good doctor. He was one of the Jewish refugee doctors who, but for Hitler, would have been looking after some big hospital in a town the size of Düsseldorf. Instead, rich and grateful patients had built a modern clinic for him in Nassau where he treated the natives for shillings and the millionaires and their wives for ten guineas a visit. He was more used to handling overdoses of sleeping pills and the ailments of the rich and old than multiple abrasions, curare poisoning, and odd wounds that looked more as if they belonged to the days of the pirates. But these were Government orders, and under the Official Secrets Act at that. Dr. Stengel hadn't asked any questions about his patients, nor about the sixteen autopsies he had had to perform, six for Americans from the big submarine, and ten, including the corpse of the owner, from the fine yacht that had been in harbor for so long.

Now he said carefully, "Miss Vitali will be all right. For the moment she is suffering from shock. She needs rest."

"What else? What was the matter with her?"

"She had swum a long way. She was not in a condition to undertake such a physical strain."

"Why not?"

The doctor moved toward the door. "And now you too must rest. You have been through much. You will take one of those hypnotics once every six hours. Yes? And plenty of sleep. You will soon be on your feet again. But for some time you must take it easy, Mr. Bond."

Take it easy. You must take it easy, Mr. Bond. Where had he heard those idiotic words before? Suddenly Bond was raging with fury. He lurched out of bed. In spite of the sudden giddiness, he staggered toward the doctor. He shook a fist in the urbane face—urbane because the doctor was used to the emotional storms of patients, and because he knew that in minutes the strong soporific would put Bond out for hours. "Take it easy! God damn you! What do you know about taking it easy? Tell me what's the matter with that girl! Where is she? What's the number of her room?" Bond's hands fell limply to his sides. He said feebly, "For God's sake tell me, Doctor. I, I need to know."

Dr. Stengel said patiently, kindly, "Someone has ill-treated her. She is suffering from burns—many burns. She is still in great pain. But"—he waved a reassuring hand—"inside she is well. She is in the next room, in No. 4. You may see her, but only for a minute. Then she will sleep. And so will you. Yes?" He held open the door.

"Thank you. Thank you, Doctor." Bond walked out of the room with faltering steps. His blasted legs were beginning to give again. The doctor watched him go to the door of No. 4, watched him open it and close it again behind him with the exaggerated care of a drunken man. The doctor went off along the corridor thinking: It won't do him any harm and it may do her some good. It is what she needs—some tenderness.

Inside the small room, the jalousies threw bands of light and shadow over the bed. Bond staggered over to the bed and knelt down beside it. The small head on the pillow turned toward him. A hand came out and grasped his hair, pulling his head closer to her. Her voice said huskily, "You are to stay here. Do you understand? You are not to go away."

When Bond didn't answer, she feebly shook his head to and fro, "Do you hear me, James? Do you understand?" She felt Bond's body slipping to the floor. When she let go his hair, he slumped down on the rug beside her bed. She carefully shifted her position and looked down at him. He was already asleep with his head cradled on the inside of his forearm.

The girl watched the dark, rather cruel face for a moment. Then she gave a small sigh, pulled the pillow to the edge of the bed that it was just above him, laid her head down so that she could see him whenever she wanted to, and closed her eyes.